essays critical and clinical

essays
critical and clinical

Gilles Deleuze

Translated by
Daniel W. Smith and Michael A. Greco

University of Minnesota Press

Minneapolis

The University of Minnesota Press gratefully acknowledges financial
assistance provided by the French Ministry of Culture for the
translation of this book.

Originally published as *Critique et Clinique*, copyright 1993 Les Éditions de Minuit.

Published by the University of Minnesota Press
111 Third Avenue South, Suite 290
Minneapolis, MN 55401-2520

http://www.upress.umn.edu

Printed in the United States of America on acid-free paper

Library of Congress Cataloging-in-Publication Data

Deleuze, Gilles.
    Essays critical and clinical / Gilles Deleuze ; translated by
Daniel W. Smith and Michael A. Greco.
        p.   cm.
    Includes index.
    ISBN 0-8166-2568-9 (alk. paper). — ISBN 0-8166-2569-7 (pbk. :
alk. paper)
    1. Style, Literary.   2. Language and languages—Style.   I. Title.
PN203.D46   1997   97-13300
809—dc21

10 09 08 07 06 05   10 9 8 7 6 5 4 3 2

Great books are written in a kind of foreign language.
—Proust, *Contre Sainte-Beuve*

Contents

Translators' Preface

Although this translation was undertaken jointly, each of the translators took responsibility for the first and final drafts of specific essays. Essays 4, 7, 9, 10, 12, and 15 were done by Michael A. Greco; the remainder, except the final essay, were done by Daniel W. Smith. The translation of Essay 18, by Anthony Uhlmann, first appeared in *Substance* 78 (1995), pp. 3–28, and is published here in revised form. The French version of this essay was originally published as the postface to Samuel Beckett, *Quad et autres pièces pour la télévision*, trans. Edith Fournier (Paris: Minuit, 1992), and we thank Jerome Lindon of Éditions de Minuit for his permission to include it in this collection. We consulted translations of earlier versions of two essays: "On Four Poetic Formulas Which Might Summarize the Kantian Philosophy," translated by Hugh Tomlinson and Barbara Habberjam, in Gilles Deleuze, *Kant's Critical Philosophy* (Minneapolis: University of Minnesota Press, 1984), and "He Stuttered," translated by Constantin V. Boundas, in *Gilles Deleuze and the Theater of Philosophy*, edited by Constantin V. Boundas and Dorothea Olkowski (New York: Routledge, 1994). Throughout the translation, we have tried to err on the side of fidelity to the French rather than felicity in the English. In conformity with Deleuze's claim that the third person is the condition for literary enunciation, for example, we have consistently translated the French *on* as "one," even in contexts where this introduces a certain stylistic tension in the English. As far as possible, we have tried to maintain a terminological consistency with earlier translations of Deleuze's books. On this score, we would like to acknowledge our indebtedness to, in particular, Constantin V. Boundas, Martin Joughin, Brian Massumi, Paul Patton, and Hugh Tomlinson, whose translations we consulted. We would like

TRANSLATORS' PREFACE

to thank Lisa Freeman and Biodun Iginla at the University of Minnesota Press for their support, encouragement, and patience during this project, as well as Lynn Marasco for her careful reading of the manuscript. Peter Canning, John Culbert, Gregg Lambert, James Lastra, Timothy Murphy, and Robert Pippin offered helpful advice on various aspects of the translation. Martin Joughin suggested the translation of the title. The translation is dedicated to Eleanor Hendriks, without whose unwavering support it would not have been possible.

Introduction

"A Life of Pure Immanence": Deleuze's "Critique et Clinique" Project

Daniel W. Smith

> *The critical (in the literary sense) and the clinical*
> *(in the medical sense) may be destined to enter into*
> *a new relationship of mutual learning.*[1]

Although *Essays Critical and Clinical* is the only book written by
Gilles Deleuze that is devoted primarily to literature, literary references
are present everywhere in his work, running almost parallel to the
philosophical references. In 1967 Deleuze published a study of Sacher-
Masoch in which he first linked together the "critical" and the "clinical." The 1969 *Logic of Sense* is in part a reading of Lewis Carroll's
work and includes supplementary material and chapters on Klossowski, Tournier, Zola, Fitzgerald, Lowry, and Artaud.[2] Literary references occupy considerable portions of the two-volume *Capitalism and
Schizophrenia*, which Deleuze wrote in the 1970s with Félix Guattari.[3]
He has written books on both Proust (1964) and Kafka (1975, with
Guattari), as well as two long essays on Carmelo Bene (1979) and
Samuel Beckett (1992).[4] His 1977 *Dialogues* with Claire Parnet includes an important chapter entitled "On the Superiority of Anglo-
American Literature."[5] *Essays Critical and Clinical* comprises eight
newly revised articles that were originally published by Deleuze be-
tween 1970 and 1993, along with ten essays that appear here for the

first time. Once again, names of philosophers (Plato, Spinoza, Kant, Nietzsche, Heidegger) appear side by side with names of literary figures (Melville, Whitman, D. H. Lawrence, T. E. Lawrence, Beckett, Artaud, Masoch, Jarry, Carroll). Although he first announced the idea for this book during a 1988 interview, it is clear that Deleuze had conceived of the "critique et clinique" project early on in his career and pursued it in various forms throughout his published work.[6]

What role do these literary analyses play in Deleuze's philosophical oeuvre? In *What Is Philosophy?* Deleuze and Guattari define philosophy as a practice of concepts, an activity that consists in the formation, invention, or creation of concepts, and indeed their work is marked throughout by an extraordinary conceptual inventiveness. But philosophy, Deleuze adds, necessarily enters into variable relations with other domains such as science, medicine, and art. Art, for instance, is an equally creative enterprise of thought, but one whose object is to create sensible aggregates rather than concepts. Great artists and authors, in other words, are also great thinkers, but they think in terms of percepts and affects rather than concepts: painters, one might say, think in the medium of lines and colors, just as musicians think in sounds, filmmakers think in images, writers think in words, and so on. Neither activity has any privilege over the other. Creating a concept is neither more difficult nor more abstract than creating new visual, sonorous, or verbal combinations; conversely, it is no easier to read an image, painting, or novel than it is to comprehend a concept. Philosophy, Deleuze insists, cannot be undertaken independently of science and art; it always enters into relations of mutual resonance and exchange with these other domains, though for reasons that are always internal to philosophy itself.[7]

Deleuze therefore writes on the arts not as a critic but as a philosopher, and his books and essays on the various arts, and on various artists and authors, must be read, as he himself insists, as works of "philosophy, nothing but philosophy, in the traditional sense of the word."[8] The cinema, for instance, produces images that move, and that move in time, and it is these two aspects of film that Deleuze sets out to analyze in *The Movement-Image* and *The Time-Image*: "What exactly does the cinema show us about space and time that the other arts don't show?"[9] Deleuze thus describes his two-volume *Cinema* as "a book of logic, a logic of the cinema" that sets out "to isolate certain cinematographic concepts," concepts that are specific to the cinema, but that can only be formed philosophically.[10] *Francis Bacon: The Logic of Sensation* likewise creates a series of philosophical concepts, each of which relates to a particular aspect of Bacon's paintings, but also finds a place in "a general logic of sensation."[11] *Essays Critical and Clinical* must be evaluated in the same manner, that is, in terms of the concepts Deleuze extracts from the literary works he examines and the links he establishes between philosophy, literature, and the other arts.[12] The book is not a mere collection of articles; though most of the essays are devoted to individual authors, the book develops a series of concepts like so many motifs that appear and reappear in different essays, which enter into increasingly complex contrapuntal relationships with each other, and which could likewise be said to find a place in a logic of literature—or rather, a logic of "Life." For if the *Cinema* volumes deal primarily with space and time, and *Francis Bacon* with the nature of sensation, Deleuze's writings on literature are primarily linked with the problematic of *Life*. "You have seen what is essential for me," he once wrote to a commentator, "this 'vitalism' or a conception of life as a non-organic power"; in a later interview, he added, "Everything I've written is vitalistic, at least I hope it is."[13]

The idea that literature has something to do with life is certainly not a novel one. In Deleuze's work, however, the notion of Life, as a philosophical concept, has a complex ontological and ethical status. In one of the last essays he published before his suicide in November 1995—a short, dense, abstract, yet strangely moving piece—Deleuze wrote of a scene from Charles Dickens's *Our Mutual Friend*. A rogue despised by everyone is brought in on the verge of death, and the people tending to him suddenly manifest a kind of respect and love for the slightest sign of life in the dying man. "No one has the least regard for the man," writes Dickens. "With them all, he has been an object of avoidance, suspicion, and aversion; but the spark of life within him is curiously separate from himself now, and they have a deep interest in it, probably because it is life, and they are living and must die."[14] As the man revives, his saviors become colder, and he recovers all his crudeness and maliciousness. Yet "between his life and his death," comments Deleuze,

> there is a moment that is no longer anything but a life playing with death. The life of an individual has given way to an impersonal and yet singular life that disengages a pure event freed from the accidents of the inner and outer life, that is, from the subjectivity and objectivity

of what happens. A *homo tantum* with whom everyone sympathizes, and who attains a kind of beatitude. This is a haecceity, which is no longer an individuation but a singularization: *a life of pure immanence,* neutral, beyond good and evil.

In the next paragraph, he notes that this same nonorganic vitality is made manifest in a newborn baby: "Small infants all resemble each other and have hardly any individuality; but they have singularities—a smile, a gesture, a grimace—which are not subjective characteristics. Infants are traversed by an immanent life that is pure power, and even a beatitude through their sufferings and weaknesses."[15] For Deleuze, Life is an impersonal and nonorganic power that goes beyond any lived experience—an ontological concept of Life that draws on sources as diverse as Nietzsche (life as "will to power"), Bergson (the *élan vital*), and modern evolutionary biology (life as "variation" and "selection"). And if Life has a direct relation to literature, it is because writing itself is "a passage of Life that traverses both the livable and the lived."[16]

But the concept of Life also functions as an ethical principle in Deleuze's thought. Throughout his works, Deleuze has drawn a sharp distinction between morality and ethics. He uses the term "morality" to define, in general terms, any set of "constraining" rules, such as a moral code, that consists in *judging* actions and intentions by relating them to transcendent or universal values ("this is good, that is evil"). What he calls "ethics" is, on the contrary, a set of "facilitative" *(facultative)* rules that *evaluates* what we do, say, think, and feel according to the immanent mode of existence it implies. One says or does this, thinks or feels that: *what mode of existence does it imply?*[17] This is the link that Deleuze sees between Spinoza and Nietzsche, whom he has always identified as his philosophical precursors. Each of them argued, in his own manner, that there are things one cannot do or think except on the condition of being weak, base, or enslaved, unless one harbors a resentment against life (Nietzsche), unless one remains the slave of passive affections (Spinoza); and there are other things one cannot do or say except on the condition of being strong, noble, or free, unless one affirms life, unless one attains active affections. An immanent ethical difference (good/bad) is in this way substituted for the transcendent moral opposition (Good/Evil). "*Beyond Good and Evil,*" wrote Nietzsche, "at least that does *not* mean 'Beyond Good and Bad.'"[18] The

"Bad" or sickly life is an exhausted and degenerating mode of existence, one that judges life from the perspective of its sickness, that devaluates life in the name of "higher" values. The "Good" or healthy life, by contrast, is an overflowing and ascending form of existence, a mode of life that is able to transform itself depending on the forces it encounters, always increasing the power to live, always opening up new possibilities of life. For Deleuze, every literary work implies a way of living, a form of life, and must be evaluated not only critically but also clinically. "Style, in a great writer, is always a style of life too, not anything at all personal, but inventing a possibility of life, a way of existing."[19]

Put differently, the question that links literature and life, in both its ontological and its ethical aspects, is the question of *health*. This does not mean that an author necessarily enjoys robust health; on the contrary, artists, like philosophers, often have frail health, a weak constitution, a fragile personal life (Spinoza's frailty, D. H. Lawrence's hemoptysis, Nietzsche's migraines, Deleuze's own respiratory ailments). This frailty, however, does not simply stem from their illnesses or neuroses, says Deleuze, but from having seen or felt something in life that is too great for them, something unbearable "that has put on them the quiet mark of death."[20] But this something is also what Nietzsche called the "great health," the vitality that supports them through the illnesses of the lived. This is why, for Deleuze, writing is never a personal matter. It is never simply a matter of our lived experiences: "You don't get very far in literature with the system 'I've seen a lot and been lots of places.'"[21] Novels are not created with our dreams and fantasies, nor our sufferings and griefs, our opinions and ideas, our memories and travels, nor "with the interesting characters we have met or the interesting character who is inevitably oneself (who isn't interesting?)."[22] It is true that the writer is "inspired" by the lived; but even in writers like Thomas Wolfe or Henry Miller, who seem to do nothing but recount their own lives, "there's an attempt to make life something more than personal, to free life from what imprisons it."[23] Nor does Deleuze read works of literature primarily as texts, or treat writing in terms of its "textuality," through he by no means ignores the effect literature has on language. His approach to literature must thus be distinguished from Jacques Derrida's deconstructive approach. "As for the method of deconstruction of texts," Deleuze once remarked, "I see clearly what it is, I admire it a lot, but it has nothing to do with my own method. I do not present myself as a commentator on texts. For me, a text is merely a small cog in an extra-textual practice. It is not a question of commentating on the text by a method of deconstruction, or by a method of textual practice, or by other methods; it is a question of seeing what *use* it has in the extra-textual practice that prolongs the text."[24] For Deleuze, the question of literature is linked not to the question of its textuality, or even to its historicity, but to its "vitality," that is, its "tenor" of Life.

How then are we to conceive of this link between literature and life, between the critical and the clinical? Deleuze first raised this question in his 1967 book *Coldness and Cruelty* in the context of a concrete problem: Why were the names of two literary figures, Sade and Masoch, used as labels in the nineteenth century to denote two basic "perversions" in clinical psychiatry? This encounter between literature and medicine was made possible, Deleuze argues, by the peculiar nature of the *symptomatological* method. Medicine is made up of at least three different activities: symptomatology, or the study of signs; etiology, or the search for causes; and therapy, or the development and application of a treatment. While etiology and therapeutics are integral parts of medicine, symptomatology appeals to a kind of limit-point, premedical or submedical, that belongs as much to art as to medicine.[25] In symptomatology, illnesses are sometimes named after typical patients (Lou Gehrig's disease), but more often it is the doctor's name that is given to the disease (Parkinson's disease, Roger's disease, Alzheimer's disease, Creutzfeldt-Jakob disease). The principles behind this labeling process, Deleuze suggests, deserve careful analysis. The doctor certainly does not "invent" the disease, but rather is said to "isolate" it: he or she distinguishes cases that had hitherto been confused by dissociating symptoms that were previously grouped together, and by juxtaposing them with others that were previously dissociated. In this way, the doctor constructs an original clinical concept for the disease: the components of the concept are the *symptoms*, the signs of the illness, and the concept becomes the name of a *syndrome*, which marks the meeting place of these symptoms, their point of coincidence or convergence. When a doctor gives his or her name to an illness, it constitutes an important advance in medicine, insofar as a proper name is linked to a given group of symptoms or signs. Moreover, if diseases are named after their symptoms rather than after their causes, it is because, even in medicine, a correct etiology depends first of all on a rigorous symptomatology: "Etiology, which is the scientific or experimental side of medicine, must be subordinated to symptomatology, which is its literary, artistic aspect."[26]

The fundamental idea behind Deleuze's "critique et clinique" project is that authors and artists, like doctors and clinicians, can themselves be seen as profound symptomatologists. Sadism and masochism are clearly not diseases on a par with Parkinson's disease or Alzheimer's disease. Yet if Krafft-Ebing, in 1869, was able to use Masoch's name to designate a fundamental perversion (much to Masoch's own consternation), it was not because Masoch "suffered" from it as a patient, but rather because his literary works isolated a particular way of existing and set forth a novel symptomatology of it, making the contract its primary sign. Freud made use of Sophocles in much the same way when he created the concept of the Oedipus complex.[27] "Authors, if they are great, are more like doctors than patients," writes Deleuze:

> We mean that they are themselves astonishing diagnosticians or symptomatologists. There is always a great deal of art involved in the grouping of symptoms, in the organization of a *table* [*tableau*] where a particular symptom is dissociated from another, juxtaposed to a third, and forms the new figure of a disorder or illness. Clinicians who are able to renew a symptomatological picture produce a work of art; conversely, artists are clinicians, not with respect to their own case, nor even with respect to a case in general; rather, they are clinicians of civilization.[28]

It was Nietzsche who first put forward the idea that artists and philosophers are physiologists, "physicians of culture," for whom phenomena are signs or symptoms that reflect a certain state of forces.[29] Indeed, Deleuze strongly suggests that artists and authors can go *further* in symptomatology than doctors and clinicians, precisely "because the work of art gives them new means, perhaps also because they are less concerned about causes."[30]

This point of view is very different from many psychoanalytic interpretations of writers and artists, which tend to see authors, through their work, as possible or real patients, even if they are accorded the benefit of "sublimation." Artists are treated as clinical cases, as if they were ill, however sublimely, and the critic seeks a sign of neurosis like a secret in their work, its hidden code. The work of art then seems to be inscribed between two poles: a regressive pole, where the work hashes out the unresolved conflicts of childhood, and a progressive pole, by which the work invents paths leading to a new solution concerning the future of humanity, converting itself into a "cultural object." From both these points of view, there is no need to "apply" psychoanalysis to the work of art, since the work itself is seen to constitute a successful psychoanalysis, either as a resolution or a sublimation. This infantile or "egoistic" conception of literature, this imposition of the "Oedipal form" on the work of art, Deleuze suggests, has been an important factor in the reduction of literature to an object of consumption subject to the demands of the literary market.[31]

Coldness and Cruelty provides one of the clearest examples of what might be termed Deleuze's "symptomatological" approach to literature. At a conceptual level, the book is an incisive critique of the clinical notion of "sadomasochism," which presumes that sadism and masochism are complementary forces that belong to one and the same pathological entity. Psychiatrists were led to posit such a "crude syndrome," Deleuze argues, partly because they relied on hasty etiological assumptions (the reversals and transformations of the so-called sexual instinct), and partly because they were "content with a symptomatology much less precise and much more confused than that which is found in Masoch himself."[32] Because the judgments of clinicians are often prejudiced, Deleuze adopts a literary approach in Coldness and Cruelty, offering a differential diagnosis of sadism and masochism based on the works from which their original definitions were derived. Three results of Deleuze's analysis are important for our purposes. On the clinical side, Deleuze shows that sadism and masochism are two incommensurable modes of existence whose symptomatologies are completely different. Each chapter of Coldness and Cruelty analyzes a particular aspect of the sadomasochistic "syndrome" (the nature of the fetish, the function of fantasy, the forms of desexualization and resexualization, the status of the father and mother, the role of the ego and superego, etc.) and in each case shows how it can be broken down into "symptoms" that are specific to the worlds of sadism and masochism. On the critical side, he shows that these clinical symptoms are inseparable from the literary styles and techniques of Sade and Masoch, both of whom, he argues, submit language to a "higher function": in Sade, an Idea of pure reason (absolute negation) is projected into the real, producing a speculative-demonstrative use of language that operates through quantitative repetition; in Masoch, by contrast, the real is suspended in a suprasensual Ideal, producing a dialectical-imaginative use of language that operates through qualitative suspense. Finally, Deleuze shows how these new modes of existence and new uses of language were linked to *political acts of resistance*: in Sade's case, these acts were linked to the French revolution, which he thought would remain sterile unless it stopped making laws and set up institutions of perpetual motion (the sects of libertines); in Masoch's case, masochistic practices were linked to the place of minorities in the Austro-Hungarian empire, and to the role of women within these minorities.[33]

Deleuze initially saw *Coldness and Cruelty* as the first installment of a series of literary-clinical studies: "What I would like to study (this book would merely be a first example) is an articulable relationship between literature and clinical psychiatry."[34] The idea was not to apply psychiatric concepts to literature, but on the contrary to extract non-preexistent clinical concepts from the works themselves. As is often the fate with such proposals, Deleuze did not exactly realize the project in its envisioned form. Yet when Deleuze asked, ten years later, "Why is there not a 'Nietzscheism,' 'Proustism,' 'Kafkaism,' 'Spinozism' along the lines of a generalized clinic?" he implied that his monographs on each of these thinkers fell, to a greater or lesser degree, within the scope of the "critique et clinique" project.[35] *Nietzsche and Philosophy*, for instance, shows how Nietzsche set out to diagnose a disease (nihilism) by isolating its symptoms (*ressentiment*, the bad conscience, the ascetic ideal), by tracing its etiology to a certain relation of active and reactive forces (the genealogical method), and by setting forth both a prognosis (nihilism defeated by itself) and a treatment (the revaluation of values). Deleuze thought that the most original contribution of his doctoral thesis, *Expressionism in Philosophy: Spinoza*, was its analysis of the composition of finite "modes" in Spinoza, which includes both a clinical diagnostic of their passive state (human bondage) and a treatment for their becoming-active (the "ethical" task).[36] In the first edition of *Proust and Signs* (1964), Deleuze interprets *A la recherche du temps perdu* as a symptomatology of various worlds of signs that mobilize the involuntary and the unconscious (the world of love, the social world, the material world, and the world of art, which comes to transform all the others).[37] Even in *Kafka: Toward a Minor Literature*, Deleuze and Guattari show how Kafka's work provided a symptomatological diagnosis of the "diabolical powers" of the future (capitalism, bureaucracy, fascism, Stalinism) that were knocking at the door. Certain essays collected in *Essays Critical and Clinical* could similarly be read as literary-clinical studies of specific writers. In all these works, what Foucault called the "author function" has all but disappeared; the proper name does not refer to a particular person as an author but to a regime of signs or concepts, a determinate multiplicity or assemblage. Deleuze speaks of Nietzsche's philosophy or Proust's novel in much the same way one speaks of Alzheimer's disease in medicine, the Doppler effect or the Kelvin effect in science, the Hamiltonian number or the Mandelbrot set in mathematics, that is, as a *nonpersonal mode of individuation.* If we were to characterize the symptomatological method used by Deleuze, we could do so in terms of these two fundamental components: the function of the proper name, and the assemblage or multiplicity designated by the name.[38]

With the publication of *Anti-Oedipus* in 1972, however, the "critique et clinique" project took a new turn, or at least brought to the fore a tendency that would become ever more pronounced as Deleuze's own work progressed. *Anti-Oedipus* offers a now-famous critique of psycho-analysis that is primarily symptomatological: psychoanalysis, Deleuze and Guattari contend, fundamentally misunderstands signs and symp-toms. Given the book's subtitle, *Capitalism and Schizophrenia,* one might expect Deleuze and Guattari to provide a symptomatological analysis of schizophrenia that would correct the errors and abuses of psychoanalysis. But in fact this is not quite the case. Schizophrenia is an acute phenomenon that poses numerous problems to the clinical method: not only is there no agreement as to the etiology of schizo-phrenia, but even its symptomatology remains uncertain. In most psy-chiatric accounts of schizophrenia (Kraepelin, Bleuler), the diagnostic criteria are given in purely *negative* terms, that is, in terms of the de-struction the disorder engenders in the subject: dissociation, autism, detachment from reality. Psychoanalysis retains this negative view-point, insofar as it relates all the syntheses of the unconscious to the father-mother-child triangle of the Oedipus complex (the ego): in neu-rosis, the ego obeys the requirements of reality and represses the drives of the id, whereas in psychosis the ego remains under the sway of the id, leading to a break with reality.[39] The problem with both psychiatry and psychoanalysis is that these negative symptoms are dispersed and scattered, and are difficult to totalize or unify in a coherent clinical entity, or even a localizable "mode of existence": "schizophrenia is a discordant syndrome, always in flight from itself."[40]

Anti-Oedipus therefore takes the "critique et clinique" project to a properly transcendental level. From the clinical viewpoint, one of its aims is to describe schizophrenia in its *positivity*, no longer as actualized in a mode of life but as the *process* of life itself. Deleuze and Guattari draw a sharp distinction between schizophrenia as a process and schizophrenia as a clinical entity (which results from an *interruption* of the process, as in the case of Nietzsche), although their use of the same term to describe both phenomena has led to numerous misunderstandings.[41] For what *Anti-Oedipus* terms "schizophrenia as a process" is nothing other than what *A Thousand Plateaus* terms "the process of Life" as a nonorganic and impersonal power. "The problem of schizophrenization as a cure consists in this: how can schizophrenia be disengaged as *a power of humanity and of Nature* without a schizophrenic thereby being produced? A problem analogous to that of Burroughs (How to incarnate the power of drugs without being an addict?) or Miller (How to get drunk on pure water?)"[42] From the critical side, Deleuze and Guattari once again appeal to the work of literary figures, especially a number of Anglo-American writers, whose work here assumes an importance it did not have in Deleuze's earlier work. "We have been criticized for overquoting literary authors," they would later comment, "but is it our fault that Lawrence, Miller, Kerouac, Burroughs, Artaud, and Beckett know more about schizophrenia than psychiatrists and psychoanalysts?"[43] If literature here takes on a schizophrenic vocation, it is because the works of these writers no longer simply present the symptomatology of a mode of life, but rather attempt to trace the virtual power of the nonorganic Life itself.

How are we to conceive of this "schizophrenic vocation" of literature? In 1970 Deleuze wrote a new essay on Proust entitled "The Literary Machine," which was added to the second edition of *Proust and Signs*. Whereas the first edition of *Proust and Signs* considered the *Recherche* from the viewpoint of its interpretation of signs, "The Literary Machine" considers the work from the viewpoint of its creation, its production of signs.[44] For art, Deleuze argues, is essentially productive: the work of art is a machine for producing or generating certain effects, certain signs, by determinable procedures. Proust suggested that his readers use his book as an optical instrument, "a kind of magnifying glass" that would provide them with "the means of reading within themselves," in much the same way that Joyce described his works as machines for producing "epiphanies."[45] There is thus a "literary effect" produced by literature, much as we speak of an optical effect or an electromagnetic effect; and the "literary machine" is an apparatus capable of creating these effects, producing signs of different orders, and thus capable of functioning effectively. The question Deleuze here poses to the literary work is not "What does it mean?" (interpretation) but rather "How does it function?" (experimentation). "The modern work of art has no problem of meaning, it has only a problem of use."[46] But the claim that "meaning is use" requires a transcendental analysis:

> No one has been able to pose the problem of language except to the extent that linguists and logicians have eliminated meaning; and the *highest* power of language was discovered only when the *work* was viewed as a machine, producing certain effects, amenable to a certain use. . . . The idea that meaning is nothing other than use becomes a principle only if we have at our disposal *immanent* criteria capable of determining legitimate uses, as opposed to illegitimate uses that would refer use to a supposed meaning and restore a kind of transcendence. Analysis termed transcendental is precisely the determination of these immanent criteria.[47]

For Deleuze, these immanent criteria can be summarized in two principles.

First, the claim that meaning is use is valid only if one begins with elements that in themselves, apart from their use, are devoid of any signification. Modern literature has tended to pose this question in terms of the problem of a world in *fragments,* a world deprived of its unity, reduced to crumbs and chaos. We live in an age that no longer thinks in terms of a primordial Unity or Logos that we have lost (Platonism), or some future Totality that awaits us as the result of a dialectic or evolution (Hegelianism), or even a Subjectivity, whether universal or not, that could bestow a cohesion or unity upon the world (Kantianism). It is only when objective contents and subjective forms have collapsed and given way to a world of fragments, to a chaotic and multiple impersonal reality, that the work of art assumes its full meaning—"that is, exactly all the meanings one wants it to have according to its functioning; the essential point being that it functions, that the machine works."[48] The elements or parts of the literary machine, in short, must be recognized by their mutual independence, *pure singularities,* "a pure and dispersed anarchic multiplicity, without unity or totality, whose elements are welded and pasted together by the real distinction or the very absence of a link."[49] This is the principle of *difference,* which constitutes the first criterion: fragments or parts whose sole relationship is sheer difference, that are related to each other only in that each of them is different. "Dissociation" here ceases to be a negative trait of the schizophrenic and becomes a positive and productive principle of both Life and Literature.

Second, the problem of the work of art is to establish a system of communication among these parts or elements that are in themselves noncommunicating. The literary work, Deleuze argues, must be seen as the unity *of* its parts, even though it does not unify them; the whole produced by the work is rather a "peripheral" totality that is added *alongside* its parts as a *new* singularity fabricated separately. Proust describes the *Recherche* as a literary apparatus that brings together heterogenous elements and makes them function together; the work thus constitutes a whole, but this whole is itself a part that merely exists alongside the other parts, which it neither unifies nor totalizes. Yet it nonetheless has an *effect* on these parts, since it is able to create nonpreexistent relations between elements that in themselves remain disconnected, and are left intact.[50] This is the empiricist principle that pervades Deleuze's philosophy, which constitutes the second criterion: *relations are always external to their terms,* and the Whole is never a principle but rather an effect that is derived from these external relations, and that constantly varies with them. Russell demonstrated the insoluble contradictions set theory falls into when it treats the set of all sets as a Whole. This is not because the notion of the Whole is devoid of sense, but it is not a set and does not have parts; it is rather what *prevents* each set from closing in on itself, forcing it to extend itself into a larger set, to infinity. The Whole, in other words, is the Open, because it is its nature to constantly produce or create the *new.*

Deleuze thus describes his philosophy as "a logic of multiplicities," but he also insists that "the multiple *must be made,*" that it is never given in itself.[51] This production of the multiple entails two tasks: obtain pure singularities, and establish relations or syntheses between them so as to produce a variable Whole that would be the "effect" of the multiplicity and its disconnected parts. These are precisely the two paradoxical features of Life as a nonorganic and impersonal power: it is a power of abstraction capable of extracting or producing singularities and placing them in continuous variation, and a power of creation capable of inventing ever new relations and conjugations between these singularities. The former defines the vitality of life; the latter, its power of innovation. Deleuze is here appealing, at least in part, to a model borrowed from biology, which defines Life (in the evolutionary sense) as a process consisting of the molecular production of variation and the a posteriori selection of these variants.[52] To be sure, Deleuze is aware of the dangers of invoking scientific propositions outside of their own domain: it is the danger of an arbitrary metaphor or a forced application. "But perhaps these dangers are averted," he writes in another context, "if we restrict ourselves to *extracting from scientific operators a particular conceptualizable character* which itself refers to non-scientific domains, and converges with science without applying it or making it a metaphor."[53] This is the "vitalism" to which Deleuze lays claim: not a mystical life force, but the abstract power of Life as a principle of creation.

From this point of view, the relation between the critical and the clinical becomes more complex. On the one hand, the term "critical" refers not only to *criticism* in the literary sense, but also to *critique* in the Kantian sense of the word. The philosophical question now concerns the determination of the *genetic elements* that condition the production of the literary work. (Deleuze, one should note, describes the "transcendental field" in a completely different manner than does Kant. Much like the genetic "code," it constitutes the conditions of real experience and not merely possible experience; and it is never larger than what it conditions, but is itself determined at the same time as it determines what it conditions.) On the other hand, the term "clinical" does not simply imply a diagnosis of a particular mode of existence, but concerns the criteria according to which one assesses the potentialities of "life" in a given work. It is no longer simply a question of ascertaining the symptomatology of particular *mode* of life, but of attaining the genetic level of the double power of Life as a *process*.

Now in fulfilling these two vitalistic powers, modern literature can be said to have had five interrelated effects—effects that, as Deleuze suggests in his essay on Klossowski, are the inevitable consequences that follow from the death of God: *the destruction of the world, the dissolution of the subject, the dis-integration of the body, the "minorization" of politics,* and *the "stuttering" of language.*[54] Or rather, it would be more accurate to say that these are five themes of Deleuze's own philosophy that, in the context of his own work, enter into a certain resonance or affinity with the work of specific writers and artists. Deleuze has undertaken a formidable *conceptual* creation in each of these domains, and in what follows I would simply like to show, in a rather summary fashion, the role each of these themes plays in the context of Deleuze's "critique et clinique" project.

1. *The Destruction of the World* (Singularities and Events). Ontologically and logically, Deleuze locates the philosophical basis for modern literature in Leibniz. Leibniz conceives of the world as a "pure emission of singularities," and individuals (monads) are constituted by the convergence and actualization of a certain number of these singularities, which become its "primary predicates." Here, for instance, are four singularities of a life: "to be the first man," "to live in a garden of paradise," "to have a woman emerge from one's rib," "to sin." These singularities cannot yet be defined as predicates, but constitute what Deleuze calls pure "events." Linguistically, they are like indeterminate infinitives that are not yet actualized in determinate modes, tenses, persons, and voices. The great originality of Deleuze's reading of Leibniz, in both *The Fold* and *The Logic of Sense,* lies in his insistence on the anteriority of this domain of singularities (the virtual) in relation to predicates (the actual).[55] "Being a sinner" is an analytic predicate of a constituted individual or subject, but the infinitive "to sin" is a virtual singularity-event in the neighborhood of which the monad "Adam" will be actualized. Such singularities constitute the genetic elements not only of an individual life, but also of the world in which they are actualized. For one can add to these four singularities a fifth one: "to resist temptation." This singularity is not impossible in itself, but it is, as Leibniz put it, *incompossible* with the world in which Adam sinned. There is here a divergence or bifurcation in the series that passes through the first three singularities; the vectors that extend from this fifth singularity to the three others do not converge, they do not pass through common values, and this bifurcation marks a border between two incompossible worlds: Adam the nonsinner belongs to a possible world that is incompossible with our own. For Leibniz, the only thing that prevents these incompossible worlds from coexisting is the theological hypothesis of a God who calculates and chooses among them in a kind of divine game: from this infinity of possible worlds, God selects the "Best," the one richest with reality, which is defined by the set of

convergent series that constitute it, and the set of monads that express it with varying degrees of clarity. Each monad, though it has neither door nor window, nonetheless expresses the *same* world in the infinite series of its predicates ("the preestablished harmony"), each of them being a different *point of view* on the single compossible world that God causes them to envelop ("perspectivism").

Literature acceded to its modernity, Deleuze suggests, not only when it turned to language as its condition, but when it freed the virtual from its actualizations and allowed it to assume a validity of its own. Deleuze often cites as an example Borges's famous story "The Garden of the Forking Paths," in which a purely virtual world is described in the labyrinthine book of a Chinese philosopher named Ts'ui Pên: "In all fiction, when a man is faced with alternatives, he chooses one at the expense of others. In the almost unfathomable Ts'ui Pên, he chooses—simultaneously—all of them. . . . Fang, let us say, has a secret. A stranger knocks at the door. Naturally there are various outcomes. Fang can kill the intruder, the intruder can kill Fang, both can be saved, both can die, etc. *In Ts'ui Pên's work, all the possible solutions occur, each one being the point of departure for other bifurcations.* . . . You have come to my house, but in one of our possible pasts you are my enemy, in another, my friend."[56] Leibniz had in fact given a similar presentation of the universe at the conclusion of the *Theodicy*—"an astonishing text," says Deleuze, "that we consider a source of all modern literature."[57] In Ts'ui Pên's labyrinth, however, God is no longer a Being who compares and chooses the richest compossible world, as in the *Theodicy;* he has now become a pure Process that passes through all these virtual possibilities, forming an infinite web of diverging and converging series. Divergences, bifurcations, and incompossibles now belong to *one and the same universe,* a chaotic universe in which divergent series trace endlessly bifurcating paths: a "chaosmos" and no longer a world.

Hindered as he was by theological exigencies, Leibniz could only hint at the principle of the "ideal game" that governs the relations among singularities considered in themselves. For the inherence of predicates in the expressive monad presupposes the compossibility of the expressed world, but both in turn presuppose the distribution of pure singularities that are a-cosmic and preindividual, and are linked together in series according to rules of convergence and divergence. This liberation of the virtual implies a fundamentally new type of narration, whose conditions Deleuze outlines in a chapter of *The Time-Image* entitled "The Powers of the False."[58] Descriptions no longer describe a preexisting actual reality; rather, as Robbe-Grillet says, they now stand for their objects, creating and erasing them at the same time. Time ceases to be chronological, and starts to pose the simultaneity of incompossible presents or the coexistence of not-necessarily-true pasts. Abstract space becomes disconnected, its parts now capable of being linked in an infinite number of ways through nonlocalizable relations (as in the Riemanian or topological spaces of modern mathematics). Concrete space is no longer either stable or unstable but *metastable*, presenting "a plurality of ways of being in the world" that are incompatible yet coexistent. Forces lose their centers of movement and fixed points of reference and are now merely related to other forces. "Perspectivism" no longer implies a plurality of viewpoints on the same world or object; each viewpoint now opens on to another world that itself contains yet others. The "harmony" of Leibniz's world gives way to an emancipation of dissonance and unresolved chords that are not brought back into a tonality, a "polyphony of polyphonies" (Boulez). Most importantly, perhaps, the formal logic of actual predicates is replaced by a properly "transcendental" logic of virtual singularities. It is under these virtual conditions (and only under these conditions) that Deleuze and Guattari speak of a "rhizome," that is, a multiplicity in which a singularity can be connected to any other in an infinite number of ways. Deleuze distinguishes, in general, between three types of syntheses among singularities: a *connective* synthesis (if . . . then), which bears upon the construction of a single series; a *conjunctive* synthesis (and . . . and), which is a method of constructing convergent series; and, most importantly, a paradoxical *disjunctive* synthesis (either . . . or), which affirms and distributes divergent series and turns disjunction into a positive and synthetic principle. (One of the essential questions posed by *Logic of Sense* concerns the conditions in which disjunction can be a synthetic principle and not merely a procedure of exclusion.)[59] Narration, in short, can describe this virtual domain only by becoming fundamentally *falsifying*: neither true nor false in content—an undecidable alternative—but false in its form, what Nietzsche called the creative power of the false (the production of truths that "falsify" established truths).[60]

Many of Deleuze's analyses of literature in *Difference and Repetition* and *Logic of Sense* concern the various techniques by which such disjunctive syntheses have been put to use in language by various writers. *The Logic of Sense,* for instance, includes an analysis of the various types of "portmanteau-words" created by Lewis Carroll, which make language ramify and bifurcate in every direction: the *contracting* word, which forms a connective synthesis over a single series ("Your Royal Highness" is contracted into "y'reince"); the *circulating* word, which forms a conjunctive syntheses between two heterogenous series (Snark = snake + shark; slithy = slimy + lithe, etc.); and the *disjunctive* word, which creates an infinite ramification of coexistent series (frumious = furious + fuming, in which the true disjunction is between "fuming-furious" and "furious-fuming," which in turn creates ramifications in other series).[61] Raymond Roussel produced his texts by making two divergent series resonate. In *La Doublure* this procedure rests on the double meaning of a homonym (the title can mean either "The Understudy" or "The Lining"): the space opened up at the heart of the word is filled by a story and by objects that themselves take on a double meaning, each participating in two stories at the same time. *Impressions of Africa* complicates the procedure, starting with a quasi homonym, "*billard/pillard*," but hiding the second story within the first.[62] Gombrowicz's *Cosmos* is similarly structured around a series of hanged animals and a series of feminine mouths, which communicate with each other by means of strange interfering objects and esoteric words. Joyce's *Ulysses* implicates a story between two series, Ulysses/Bloom, employing a multitude of procedures that almost constitute an archaeology of the modes of narration: a prodigious use of esoteric and portmanteau words, a system of correspondences between numbers, a "questionnaire" method of questions/responses, the institution of trains of multiple thoughts. *Finnegans Wake* takes the technique to its limit, invoking a letter that makes *all* the divergent series constitutive of the "chaosmos" communicate in a transversal dimension.[63] Such a universe goes beyond any lived or livable experience; it exists only in thought and has no other result than the work of art. But it is also, writes Deleuze, "that by which thought and art are real, and disturb the reality, morality, and economy of the world."[64]

2. *The Dissolution of the Subject* (Affects and Percepts). In such a chaotic and bifurcating world, the status of the individual changes as well: the monadology becomes a nomadology. Rather than being closed upon the compossible and convergent world they express from within

(the monadic subject), beings are now torn open and kept open through the divergent series and incompossible ensembles that continually pull them outside themselves (the nomadic subject). "Instead of a certain number of predicates being excluded by a thing by virtue of the identity of its concept, each 'thing' is open to the infinity of singularities through which it passes, and at the same time it loses its center, that is to say, its identity as a concept and as a self."[65] An individual is a multiplicity, the actualization of a set of virtual singularities that function together, that enter into symbiosis, that attain a certain consistency. But there is a great difference between the singularities that define the virtual plane of immanence and the individuals that actualize them and transform them into something transcendent. A wound is actualized in a state of things or in the lived experience of an individual; but in itself it is a pure virtuality on the plane of immanence that sweeps one along in *a* life. "My wound existed before me," writes Joe Bousquet, a French poet shot in World War I. "I was born to embody it."[66] The question Deleuze poses with regard to the subject is "How can the individual transcend its form and its syntactical link with a world in order to attain the universal communication of events?"[67] What he calls "schizophrenization" is a limit-process in which the identity of the individual is dissolved and passes entirely into the virtual chaosmos of included disjunctions. The schizophrenic quickly shifts from one singularity to another, never explaining events in the same manner, never invoking the same genealogy ("I, Antonin Artaud, am my son, my father, my mother, and myself"), never taking on the same identity (Nijinsky: "I am God. I was not God. I am a clown of God. I am Apis. I am an Egyptian. I am a Negro. I am a Chinaman. I am a Japanese . . .")."[68] If Deleuze sees a fundamental link between Samuel Beckett's work and schizophrenia, it is because Beckett likewise situates his characters entirely in the domain of the virtual or the possible: rather than trying to *realize* a possibility, they remain within the domain of the possible and attempt to *exhaust* logically the whole of the possible, passing through all the series and permutations of its included disjunctions (the permeation of "sucking stones" in *Molloy*, the combinatorial of five biscuits in *Murphy*, the series of footwear in *Watt*). In the process, they exhaust themselves physiologically, losing their names, their memory, and their purpose in "a fantastic decomposition of the self."[69]

Even without attaining this limit, however, the self is not defined by its identity but by a process of "becoming." Deleuze and Guattari analyze this concept in a long and complex chapter of A *Thousand Plateaus*.[70] The notion of becoming does not simply refer to the fact that the self does not have a static being and is in constant flux. More precisely, it refers to an objective zone of indistinction or indiscernibility that always exists between any two multiplicities, a zone that immediately *precedes* their respective natural differentiation.[71] In a bifurcating world, a multiplicity is defined not by its center but by the limits and borders where it enters into relations with other multiplicities and changes nature, transforms itself, follows a *line of flight*. The self is a threshold, a door, a becoming between two multiplicities, as in Rimbaud's formula "I is another." One can enter a zone of becoming with anything, provided one discovers the literary or artistic means of doing so. Nowhere is this idea of becoming better exemplified than in Herman Melville's *Moby-Dick*, which Deleuze and Guattari consider to be "one of the greatest masterpieces of becoming."[72] The relation between Captain Ahab and the white whale is neither an imitation or mimesis, nor a lived sympathy, nor even an imaginary identification. Rather, Ahab *becomes* Moby-Dick, he enters a zone of indiscernibility where he can no longer distinguish himself from Moby-Dick, to the point where he strikes himself in striking the whale. And just as Ahab is engaged in a becoming-whale, so the animal simultaneously becomes something other: an unbearable whiteness, a shimmering pure white wall. "To me, the white whale is that wall, shoved near to me. Sometimes I think there is naught beyond. But 'tis enough."[73] What is the reality of this becoming? It is obvious that Ahab does not "really" become a whale, any more than Moby-Dick "really" becomes something else. In a becoming, one term does not become another; rather, each term encounters the other, and the becoming is something between the two, outside the two. This "something" is what Deleuze calls a pure *affect* or *percept,* which is irreducible to the affections or perceptions of a subject. "Percepts are not perceptions, they are packets of sensations and relations that outlive those who experience them. Affects are not feelings, they are becomings that go beyond those live through them (they become other)."[74] In *Moby-Dick,* both Ahab and the whale lose their texture as subjects in favor of "an infinitely proliferating patchwork" of affects and percepts that escape their form, like the pure whiteness of the wall, or "the furrows that twist from Ahab's brow to that of the Whale."[75] "We attain to the percept and the affect only as to autonomous and sufficient beings that no longer owe anything to those who experience or have experienced them."[76]

What does it mean to speak of a pure affect as an "autonomous being"? In his remarkable chapters on "the affection-image" in *The Movement-Image*, Deleuze takes as one of his examples the climactic scene of G. B. Pabst's film *Pandora's Box*. Jack the Ripper, looking dreamily into Lulu's compassionate face in the light of a lamp, suddenly sees the gleam of a bread knife over her shoulder; his face, in close-up, gasps in terror, his pupils grow wider, "the fear becomes a paroxysm"; then his face relaxes again as he accepts his destiny, given the irresistible call of the weapon and the availability of Lulu as a victim. This scene, Deleuze suggests, can be grasped in two ways. On the one hand, it defines an "actual" state of affairs, localized in a certain place and time, with individualized characters (Lulu, Jack), objects with particular uses (the lamp, the knife), and a set of *real connections* between these objects and characters. On the other hand, it can also be said to define a set of qualities in a pure state, outside their spatiotemporal coordinates, with their own ideal singularities and *virtual conjunctions:* Lulu's compassionate look, the brightness of the light, the gleam of the blade, Jack's terror, resignation, and ultimate decisiveness.[77] These are what Deleuze call pure "possibles," that is, singular qualities or powers.

In Pabst's film, brightness, terror, decisiveness, and compassion are very different qualities and powers: the first is a quality *of* a sensation; the second is the quality *of* a feeling; the third, *of* an action; and the last, *of* a state. But these qualities are not themselves either sensations, feelings, actions, or states; they express rather the quality of a possible sensation or feeling. Brightness is not the same as a particular sensation, nor is decisiveness the same as a particular action; they are rather qualities that will be actualized under certain conditions in a particular sensation (the knife blade in the light of the lamp) or a particular action (the knife in Jack's hand). They correspond to what C. S. Peirce called "Firstness," the category of the Possible, which considers qualities in themselves as positive possibilities, without reference to anything else, independently of their actualization in a particular state of affairs. According to Deleuze, Peirce seems to have been influenced here by Maine de Biran, who had already spoken of pure affections, "unplaceable because they have no relation to a determinate space, present in the sole form of a 'there is . . .' because they have no relation to a subject (the pains of a hemiplegic, the floating images of falling asleep, the visions of madness)." "Secondness," by contrast, is the category of the Real, in which these qualities have become "forces" that are related to each other (exertion-resistance, action-reaction, excitation-response, situation-behavior, individual-milieu) and are actualized in determinate space-times, geographical or historical milieus, and individual people.[78]

Now, what Deleuze calls an affect is precisely the "complex entity" that, at each instant, secures the virtual conjunction of a set of such singular qualities or powers (the brightness, the terror, the compassion). Art does not actualize these virtual affects; it gives them "a body, a life, a universe."[79] The strength of Deleuze's discussion in *The Movement-Image* lies in its analysis of the way in which, in the cinema, such qualities or powers are obtained through the *close-up:* when we see the face of a fleeing coward in close-up, we see "cowardice" in person, freed from its actualization in a particular person. "The possibility of drawing near to the human face," writes Ingmar Bergman, "is the primary originality and distinctive quality of the cinema."[80] Ordinarily, the face of a human subject plays a role that is at once individuating, socializing, and communicative; in the close-up, however, the face becomes an autonomous entity that tends to destroy this triple function: social roles are renounced, communication ceases, individuation is suspended. The organization of the face is undone in favor of its own material traits ("parts which are hard and tender, shadowy and illuminated, jagged and curved, dull and shiny, smooth and grainy"), which become the building material, the "hylé," of an affect, or even a system of affects.[81] Sometimes a face can be *reflective,* immutable and without becoming, fixed on a thought or object, expressing a pure *Quality* that marks a minimum of movement for a maximum of unity (Lulu's compassion); sometimes, by contrast, a face can be *intensive,* feeling a pure *Power* that passes through an entire series of qualities, each of them assuming a momentary independence, but then crossing a threshold that emerges onto a new quality (Jack the Ripper's series of ascending states of terror). Between these two poles, there can be numerous intermixings. But this is the way in which the face participates in the nonorganic Life of things, pushing the face to its point of nudity and even inhumanity, as if every face enveloped an unknown and unexplored landscape. For Deleuze, the affective film par excellence is Carl Dreyer's *The Passion of Joan of Arc,* which is made up almost exclusively of short close-ups. Joan of Arc's trial is an event actualized in a historical situation, with individuated characters and roles (Joan, the bishop, the judges), with the affections of these characters (the bishop's anger, Joan's martyrdom). But the ambition of Dreyer's film is to extract the "Passion" from the trial: "All that will be preserved from the roles and situations will be what is needed for the affect to be extracted and to carry out its conjunctions—this 'power' of anger or of ruse, this 'quality' of victim or martyrdom."[82] Bergman perhaps pushed the affection-image of the face to its extreme limit: in the superimposition of faces in *Persona,* the image absorbs two beings and dissolves them in a void, having as its sole affect a mute Fear, the fear of the face when confronted with its own "effacement."[83]

Literature has its own means of extracting affects. "A great novelist," write Deleuze and Guattari, "is above all an artist who invents unknown or unrecognized affects and brings them to light as the becoming of his characters."[84] It is not that they are proposing an aesthetic of pure qualities, for affects must always be considered from the standpoint of the becomings that seize hold of them. "Pure affects imply an enterprise of desubjectivation."[85] The aim of literature, for Deleuze, is not the development of forms or the formation of subjects, but the displacement or catapulting of becomings into affects and percepts, which in turn are combined into "blocks of sensation" through their virtual conjunction. In Emily Brontë's *Wuthering Heights,* for example, Catherine and Heathcliff are caught up in a double becoming ("I *am* Heathcliff") that is deeper than love and higher than the "lived," a profound passion that traces a zone of indiscernibility between the two characters and creates a block of becoming that passes through an entire series of intensive affects.[86] In Kafka's *Metamorphosis,* Gregor Samsa is caught up, like Ahab, in a becoming-animal, but he finds himself Oedipalized by his family and goes to his death.[87] In Chrétien de Troyes's novels, one finds catatonic knights seated on their steeds, leaning on their lances, awaiting chivalry and adventure. Like Beckett's characters, "the knight of the novel of courtly love spends his time forgetting his name, what he is doing, what people say to him, he doesn't know where he is going or to whom he is speaking"—an amnesiac, an ataxic, a catatonic, a schizophrenic, a series of pure affects that constitutes the becoming of the knight.[88] It is at this level of the affect, as a genetic element, that life and literature converge on each other: "Life alone creates such zones where living beings whirl around, and only art can reach and penetrate them in its enterprise of co-creation."[89]

What we have said of affects applies equally to *percepts*. Just as the affect goes beyond the affections of a character, so the percept goes beyond the character's perceptions of the landscape. A percept, says Deleuze, is "a perception in becoming," a potentialization that raises sight to the nth power and breaks with the human perception of determinate milieus.[90] The character's relation to the landscape, writes François Zourabichvili, "is no longer that of an autonomous and pre-existent inner life and an independent external reality supposed to reflect this life"; rather, the landscape "involves one in a becoming where the subject is no longer coextensive with itself."[91] In *Moby-Dick*, Captain Ahab has perceptions of the sea, but he has them only because he has entered into a relationship with Moby-Dick that makes him become-whale, and forms a compound of sensations that no longer has need of either Ahab or the whale: the Ocean as a pure percept. In *Seven Pillars of Wisdom*, T. E. Lawrence has perceptions of the Arabian desert, but he has entered into a becoming-Arab that populates the hallucinatory haze of the desert with the affects of shame and glory: the Desert as percept. In Virginia Woolf's *Mrs. Dalloway*, Mrs. Dalloway has perceptions of the town, but this is because she has passed into the town like "a knife through everything," to the point where she herself has become imperceptible; she is no longer a person, but a becoming ("She would not say of herself, I am this, I am that"): the Town as a percept.[92] What the percept makes visible are the invisible forces that populate the universe, that affect us and make us become: characters pass into the landscape and themselves become part of the compound of sensations. These percepts are what Woolf called "moments of the world," and what Deleuze terms "haecceities," in which the mode of individuation of "a life" does not differ in nature from that of "a climate," "a wind," "a fog," or "an hour of a day." They are assemblages of nonsubjectified affects and percepts that enter into virtual conjunction. "The street enters into composition with the horse, just as the dying rat enters into composition with the air, and the beast and the full moon enter into composition with each other."[93] The landscape is no longer an external reality, but has become the very element of a "passage of Life." As Deleuze and Guattari put it, "We are not *in* the world, we become *with* the world."[94]

How can such a "moment of the world" be made to exist by itself, to achieve an autonomous status? In his chapter "The Perception-Image" in *The Movement-Image*, Deleuze shows how Vertov's "kino-eye" attempted to attain, through cinematic means, a perception as it was "before" humans, the pure vision of a nonhuman eye (the camera) that would be in matter itself, making possible the construction of an "any-space-whatever" released from its human coordinates. Similarly, in painting, Cézanne spoke of the need to always paint at close range, to *no longer see* the wheat field, to be too close to it, to lose oneself in the landscape, without landmarks, to the point where one no longer sees forms or even matters, but only forces, densities, intensities: the forces of folding in a mountain, the forces of germination in an apple, the thermal and magnetic forces of a landscape. This is what Cézanne called the world before humanity, "dawn of ourselves," "iridescent chaos," "virginity of the world": a collapse of visual coordinates in a universal variation or interaction. Afterward, the earth can emerge, "stubborn geometry," "the measure of the world," "geological foundations"—though with the perpetual risk that the earth in turn may once again disappear in a "catastrophe."[95] Paul Klee described the act of painting in similar terms: "not to render the visible, but to *render visible*"—that is, to render visible forces that are not visible in themselves. In music, Messiaen spoke of his sonorous percepts as "melodic landscapes" populated by "rhythmic characters."[96] In literature, Woolf's formula was "to saturate every atom": "to eliminate all waste, deadness, superfluity," everything that adheres to our lived perceptions; but also to saturate the percept, "to put everything into it," to include everything.[97] Whatever the technical means involved, such percepts can only be constructed in art, since *they belong to an eye that we do not have*. "In each case style is needed—the writer's syntax, the musician's modes and rhythms, the painter's lines and colors—to raise lived perceptions to the percept and lived affections to the affect."[98]

Affects and percepts are thus the genetic and immanent elements constitutive of *a* life. "The individuation of a life," write Deleuze and Guattari, "is not the same as the individuation of the subject that leads it or serves as its support."[99] A "life" is constructed on *an immanent plane of consistency* that knows only relations between affects and percepts, and whose composition, through the creation of blocks of sensations, takes place in the indefinite and virtual time of the pure event (Aeon). A "subject" is constructed on *a transcendent plane of organization* that already involves the development of forms, organs, and functions, and takes place in a measured and actualized time (Chronos). It is true that the opposition between these two types of planes is abstract, since one continually and unnoticeably passes from one to the other; it is perhaps better to speak of two movements or tendencies, since there is no subject that is not caught up in a process of becoming, and affects and percepts presuppose at least a minimal subject from which they are extracted, or as an "envelope" that allows them to communicate.[100] In *A Thousand Plateaus*, Goethe and Kleist are presented as almost paradigmatic examples of these two tendencies in literature. Goethe, like Hegel, insisted that writing should aim at the regulated formation of a Subject, or the harmonious development of a Form; hence his emphasis on themes such as the sentimental education, the inner solidity of the characters, the harmony between forms, the continuity of their development, and so forth. In Kleist, by contrast, feelings are uprooted from the interiority of the subject and are projected outward into a milieu of pure exteriority: love and hate are pure affects (*Gemüt*) that pierce the body like weapons; they are instances of the becomings of the characters (Achilles' becoming-woman, Penthesilea's becoming-dog). There is no subject in Kleist, but only the affects and percepts of a life that combine into "blocks of becoming," blocks that may petrify in a catatonic freeze, and then suddenly accelerate to the extreme velocity of a flight of madness ("Catatonia is: 'This affect is too strong for me'; and a flash is: 'The power of this affect is sweeping me away'").[101] Proust, who is perhaps the most frequent point of reference in Deleuze's works, combines these two tendencies in an almost exemplary manner. In the course of "lost time," Proust progressively extracts affects and percepts from his characters and landscapes, so that the "plane of composition" of the *Recherche* emerges only gradually, as the work progresses, slowly sweeping everything along in its path, until it finally appears for itself in "time regained": the forces of pure time that have now become perceptible in themselves.[102] For Deleuze, it is only by passing through the "death of the subject" that one can achieve a true individuality and acquire a proper name. "It's a strange business, speaking for yourself, in your own name, because it doesn't at all come with seeing yourself as an ego or a person or a subject. Individuals find a real name for themselves only through the harshest exercise in depersonalization, by opening themselves to the multiplicities everywhere within them, to the intensities running through them. . . . *Experimentation on ourself is our only identity.*"[103]

3. *The Dis-integration of the Body* (Intensities and Becomings). The dissolution of the logical identity of the subject has as its correlate the physical dis-integration of the organic body. Beneath the organic body, and as its condition, there lies what Artaud discovered and named: the *body without organs,* which is a purely intensive body. The body without organs is one of Deleuze's most notorious concepts; it appears for the first time in *The Logic of Sense,* is developed conceptually in *Anti-Oedipus,* and is the object of a programmatic chapter of *A Thousand Plateaus* entitled "How Do You Make Yourself a Body without Organs?"[104] Deleuze finds its biological model in the egg, which is an intensive field, literally without organs, defined solely by axes and vectors, gradients and thresholds, displacements and migrations.[105] But here again, Deleuze appeals to embryology only in order to extract a philosophical concept from it: the body without organs is the model of Life itself, a powerful nonorganic and intensive vitality that traverses the organism; by contrast, the organism, with its forms and functions, is not life, but rather that which imprisons life. But for Deleuze, the body without organs is not something that exists "before" the organism; it is *the intensive reality of the body,* a milieu of intensity that is "beneath" or "adjacent to" the organism and continually in the process of constructing itself. It is what is "seen," for example, in the phenomena known as internal or external "autoscopia": it is no longer *my* head, but I feel myself inside *a* head; or I do not see myself in the mirror, but I feel myself in the organism I see, and so on.

In *Anti-Oedipus,* Deleuze and Guattari make use of the concept of the body without organs to describe the experience of schizophrenics, for whom the body without organs is something that is primarily *felt* under the integrated organization of the organism, as if the organs were experienced as pure *intensities* capable of being linked together in an infinite number of ways. In *Naked Lunch,* Burroughs provides a vivid literary description of such a vital schizoid body:

> No organ is constant as regards either function or position . . . sex organs sprout everywhere . . . rectums open, defecate, and close . . . the entire organism changes color and consistency in split-second adjustments. . . . The human body is scandalously inefficient. Instead of a mouth and an anus to get out of order why not have one all-purpose

hole to eat *and* eliminate? We could seal up nose and mouth, fill in the stomach, make an air hole direct into the lungs where it should have been in the first place.[106]

In *Lenz*, George Büchner describes the stroll of a schizophrenic whose intensive organs enter into a becoming with all the elements of nature, to the point where the distinction between self and nonself, man and nature, inside and outside, no longer has any meaning.[107] D. H. Lawrence painted the picture of a similar body without organs in *Fantasia of the Unconscious*, with the sun and the moon as its two poles, and its various planes, sections, and plexuses.[108] But schizophrenics also experience states in which this anorganic functioning of the organs stops dead, as the intensities approach the limit where intensity equals zero. It is here that the body without organs becomes a model of Death, coextensive with Life. Authors of horror stories know this well, when they appeal to the terror not of the organic corpse, but of the catatonic schizophrenic: the organism remains, with its vacant gaze and rigid postures, but the vital intensity of the body is suspended, frozen, blocked. These two poles of the body without organs—the vital anorganic functioning of the organs and their frozen catatonic stasis, with all the variations of attraction and repulsion that exist between them —translate the entire anguish of the schizophrenic. For schizophrenics experience these naked intensities in a pure and almost unendurable state: beneath the hallucinations of the senses ("I see," "I hear") and the deliriums of thought ("I think"), there is something more profound, a feeling of intensity, that is, a *becoming* or a transition ("I feel"). A gradient is crossed, a threshold is surpassed or retreated from, a migration is brought about: "I feel that I am becoming woman," "I feel that I am becoming god," "I feel that I am becoming pure matter." When Judge Schreber, in a famous case analyzed by Freud, says he is becoming a woman and can feel breasts on his naked torso, he is expressing a lived emotion that neither resembles nor represents breasts but rather designates a zone of pure intensity on his body without organs.[109]

Now according to Deleuze and Guattari, what we call a "delirium" is the general matrix by which the intensities and becomings of the body without organs directly invest the sociopolitical field. One of the essential theses of *Anti-Oedipus* is that delirious formations are not reducible to the father-mother-child coordinates of the Oedipus complex; they are neither familial nor personal but world-historical: it's the Russians that worry the schizo, or the Chinese; his mouth is dry, someone buggered him in the subway, there are spermatozoa swimming everywhere; it's Franco's fault, or the Jews'. . . . The great error of psychoanalysis was to have largely ignored the social, political, geographical, tribal, and, above all, *racial* content of delirium, or to have reduced it to the familial or personal. More importantly, for Deleuze, these delirious formations constitute "kernels of art," insofar as the artistic productions of the "mad" can themselves be seen as the construction of a body without organs with its own geopolitical and racial coordinates.[110] Artaud's "theater of cruelty" cannot be separated from his confrontation with the "races," and his confrontation with forces and religions of Mexico, all of which populate his body without organs. Rimbaud's "season in hell" cannot be separated from a becoming-Mongol or a becoming-Scandinavian, a vast "displacement of races and continents," the intensive feeling of being "a beast, a Negro, of an inferior race inferior for all eternity" ("'I am from a distant race: my ancestors were Scandinavians; they used to pierce their sides and drink their own blood.—I will make gashes on my entire body and tattoo it. I want to be as hideous as a Mongol.' . . . I dreamed of crusades, of unrecorded voyages of discovery, of republics with no history, of hushed-up religious wars, revolutions in customs, displacements of races and continents").[111] Zarathustra's "Grand Politics" cannot be separated from the life of the races that leads Nietzsche to say, "I'm not German, I'm Polish."[112] Delirium does not consist in identifying one's ego with various historical figures, but of identifying thresholds of intensity that are traversed on the body without organs with proper names. Nietzsche, for example, does not suddenly lose his reason and identify himself with strange personages; rather, his delirium passes through a series of intensive states that receive various proper names, some of which designate his allies, or manic rises in intensity (Prado, Lesseps, Chambige, "honest criminels"), others his enemies, or depressive falls in intensity (Caiaphus, William, Bismarck, the "antisemites")—a chaos of pure oscillations invested by "all the names of history" and not, as psychoanalysis would have it, by "the name of the father." Even when he is motionless, the schizophrenic undertakes vast voyages, but they are voyages in intensity: he crosses the desert of his body without organs, and along the way struggles against other races, destroys civilizations, becomes a woman, becomes God.

Deleuze and Guattari seem to go ever further. If the body without organs is the model of Life, and delirium is the process by which its intensities directly invest history and geography, then every literary work—and not merely the productions of the mad—can be analyzed clinically as constituting a kind of delirium. The question one must ask is, What are the regions of History and the Universe, what are the nations and races, that are invested by a given work of art? One can make a map of the rhizome it creates, a cartography of its body without organs. In *A Thousand Plateaus,* Deleuze and Guattari propose a brief cartographic sketch of American literature: in the East, there was a search for an American code and a recoding with Europe (Henry James, Eliot, Pound); in the South, an overcoding of the ruins of the slave system (Faulkner, Caldwell, O'Connor); in the North, a capitalist decoding (Dos Passos, Dreiser); but in the West, there was a profound line of flight, with its ever receding limits, its shifting and displaced frontier, its Indians and cultures, its madness (Kerouac, Kesey, the Beats). It is from this clinical viewpoint that Deleuze writes of the superiority of Anglo-American literature.[113] D. H. Lawrence reproached French literature for being *critical* of life rather than *creative* of life, filled with a mania for judging and being judged. But Anglo-American writers know how to leave, to push the process further, to follow a line of flight, to enter into a becoming that escapes the *ressentiment* of persons and the dominance of established orders. Yet Deleuze and Guattari constantly point to the ambiguity of such lines of flight. For is it not the destiny of literature, American and otherwise, to fail to complete the process, such that the line of flight becomes blocked or reaches an impasse (Kerouac's sad end, Céline's fascist ravings), or even turns into a pure line of demolition (Woolf's suicide, Fitzgerald's crack-up, Nietzsche's and Hölderlin's madness)?[114] Kerouac took a revolutionary "flight" (*On the Road*) with the soberest of means, but later immersed himself in a dream of a Great America and went off in search of his Breton ancestors of a superior race. Céline, after his great experimentations, became the victim of a delirium that communicated more and more with fascism and the paranoia of his father. In *Anti-Oedipus,* Deleuze and Guattari suggest that a "universal clinical theory" of literature as delirium would have to situate works of art between two poles: a "paranoic" pole, or literature as a disease, in which the intensities of the body without organs are invested in fascizing, moralizing, nationalist, and racist tendencies ("I am one of your kind, a superior race, an Aryan"); and a "schizophrenic" pole, or literature as the measure of health, which always pushes the process further, following the line of flight, invoking an impure and bastard race that resists everything that crushes and imprisons life ("I am a beast, a nigger . . . I am of an inferior race for all eternity").

4. *The "Minorization" of Politics* (Speech Acts and Fabulation). It is here that we confront Deleuze's conception of the political destiny of literature. Just as writers do not write with their egos, neither do they write "on behalf of" an already existing people or "address" themselves to a class or nation. When great artists such as Mallarmé, Rimbaud, Klee, Berg, or the Straubs evoke a people, what they find rather is that "the people are missing."[115] For Deleuze, this implies a new conception of the "revolutionary" potential of literature. The two great modern revolutions, the American and the Soviet, shared a belief in the finality of universal history in which "the people are already there," even if they exist in an oppressed or subjugated state, blind and unconscious, awaiting their actualization, their "becoming-conscious." America sought to create a revolution whose strength would lie in a *universal immigration,* a melting pot in which émigrés from all countries would be fused in a unanimist community, just as Russia sought to make a revolution whose strength would lie in a *universal proletarization,* a communist society of comrades without property or family. Hence the belief that literature, or even the cinema (Eisenstein's *October,* Griffith's *Birth of a Nation*), could become an art of the masses, a supremely revolutionary or democratic art. But the failure of the two revolutions, heralded by numerous factors (the Civil War and the fragmentation of the American people; Stalinism and the liquidation of the Soviets, which replaced the unanimity of peoples with the tyrannical unity of a party, and the subsequent breakup of the Soviet empire), would come to compromise this unanimist belief. In the cinema, it was the rise of Hitler that sounded the final death knell. Benjamin, and then Syberberg, showed how, in Nazism, the cinema, as the art of automatic movement, did not coincide with the "masses become subjects" but with the masses subjected and reduced to psychological automatons: politics as "art," Hitler as filmmaker (Riefenstahl's *Triumph of the Will*). If art was to find a political task, Deleuze argues, it would have to be on a new basis, that is, on the basis of this very fragmentation and breakup: not that of addressing an already existing people,

but of contributing to the invention of a people who are *missing*. Whitman had already noted that, in America, both the people and the writer confront a double problem: a collection of noncommunicating fragments or immigrants, and a tissue of shifting relations between them that must constantly be created or acquired. But these conditions were perhaps clearer in the third world, hidden as they were in the West by the mechanisms of power and the systems of majority. For when a colonizer proclaims, "There has never been a people here," the people necessarily enter into the conditions of a becoming, they must *invent themselves* in new conditions of struggle, and the task of a political literature is to contribute to the invention of this unborn people who do not yet have a language.[116]

If the people are missing, says Deleuze, it is precisely because they exist in the condition of a *minority*. In *Capitalism and Schizophrenia*, Deleuze and Guattari offer an analysis of the present state of capitalism not in terms of its contradictions and classes, but rather in terms of its "lines of flight" and its minorities.[117] The concept of the "minor" developed by Deleuze and Guattari is a complex one, having references that are musical, literary, and linguistic as well as juridical and political. In the political context, they argue, the difference between a majority and a minority is not a quantitative one. A majority is not defined by its large numbers, but by an ideal constant or standard measure by which it can be evaluated (for instance, white, Western, male, adult, reasonable, heterosexual, residing in cities, speaking a standard language . . .); any determination that deviates from this axiomatic model, by definition and regardless of number, will be considered minoritarian. "Man" constitutes a majority, for instance, even though men are less numerous than women or children; and minorities are frequently larger in number than the majority.[118] For Deleuze and Guattari, the true theoretical opposition is between those elements that enter into the class axiomatic of capitalism and those that elude or free themselves from this axiomatic (as "undecidable propositions" of the axiomatic, or nondenumerable multiplicities). It is true that minorities are "objectively" definable states—definable in terms of language, ethnicity, or sex, with their own territorialities. It is also true that minorities must necessarily struggle to become a majority—to be recognized, to have rights, to achieve an autonomous status, and so on (women's struggle for the vote, for abortion, for jobs; the struggle of the third world; the struggle of oppressed minorities in the East and West). But for Deleuze and Guattari, these struggles are also the index of another, coexistent and almost subterranean combat. For the majority is in fact an abstract standard that constitutes the analytic fact of "Nobody"; everyone, under some aspect or another, is caught up in a becoming-minor. Moreover, in a certain manner, one could say that it is the majority that implies a state of domination, and not the reverse, since it entails a subjection to the model; and that it is the process of becoming-minoritarian, as a universal figure, that constitutes what is called "autonomy."[119] A minority by definition has no model; *it is itself a becoming or a process*, in constant variation, and the power of a minority is not measured by its ability to enter and make itself felt within the majority system. Minorities have the potential of promoting compositions (connections, convergences, divergences) that do not pass by way of the captialist economy any more than they do the state formation. In their "Treatise on Nomadology—The War Machine," one of the most original and important texts in *A Thousand Plateaus*, Deleuze and Guattari attempt to describe the organizational conditions of social formations constructed along a line of flight, which are by nature variable and nomadic.[120] This is what they term the "minorization" of politics, insofar as minorities must be thought of as seeds or crystals of becoming whose value is to trigger uncontrollable movements within the mean or the majority.

If modern political literature and cinema can play a role in the constitution of minorities, it is because they are no longer undertaken on the basis of a "people" who are already there, awaiting their becoming conscious and the possibility of revolution. Rather, they are constituted on a set of impossibilities in which the people are missing, in which the only consciousness is the consciousness of violence, fragmentation, the betrayal of every revolution, the shattered state of the emotions and drives: an impasse in every direction. For Deleuze, this is what constitutes the new object of a political literature or cinema: the *intolerable,* that is, a lived actuality that at the same time testifies to the impossibility of living in such conditions. And minority writers and filmmakers, faced with an illiterate public and rampant deculturation, confront the same set of impasses in their work. On the one hand, they cannot simply appeal to the collective fictions and archaic myths of their people, since, as in Rocha's film *Black God and White Devil,* it is often these same myths (of prophetism and banditism) that cause the colonized to turn against themselves—and to intensify—the capitalist violence they

suffer from without (in this case, out of a need for idolization). Cultur-
ally, one could say that minorities are doubly colonized: by the stories,
films, television programs, and advertisements that are imposed on
them from without, but also by their own myths that have passed into
the service of the colonizer from within. Yet on the other hand, neither
can writers be content to produce individual utterances as invented
stories or fictions, for by appealing to their own privileged experience
("I in my position as . . ."), they break with the condition of the colonized and necessarily pass over to the side of the colonizers—even if
only aesthetically, through artistic influences. As Jean-Louis Comolli
puts it, writers and filmmakers take as their object a double impossibility: "the impossibility of escaping from the group and the impossibility
of being satisfied with it."[121]

Between these two impossibilities, however, Deleuze points to a
narrow path, one in which the artist takes real (and not fictional) characters and makes use of them as "intercessors," putting them in conditions in which they are caught in the "flagrant act" of "making up fictions," of "creating legends" or "story-telling" (Pierre Perrault, Glauber
Rocha, Jean Rouch). In the midst of an intolerable and unlivable situation, a becoming passes *between* the "people" who are missing and the
"I" of the author who is now absent, releasing a "pure speech act"
that is neither an impersonal myth nor a personal fiction, but a *collective utterance*—an utterance that expresses the impossibility of living
under domination, but thereby constitutes an act of resistance, and
functions as the prefiguration of the people who are missing. The author takes a step toward real characters, but these characters in turn
take a step toward the author: a double becoming. Such collective utterances constitute what Pasolini termed *free indirect discourse,* that is,
a newly created speech act that sets itself up as an autonomous form, a
pure event that effectuates two acts of subjectivation simultaneously,
as if the author could express himself only by becoming another
through a real character, and the character in turn could act and speak
only if his gestures and words were being reported by a third party.[122]
When an author produces a statement in this way, it occurs necessarily
as a function of a national, political, and social community—even if
the objective conditions of this community are not yet given for the
moment *except* in the literary enunciation. In literature, Deleuze frequently appeals to the texts of Kafka (in central Europe) and Melville
(in America) that present literature as the collective utterance of a

minor people who find their expression in and through the singularity of the writer, who in his very solitude is all the more in a position to express potential forces, and to be a true collective agent, a leaven or catalyst (as Klee says, "We can do no more").[123] Under these conditions, the speech act appears as a true *genetic element*, a virtuality that is capable of linking up, little by little, with other speech acts so as to constitute the free indirect discourse of a people or a minority, even if they as yet exist only as the potential of "diabolical powers to come or revolutionary forces to be constructed."[124]

In a different context, this is what Bergson termed "fabulation," which he saw as a visionary faculty that consists in creating gods and giants, "semi-personal powers or effective presences"; though it is first exercised in religion, Deleuze suggests that this is a faculty that is freely developed in art and literature, a mythmaking or fabulating function that brings *real* parties together to produce collective utterances or speech acts as the germ of a people to come. "We ought to take up Bergson's notion of fabulation," writes Deleuze, "and give it a political meaning."[125] Minority writers may find themselves surrounded by the ideology of a colonizer, the myths of the colonized, the discourse of intellectuals, and the information of the communications media that threatens to subsume them all; this is the material they have to work on. But "fabulation" is a function that extracts from them a pure speech act, a creative storytelling that is, as it were, the obverse side of the dominant myths and fictions, an act of resistance whose political impact is immediate and inescapable, and that creates a line of flight on which a minority discourse and a people can be constitued. "A minority never exists ready-made, it is only formed on lines of flight, which are also its way of advancing or attacking."[126] This fundamental affinity between the work of art and a people who are missing may never be entirely clear. There is no work of art that does not appeal to a people that does not yet exist. But artists, it is true, can only *invoke* a people; although their need for a people goes to the very heart of what they do, they cannot *create* a people, and an oppressed people cannot concern itself with art. Yet when a people creates itself, Deleuze suggests, through its own resources and sufferings, it does so in a way that links up with something in art, or rather that links up art with what it was lacking. Fabulation in this sense is a function common to both the people and art.

5. The "Stuttering" of Language (Syntax and Style). Finally, for Deleuze, the process of "becoming-minor" also describes the effect that literature has on language. Proust said that great literature opens up a kind of foreign language within the language in which it is written, as if the writer were writing as a foreigner or minority within his own language.[127] This foreign language is not another language, even a marginalized one, but rather the becoming-minor of language itself. Or as Deleuze puts it in his essay "He Stuttered," the writer introduces into language a stuttering, which is not simply a stuttering in speech, but a stuttering of the language itself.[128] In this linguistic context, Deleuze and Guattari argue that the terms *major* and *minor* do not qualify two different languages, but rather two different treatments of language, two usages or functions of the same language, and link up in a direct manner with the political question of minorities.

This is not to deny the reality of the distinction between a major language and a minor language, between a language of power and a language of the people. Minorities and immigrants are often bilingual or multilingual, living in a "major" language that they often speak poorly, and with which they have difficult political relations; in some cases, they may no longer even know their own "minor" language or mother tongue. But this distinction requires a *genetic* account: under what conditions does a language assume power in a country, or even on a worldwide scale? Conversely, by what means can one ward off linguistic power? It is not enough to say that victors impose their language on the vanquished (though this is usually the case), for the mechanisms of linguistic power are more subtle and diffuse, passing through extensible and reversible functions, which are the object of active political struggles and even microstruggles. Henri Gobard, in his book *L'aliénation linguistique,* for which Deleuze wrote a short preface, has attempted to go beyond the simple major-minor duality by distinguishing four different types of language: *vernacular* (maternal or territorial languages of rural origin), *vehicular* (languages of commerce and diplomacy, which are primarily urban), *referential* (national or cultural languages that operate through a recollection or reconstruction of the past), and *mythic* (languages that refer to a spiritual, magical, or religious domain).[129] More precisely, these distinctions refer to different *functions* that can be assumed (or lost) by diverse languages in concrete situations, or by a single language over the course of time, each with its own mechanisms of power. For instance, Latin, as a language of power, was a vehicular language in Europe before becoming a referential or cultural language, and then a mythic one. When fundamentalists protest against having the Mass said in a vernacular language, they are trying to prevent Latin from being robbed of its mythic or religious functions; similarly, classicists bemoan the fact that Latin has been stripped of its referential or cultural function, since the educational forms of power it once exercised have been replaced by other forms. The present imperialism of American English, as a worldwide linguistic power, is due not only to its status as today's vehicular language, but also to the fact that it has managed to infiltrate various cultural, mythic, and even vernacular functions in other languages (hence the purist's denunciations of "Franglais," English contaminations of the contemporary French vernacular).

But these various mechanisms of power, by which one language acquires an imperialist power over others, are at the same time accompanied by a very different tendency. For the more a language acquires the characteristics of a major language, the more it tends to be affected by internal variations that transpose it into a "minor" language. English, because of its very hegemony, is constantly being worked on from within by the minorities of the world, who nibble away at that hegemony and create the possibility of new mythic functions, new cultural references, new vernacular languages with their own uses: British English is set in variation by Gaelic and Irish English; American English is set in variation by black English and various "ghetto languages," which cannot be defined simply as a sum of mistakes or infractions against "standard" English. Minor languages are not simply sublanguages (dialects or idiolects), but express the potential of the major language to enter into a becoming-minoritarian in all its dimensions and elements. Such movements, to be sure, have their own political ambiguities, since they can mix together revolutionary aspirations with reactionary and even fascistic tendencies (archaisms, neoterritorialities, regionalisms). Moreover, from a political viewpoint, "it is difficult to see how the upholders of a minor language can operate if not by giving it (if only by writing in it) a constancy and homogeneity making it a locally major language capable of forcing official recognition (hence the political role of writers who assert the rights of a minor language)."[130] The acquisition of power by a language and the becoming-minor of that language, in other words, are coexistent movements that are constantly passing and converting into each other in both directions. In this manner, Deleuze and Guattari, following Gobard, propose a kind of "geo-linguistics," a "micro-politics" of language (in Foucault's sense), in which the internal functions of language are inseparable from incessant movements of deterritorialization and reterritorialization.

What then does it mean to speak of a "minor literature"? Many of the writers that interest Deleuze are indeed those that find themselves in situations of bi- or multilingualism: Kafka, a Czech Jew writing in German; Beckett, an Irishman writing in French and English; Luca, a Romanian writing in French. And it was Kafka who spoke most forcefully of the set of linguistic "impossibilities" that this situation imposed on him as a writer: the impossibility of *not* writing, "because national consciousness, uncertain or oppressed, necessarily exists by means of literature"; the impossibility of writing *other* than in the dominant language of German, because the Prague Jews had forgotten or repressed their native Czech vernacular, viewed Yiddish with disdain or suspicion, and could only dream of Hebrew as the mythic language of Zionism; the impossibility of writing *in* German, not only because of its standardized and vehicular status as a "paper language," but also because the "deterritorialized" elements introduced by Prague German into Middle-High German of Vienna and Berlin threatened its cultural function ("a withered vocabulary, an incorrect use of prepositions, the abuse of the pronomial, the employment of malleable verbs," and so on).[131] For Deleuze, however, the situation described by Kafka is the situation faced by all writers, even those who are not bilingual; creation, he says, necessarily takes place in such choked passages: "We have to see creation as tracing a path between impossibilities. . . . A creator who isn't grabbed around the throat by a set of impossibilities is no creator. A creator's someone who creates their own impossibilities, and thereby creates possibilities. . . . Without a set of impossibilities, you won't have a line of flight, the exit that is creation, the power of falsity that is truth."[132] And Kafka's solution to this problem, his way out of the impasse, also has a validity that extends beyond his own situation. Rather than writing in Czech, Yiddish, or Hebrew, he chose to write in the German language of Prague, with all its poverty, and to push it even further in the direction of deterritorialization, "to the point of sobriety." Rather than writing in a minor language, he instead invented a minor *use* of the major language.

A minor literature, in other words, is not necessarily a literature written in a minor or marginalized language; for Deleuze, the term "minor" does not refer to specific literatures but rather to the revolutionary conditions for every literature, even (and especially) in the midst of a great or established literature: "Only the possibility of setting up a minor practice of a major language from within allows one to define popular literature, marginal literature, and so on."[133] As Deleuze and Guattari argue in a chapter of *A Thousand Plateaus* entitled "Postulates of Linguistics," the essential distinction is between two different treatments or uses of language, a major and a minor use. Language is by nature a heterogenous and variable reality, but the variables of language can be treated in two different manners. Either one can carve out a homogeneous or standard system from a language by extracting a set of *constants* from the variables or by determining *constant relations* between them, thereby relegating pragmatics to external factors (Chomsky); or one can relate the variables of language to inherent lines of *continuous variation,* thereby making pragmatics the presupposition of all the other dimensions of language (Labov). The performative "I swear!," for example, is a very different statement depending on whether it is said by a son to his father, by a lover to his fiancée, or by a witness to a judge. But this variability can be interpreted in two different ways: *either* the statement can be said to remain constant in principle, its variations being produced by de facto and nonlinguistic circumstances external to the linguistic system; *or* one could also say that each effectuation of the statement is an actualized variable of a virtual line of continuous variation *immanent* to the system, a line that remains continuous regardless of the discontinuous leaps made by the statement, and that uproots the statement from its status as a constant and produces its placing-in-variation. The first is the major treatment of language, in which the linguistic system appears in principle as a system in equilibrium, defined by its syntactical, semantic, or phonological constants; the second is the minor treatment, in which the system itself appears in perpetual disequilibrium or bifurcation, defined by pragmatic *use* of these constants in relation to a continuous internal variation. It may be that the *scientific* study of language, in order to guarantee the constancy of its object, requires the extraction of a systematic structure from language (though *A Thousand Plateaus* contains an interesting analysis of "minor sciences" that do not operate by means of this type of formalization).[134] But Deleuze and Guattari suggest that this scientific model of language is inextricably linked with its political model, and the mechanisms by which a language becomes a language of power, a dominant or major language, homogenized, centralized, and standardized. When schoolteachers teach their students a rule of grammar, for example, they are not simply communicating a piece of information to them, but are transmitting an order or a command, since the ability to formulate grammatically correct sentences ("competence") is a prerequisite for any submission to social laws. "The scientific enterprise of extracting constants and constant relations," Deleuze and Guattari write, "is always coupled with the political enterprise of imposing them on speakers."[135] This is why the problem of becoming-minor is both a political and an artistic problem: "the problem of minorities, the problem of a minor literature, but also a problem for all of us: How to tear a minor literature away from its own language, allowing it to challenge the language and making it follow a sober revolutionary path?"[136]

For Deleuze, then, the "minor" use of language involves taking any linguistic variable—phonological, syntactical or grammatical, semantic—and placing it in variation, following the virtual line of continuous variation that subtends the entire language, and that is itself apertinent, asyntactic or agrammatical, and asemantic. It is through this minor use of language that literature brings about a decomposition or even destruction of the maternal language, but also the creation of a new minor language within the writer's own language. Many of the essays collected in *Essays Critical and Clinical* analyze the specific procedures utilized by various authors to make language "stutter" in its syntax or grammar: the schizophrenic procedures of Roussel, Brisset, and Wolfson, which constitute the very process of their psychoses; the poetic procedures of Jarry and Heidegger, who transform and transmute a living language by reactivating a dead language inside it; e. e. cummings's agrammaticalities ("he danced his did"), which stand at the limit of a series of ordinary grammatical variables; and the deviant syntax of Artaud's *cris-souffles* ("ratara ratara ratara / Atara tatara rana / Otara otara katara"), which are pure intensities that mark a limit of language.[137] (In other contexts, Deleuze analyses the phonetic stuttering of language in the theater, as in Robert Wilson's whispering, without definite pitch, or Carmelo Bene's ascending and descending variations).[138] Such writers take the elements of language and submit them to a treatment of continuous variation, out of which they extract new linguistic possibilities; they invent a minor use of language, much as in music, where the minor mode is derived from dynamic combinations in perpetual disequilibrium. In a sense, this procedure of placing-in-variation is the most natural thing in the world: it is what we call a "style." Style is a set of variations in language, a kind of modulation, and it is through style that language is pushed toward its own limit, and strains toward something that is no longer linguistic, but which language alone makes possible (such as the affects and percepts that have no existence apart from the words and syntax of the writer).[139] "This is what style is," write Deleuze and Guattari, "the moment when language is no longer defined by what it says, but by what causes it to move, to flow. . . . For literature is like schizophrenia: a process and not a goal . . . a pure process that fulfills itself, and that never ceases to reach fulfillment as it proceeds—art as 'experimentation.'" Likewise, reading a text is never an act of interpretation, it "is never a scholarly exercise in search of what is signified, still less a highly textual exercise in search of a signifier"; it too is an act of experimentation, "a productive use of the literary machine . . . a schizoid exercise that extracts from the text its revolutionary force."[140]

Deleuze's "critique et clinique" project, in the end, can be characterized by three fundamental components: (1) the function of the proper name; (2) the nonpersonal "multiplicity" or "assemblage" designated by the name; and (3) the active "lines of flight" of which these multiplicities are constituted. The first two components define what we have called the symptomatological method. For Deleuze, writers are like clinicians or diagnosticians who isolate a particular "possibility of life," a certain way of being or mode of existence whose symptomatology is set forth in their work. In these conditions, the proper name refers not to the person of the author, but to the constellation of signs and symptoms that are grouped together in the work itself. The literary technique and style of the writer (the critical) is directly linked to the creation of a differential table of vital signs (the clinical), so that one can speak of a clinical "beckettism," "proustism," or "kafkaism" just as one speaks of a clinical "sadism" or "masochism." But the symptomatological method is only one aspect of Deleuze's project. The deeper philosophical question concerns the conditions that make possible this production of new modes of existence, that is, the ontological principle of Life as a nonorganic and impersonal power. We have seen the two aspects of this active power of Life: on the one hand, it is a power of abstraction capable of producing elements that are in themselves asignifying, acosmic, asubjective, anorganic, agrammatical, and asyntactic (singularities and events, affects and percepts, intensities and becomings) and placing them in a state of continuous variation; on the other hand, it is a power of invention capable of creating ever new relations between these differential or genetic elements (syntheses of singularities, blocks of becomings, continuums of intensities). These two ontological powers of Life—the production of variation and the selection and synthesis of variants—are for Deleuze the indispensable conditions of every creation.

Deleuze describes the artistic activity of the writer in the same terms. "The aim of writing," he says, "is to carry life to the state of a non-personal power."[141] The writer, like each of us, begins with the multiplicities that have invented him or her as a formed subject, in an actualized world, with an organic body, in a given political order, having learned a certain language. But at its highest point, writing, as an activity, follows the abstract movement of a line of flight that extracts or produces differential elements from these multiplicities of lived experience and makes them function as variables on an immanent "plane of composition." "This is what it's like on the plane of immanence: multiplicities fill it, singularities connect with one another, processes or becomings unfold, intensities rise and fall."[142] The task of the writer is to establish nonpreexistent relations between these variables in order to make them function together in a singular and nonhomogeneous whole, and thus to participate in the construction of "new possibilities of life": the invention of new compositions in language (style and syntax), the formation of new blocks of sensation (affects and percepts), the production of new modes of existence (intensities and becomings), the constitution of a people (speech acts and fabulation), the creation of a world (singularities and events). The negative terms we have used to describe the above rubrics (destruction, dissolution, disintegration, and so on) are therefore only partial characterizations, since they are merely the necessary propaedeutic to this positive activity of creation and invention. "To be present at the dawn of the world . . ."

It is this ontological and creative power of Life, finally, that functions as the ethical principle of Deleuze's philosophy. For what constitutes the health or activity of a mode of existence is precisely its capacity to construct such lines of flight, to affirm the power of life, to transform itself depending on the forces it encounters (the "ethical" vision of the world). A reactive or sickly mode of existence, by contrast, cut off from its power of action or transformation, can only judge life in terms of its exhaustion or from the viewpoint of the higher values it erects against Life (the "moral" vision of the world). "Critique et clinique," from start to finish, is as much an ethical project as it is an aesthetic one. In this regard, perhaps the most important piece included in *Essays Critical and Clinical,* in terms of Deleuze's own oeuvre, is the programmatic essay entitled "To Have Done with Judgment."[143] For Deleuze, it is never a question of *judging* a work of art in terms of transcendent or universal criteria, but of *evaluating* it clinically in terms of its "vitality," its "tenor of Life": Does the work carry the process of Life to this state of an impersonal power? Or does it interrupt the process, stop its movement, and become blocked in the *ressentiment* of persons, the rigors of organic organization, the clichés of a standard language, the dominance of an established order, the world "as it is," the judgment of God? The renunciation of judgment does not deprive one of the means of distinguishing the "good" and the "bad." On the contrary, good and bad are both states of the becoming of Life, and can be evaluated by criteria that are strictly immanent to the mode of existence or work of art itself.[144] Life does not function in Deleuze's philosophy as a transcendent principle of judgment but as an immanent process of production or creation; it is neither an origin nor a goal, neither an *arche* nor a *telos,* but a pure process that always operates in the middle, *au milieu,* and proceeds by means of experimentations and unforeseen becomings. Judgment operates with preexisting criteria that can never apprehend the creation of the new, and what is of value can only come into existence by "defying judgment."

It is sometimes said that we must learn from life and not bury ourselves in books, and in a certain sense this is no doubt true. Yet we must also say that art and literature have no other object than Life, and that a "passage of Life" can only be seen or felt in a process of creation, which gives the nonorganic and impersonal power of Life a consistency and autonomy of its own, and draws us into its own becoming. "Art is never an end in itself," write Deleuze and Guattari. "It is only an instrument for tracing lines of lives, that is to say, all these real becomings that are not simply produced *in* art, all these active flights that do not consist in fleeing *into* art . . . but rather sweep it away with them toward the realms of the asignifying, the asubjective."[145] This is the point at which "critique" and "clinique" become one and the same thing, when life ceases to be personal and the work ceases to be merely literary or textual: a life of pure immanence.[146]

Preface to the French Edition

This collection of texts, some of which appear here for the first time, others of which have already been published elsewhere, is organized around certain problems. The problem of *writing:* writers, as Proust says, invent a new language within language, a foreign language, as it were. They bring to light new grammatical or syntactic powers. They force language outside its customary furrows, they make it *delirious* [*délirer*]. But the problem of writing is also inseparable from a problem of *seeing* and *hearing:* in effect, when another language is created within language, it is language in its entirety that tends toward an "asyntactic," "agrammatical" limit, or that communicates with its own outside.

The limit is not outside language, it is the outside *of* language. It is made up of visions and auditions that are not of language, but which language alone makes possible. There is also a painting and a music characteristic of writing, like the effects of colors and sonorities that rise up above words. It is through words, between words, that one sees and hears. Beckett spoke of "drilling holes" in language in order to see or hear "what was lurking behind." One must say of every writer: he is a seer, a hearer, "ill seen ill said," she is a colorist, a musician.

These visions, these auditions are not a private matter but form the figures of a history and a geography that are ceaselessly reinvented. It is delirium that invents them, as a *process* driving words from one end of the universe to the other. They are events at the edge of language. But when delirium falls back into the *clinical state,* words no longer open out onto anything, we no longer hear or see anything through them except a night whose history, colors, and songs have been lost. Literature is a health.

These problems mark out a set of paths. The texts presented here, and the authors considered, are such paths. Some pieces are short, others are longer, but they all intersect, passing by the same places, coming together or dividing off, each of them giving a view upon the others. Some of them are impasses closed off by illness. Every work is a voyage, a journey, but one that travels along this or that external path only by virtue of the internal paths and trajectories that compose it, that constitute its landscape or its concert.

1
Literature and Life

To write is certainly not to impose a form (of expression) on the matter of lived experience. Literature rather moves in the direction of the ill-formed or the incomplete, as Gombrowicz said as well as practiced. Writing is a question of becoming, always incomplete, always in the midst of being formed, and goes beyond the matter of any livable or lived experience. It is a process, that is, a passage of Life that traverses both the livable and the lived. Writing is inseparable from becoming: in writing, one becomes-woman, becomes-animal or vegetable, becomes-molecule to the point of becoming-imperceptible. These becomings may be linked to each other by a particular line, as in Le Clezio's novels; or they may coexist at every level, following the doorways, thresholds, and zones that make up the entire universe, as in Lovecraft's powerful oeuvre. Becoming does not move in the other direction, and one does not become Man, insofar as man presents himself as a dominant form of expression that claims to impose itself on all matter, whereas woman, animal, or molecule always has a component of flight that escapes its own formalization. The shame of being a man—is there any better reason to write? Even when it is a woman who is becoming, she has to become-woman, and this becoming has nothing to do with a state she could claim as her own. To become is not to attain a form (identification, imitation, Mimesis) but to find the zone of proximity, indiscernibility, or indifferentiation where one can no longer be distinguished from *a* woman, *an* animal, or *a* molecule—neither imprecise nor general, but unforeseen and nonpreexistent, singularized out of a population rather than determined in a form. One can institute a zone of proximity with anything, on the condition that one creates the literary means for doing so. André Dhôtel, for instance, makes use of the aster: something passes between the sexes, the genera, or the kingdoms.[1] Becoming is always "between" or "among": a woman between women, or an animal among others. But the power of the indefinite article is effected only if the term in becoming is stripped of the formal characteristics that make it say *the* ("the animal in front of you . . ."). When Le Clezio becomes-Indian, it is always as an incomplete Indian who does not know "how to cultivate corn or carve a dugout canoe"; rather than acquiring formal characteristics, he enters a zone of proximity.[2] It is the same, in Kafka, with the swimming champion who does not know how to swim. All writing involves an athleticism, but far from reconciling literature with sports or turning writing into an Olympic event, this athleticism is exercised in flight and in the breakdown of the organic body—an athlete in bed, as Michaux put it. One becomes animal all the more when the animal dies; and contrary to the spiritualist prejudice, it is the animal who knows how to die, who has a sense or premonition of death. Literature begins with a porcupine's death, according to Lawrence, or with the death of a mole, in Kafka: "our poor little red feet outstretched for tender sympathy."[3] As Moritz said, one writes for dying calves.[4] Language must devote itself to reaching these feminine, animal, molecular detours, and every detour is a becoming-mortal. There are no straight lines, neither in things nor in language. Syntax is the set of necessary detours that are created in each case to reveal the life in things.

To write is not to recount one's memories and travels, one's loves and griefs, one's dreams and fantasies. It is the same thing to sin through an excess of reality as through an excess of the imagination. In both cases it is the eternal daddy-mommy, an Oedipal structure that is projected onto the real or introjected into the imaginary. In this infantile conception of literature, what we seek at the end of the voyage, or at the heart of a dream, is a father. We write for our father-mother. Marthe Robert has pushed this infantilization or "psychoanalization" of literature to an extreme, leaving the novelist no other choice than the Bastard or the Foundling.[5] Even becoming-animal is not safe from an Oedipal reduction of the type "my cat, my dog." As Lawrence says, "If I am a giraffe, and the ordinary Englishmen who write about me are nice, well-behaved dogs, there it is, the animals are different. . . . The animal I am you instinctively dislike."[6] As a general rule, fantasies simply treat the indefinite as a mask for a personal or a possessive: "*a* child is being beaten" is quickly transformed into "my father beat me." But literature takes the opposite path, and exists only when it discovers beneath apparent persons the power of an impersonal—which is not a generality but a singularity at the highest point: a man, a woman, a beast, a stomach, a child . . . It is not the first two persons that function as the condition for literary enunciation; literature begins only when a third person is born in us that strips us of the power to say "I" (Blanchot's "neuter").[7] Of course, literary characters are perfectly individuated, and are neither vague nor general; but all their individual traits elevate them to a vision that carries them off in an indefinite, like a becoming that is too powerful for them: Ahab and the vision of Moby-Dick. The Miser is not a type, but on the contrary his individual traits (to love a young woman, etc.) make him accede to a vision: he *sees* gold, in such a way that he is sent racing along a witch's line where he gains the power of the indefinite—*a* miser . . . , *some* gold, more gold . . . There is no literature without fabulation, but as Bergson was able to see, fabulation—the fabulating function—does not consist in imagining or projecting an ego. Rather, it attains these visions, it raises itself to these becomings and powers.

We do not write with our neuroses. Neuroses or psychoses are not passages of life, but states into which we fall when the process is interrupted, blocked, or plugged up. Illness is not a process but a stopping of the process, as in "the Nietzsche case." Moreover, the writer as such is not a patient but rather a physician, the physician of himself and of the world. The world is the set of symptoms whose illness merges with man. Literature then appears as an enterprise of health: not that the writer would necessarily be in good health (there would be the same ambiguity here as with athleticism), but he possesses an irresistible and delicate health that stems from what he has seen and heard of things too big for him, too strong for him, suffocating things whose passage exhausts him, while nonetheless giving him the becomings that a dominant and substantial health would render impossible.[8] The writer returns from what he has seen and heard with bloodshot eyes and pierced eardrums. What health would be sufficient to liberate life wherever it is imprisoned by and within man, by and within organisms and genera? It is like Spinoza's delicate health, while it lasted, bearing witness until the end to a new vision whose passage it remained open to.

Health as literature, as writing, consists in inventing a people who are missing. It is the task of the fabulating function to invent a people. We do not write with memories, unless it is to make them the origin and collective destination of a people to come still ensconced in its betrayals and repudiations. American literature has an exceptional power to produce writers who can recount their own memories, but as those of a universal people composed of immigrants from all countries. Thomas Wolfe "inscribes all of America in writing insofar as it can be found in the experience of a single man."[9] This is not exactly a people called upon to dominate the world. It is a minor people, eternally minor, taken up in a becoming-revolutionary. Perhaps it exists only in the atoms of the writer, a bastard people, inferior, dominated, always in becoming, always incomplete. *Bastard* no longer designates a familial state, but the process or drift of the races. I am a beast, a Negro of an inferior race for all eternity. This is the *becoming* of the writer. Kafka (for central Europe) and Melville (for America) present literature as the collective enunciation of a minor people, or of all minor peoples, who find their expression only in and through the writer.[10] Though it always refers to singular agents [*agents*], literature is a collective assemblage [*agencement*] of enunciation. Literature is delirium, but delirium is not a father-mother affair: there is no delirium that does not pass through peoples, races, and tribes, and that does not haunt universal history. All delirium is world-historical, "a displacement of races and continents."[11] Literature is delirium, and as such its destiny is played out between the two poles of delirium. Delirium is a disease, the disease par excellence, whenever it erects a race it claims is pure and dominant. But it is the measure of health when it invokes this oppressed bastard race that ceaselessly stirs beneath dominations, resisting everything that crushes and imprisons, a race that is outlined in relief in literature as process. Here again, there is always the risk that a diseased state will interrupt the process or becoming; health and athleticism both confront the same ambiguity, the constant risk that a delirium of domination will be mixed with a bastard delirium, pushing literature toward a larval fascism, the disease against which it fights—even if this means diagnosing the fascism within itself and fighting against itself. The ultimate aim of literature is to set free, in the delirium, this creation of a health or this invention of a people, that is, a possibility of life. To write for this people who are missing . . . ("for" means less "in the place of" than "for the benefit of").

We can see more clearly the effect of literature on language. As Proust says, it opens up a kind of foreign language within language, which is neither another language nor a rediscovered patois, but a becoming-other of language, a minorization of this major language, a delirium that carries it off, a witch's line that escapes the dominant system. Kafka makes the swimming champion say: I speak the same language as you, and yet I don't understand a single word you're saying. Syntactic creation or style—this is the becoming of language. The creation of words or neologisms is worth nothing apart from the effects of syntax in which they are developed. So literature already presents two aspects: through the creation of syntax, it brings about not only a decomposition or destruction of 'the maternal language, but also the invention of a new language within language. "The only way to defend language is to attack it. . . . Every writer is obliged to create his or her own language . . ."[12] Language seems to be seized by a delirium, which forces it out of its usual furrows. As for the third aspect, it stems from the fact that a foreign language cannot be hollowed out in one language without language as a whole in turn being toppled or pushed to a limit, to an outside or reverse side that consists of Visions and Auditions that no longer belong to any language. These visions are not fantasies, but veritable Ideas that the writer sees and hears in the interstices of language, in its intervals. They are not interruptions of the process, but breaks that form part of it, like an eternity that can only be revealed in a becoming, or a landscape that only appears in movement. They are not outside language, but the outside of language. The writer as seer and hearer, the aim of literature: it is the passage of life within language that constitutes Ideas.

These three aspects, which are in perpetual movement, can be seen clearly in Artaud: the fall of letters in the decomposition of the maternal language (R, T . . .); their incorporation into a new syntax or in new names with a syntactic import, creators of a language ("eTReTé"); and, finally, breath-words, the asyntactical limit toward which all language tends. And even in Céline—we cannot avoid saying it, so acutely do we feel it: *Journey to the End of the Night,* or the decomposition of the maternal language; *Death on the Installment Plan,* with its new syntax as a language within language; and *Guignol's Band,* with its suspended exclamations as the limit of language, as explosive visions and sonorities. In order to write, it may perhaps be necessary for the maternal language to be odious, but only so that a syntactic creation can open up a kind of foreign language in it, and language as a whole can reveal its outside, beyond all syntax. We sometimes congratulate writers, but they know that they are far from having achieved their becoming, far from having attained the limit they set for themselves, which ceaselessly slips away from them. To write is also to become something other than a writer. To those who ask what literature is, Virginia Woolf responds: To whom are you speaking of writing? The writer does not speak about it, but is concerned with something else.

If we consider these criteria, we can see that, among all those who make books with a literary intent, even among the mad, there are very few who can call themselves writers.

2

Louis Wolfson; or, The Procedure

Louis Wolfson, author of the book *Le schizo et les langues*, calls himself "the student of schizophrenic language," "the mentally ill student," "the student of demented idioms," or, in his reformed writing, "*le jeune öme sqizofrène.*"[1] This schizophrenic impersonal form has several meanings, and for its author does not simply indicate the emptiness of his own body. It concerns a combat in which the hero can apprehend himself only through a kind of anonymity analogous to that of the "young soldier." It also concerns a scientific undertaking in which the student has no identity except as a phonetic or molecular combination. Finally, for the author, it is less a matter of narrating what he is feeling and thinking than of saying in exact terms what he is doing. One of the great originalities of this book is that it sets forth a protocol of experimentation or activity. Wolfson's second book, *Ma mère musicienne est morte*, will be presented as a double book precisely because it is interspersed with the protocols of his cancerous mother's illness.[2]

The author is American but the books are written in French, for reasons that will soon become obvious. For what the student spends his time doing is translating, and he does so in accordance with certain rules. His procedure is as follows: given a word from the maternal language, he looks for a foreign word with a similar meaning that has common sounds or phonemes (preferably in French, German, Russian, or Hebrew, the four principal languages studied by the author). For example, *Where?* will be translated as *Wo? Hier? où? ici?*, or better yet, as *Woher*. *Tree* will produce *Tere*, which phonetically becomes *Dere* and leads to the Russian *Derevo*. Thus, an ordinary maternal sentence will be analyzed in terms of its phonetic elements and movements so that it can be converted into a sentence, in one or more foreign languages, which is similar to it in sound and meaning. The operation must be done as quickly as possible, given the urgency of the situation; but it also requires a significant amount of time, given the resistances offered by each word, the inexact meanings that emerge at every stage of the conversion, and above all the necessity of drawing up phonetic rules for each case that are applicable to other transformations (the adventures of *believe,* for example, will take up forty pages). It is as if there are two circuits of transformation that coexist and interpenetrate each other, the first taking up as little time as possible, the second covering as much linguistic space as possible.

Such is the general procedure: the phrase *Don't trip over the wire* becomes *Tu'nicht tréb über èth hé Zwirn.* The initial sentence is in English, but the final one is a simulacrum of a sentence that borrows from various languages: German, French, Hebrew—a "tour de babil." It not only makes use of rules of transformation (from *d* to *t,* from *p* to *b,* from *v* to *b*), but also rules of inversion (since the English *wire* is not sufficiently invested by the German *Zwirn,* the Russian *prolovka* will be invoked, which turns *wir* into *riv,* or rather *rov*).

Now in order to overcome resistances and difficulties of this kind, the general procedure has to be perfected in two different directions. On the one hand, it moves toward an amplified procedure, grounded in "the idea of genius to associate words more freely." The conversion of an English word, for example, *early,* can now be sought in French words and phrases that are associated with "tôt" and include the consonants *R* or *L* (*suR-Le-champ, de bonne heuRe, matinaLement, diLigemment, dévoRer L'espace*); or *tired* will be converted at the same time into the French *faTigué, exTénué, CouRbaTure, RenDu,* the German *maTT, KapuTT, eRschöpfT, eRmüdeT,* and so on. On the other hand, it moves toward an evolved procedure. In this case, it is no longer a matter of analyzing or even abstracting certain phonetic elements from an English word, but of forming the word in several independent modes. Thus, among the terms frequently encountered on food labels, we not only find *vegetable oil,* which does not pose many problems, but also *vegetable shortening,* which remains irreducible to the ordinary method: what causes the difficulty is *SH, R, T,* and *N.* It will therefore be necessary to render the word monstrous and grotesque, to make it echo three times, to triple its initial sound (*shshshortening*) in order to block the first *SH* with *N* (the Hebrew *chemenn*), the second *SH* with an equivalent of *T* (the German *Schmalz*), and the third *SH* with *R* (the Russian *jir*).

Psychosis is inseparable from a variable linguistic procedure. The procedure is the very process of the psychosis. The entire procedure of the student of languages presents striking analogies with the famous "procedure," itself schizophrenic, of the poet Raymond Roussel. Roussel worked within his maternal language, French; he too converted an initial sentence into another sentence with similar sounds and phonemes, but one with a completely different meaning (*les lettres du blanc sur les bandes du vieux billard* and *les lettres du blanc sur les bandes du vieux pillard*). A first direction gave the amplified procedure, in which words associated in the first series took on another, related meaning in the second (*queue de billard* and *robe à traîne du pillard*). A second direction led to the evolved procedure, in which the original sentence was converted into autonomous components (*j'ai du bon tabac = jade tube onde aubade*). Another famous case was that of Jean-Pierre Brisset. His procedure fixed the meaning of a phonetic or syllabic element by comparing the words, from one or more languages, that shared this element; the operation was then amplified and evolved in order to provide the evolution of the meaning itself, in accordance with various syllabic compositions (hence the prisoners were first of all drenched in dirty water, *dans l'eau sale*, they were *dans la sale eau pris*, thus becoming *salauds pris,* who were then sold in *la salle aux prix*).[3]

In each of these three cases, a kind of foreign language is extracted from the maternal language, on the condition that the sounds or phonemes always remain similar. In Roussel, however, it is the referent of the words that is put in question, and the meaning does not remain the same; moreover, the other language is merely homonymous and remains French, though it acts like a foreign language. In Brisset, who puts the signification of propositions in question, other languages are called upon, but only in order to demonstrate the unity of their meanings as much as the identity of their sounds (*diavolo* and *dieu-äieul*, or *di-a vau l'au*). As for Wolfson, whose problem is the translation of languages, the various languages are combined together in a disordered manner in order to conserve the same meanings and the same sounds, but only by systematically destroying the maternal language of English from which they were extracted. By slightly modifying the meaning of

these categories, one could say that Roussel constructs a language homonymous with French, Brisset, a synonymous language, and Wolfson,
a language paronymous with English. According to one of Wolfson's
intuitions, this is perhaps the secret aim of linguistics—to kill the maternal language. The grammarians of the eighteenth century still believed
in a mother tongue; the linguists of the nineteenth century voiced
certain doubts, and changed the rules of both maternity and filiation,
sometimes invoking languages that were little more than sisters. Perhaps an infernal trio was needed to push this initiative to its limit. In
Roussel, French is no longer a maternal language, because in its words
and letters it conceals various exoticisms that give rise to "impressions
of Africa" (in keeping with France's colonial mission); in Brisset, there
is no longer a mother tongue, all languages are sisters, and Latin is not
a language (in keeping with a democratic vocation); and in Wolfson,
American English does not even have British English as its mother,
but becomes an exotic mixture or a "potpourri of various idioms" (in
keeping with the American dream of bringing together immigrants
from around the world).

Wolfson's book, however, is not a literary work, and does not
claim to be a poem. What turns Roussel's procedure into a work of art
is the fact that the interval between the original sentence and its conversion is filled with marvelously proliferating stories, which make the
starting point recede until it is entirely hidden. For example, the event
woven by the hydraulic *métier à aubes* takes up the *métier qui force à
se lever de grand matin*. These are grandiose visions—pure events that
play within language, and surpass the conditions of their apparition
and the circumstances of their actualization, just as a piece of music
exceeds the circumstances of its performance and the execution given
to it. The same holds true for Brisset: to extract the unknown face of
the event or, as he says, the other face of language. Moreover, it is the
intervals between one linguistic combination and the next that gener-
ate the great events that fill these intervals, like the birth of a neck, the
appearance of teeth, the formation of sex organs. But there is nothing
similar in Wolfson: between the word to be converted and the words of
the conversion, and in the conversions themselves, there is nothing but
a void, an interval that is lived as pathogenic or pathological. When
he translates the article *the* into the two Hebrew terms *eth* and *he*,
he comments: the maternal word is "split in two by the equally split

brain" of the student of languages. The transformations never reach the grandiose level of an event, but remain mired in their accidental circumstances and empirical actualizations. The procedure thus remains a protocol. The linguistic procedure operates in a void, and never links up with a vital process capable of producing a vision. This is why the transformation of *believe* takes up so many pages, marked by the comings and goings of those who pronounce the word, and by the intervals between the different actualized combinations (*Pieve-peave, likegleichen, leave-Verlaub* . . .). Voids subsist and spread everywhere, so that the only event that arises, turning its black face toward us, is the end of the world or the atomic explosion of the planet, which the student fears will be delayed by arms reductions. In Wolfson, the procedure is itself its own event, and has no other expression than the conditional, the past conditional, which is needed to establish a hypothetical place between an external circumstance and an improvised actualization: "The alienated linguistic student would take an E from the English *tree* and would have mentally inserted it between the T and the R, had he not realized that when a vowel is placed after a T sound, the T becomes D. . . . During this time, the mother of the alienated student followed him around, and occasionally came to his side and uttered something completely useless."[4] Wolfson's style, his propositional schema, thus links the schizophrenic impersonal with a verb in the conditional, which expresses the infinite expectation of an event capable of filling up the intervals or, on the contrary, of hollowing them out in an immense void that swallows up everything. The demented student of languages would do or would have done . . .

Wolfson's book, moreover, is not a scientific work, despite the truly scientific intention of the phonetic transformations it brings about. This is because a scientific method implies the determination or even the formation of formally legitimate totalities. Now it is obvious that the totality of the referent of the student of language is illegitimate; not only because it is constituted by the indefinite set of everything that is not English, a veritable "tour de babil," as Wolfson says, but because the set is not defined by any syntactic rule that would make it correspond to the meanings or sounds, and would order the transformations of the set in terms of a starting point that has a syntax and is defined as English. Thus, the schizophrenic lacks a "symbolism" in two different ways: on the one hand, by the subsistence of pathogenic intervals that nothing can fill; and on the other hand, by the emergence of a false totality that nothing can define. This is why he lives his own thought ironically as a double simulacrum of a poetic-artistic system and a logical-scientific method. It is this power of the simulacrum or irony that makes Wolfson's book such an extraordinary book, illuminated with that peculiar joy and sunlight characteristic of simulations, in which we feel this very particular resistance germinating in the heart of the illness. As the student says, "How nice it was to study languages, even in his crazy, if not imbecilic, manner." For "it is not rare that things go that way in life: at least a little ironically."

In order to kill the maternal language, the combat must be waged at every moment—and above all, the combat against the mother's voice, "very high and piercing and perhaps equally triumphant." He will be able to transform a part of what he hears only if he has already avoided and eliminated most of it. As soon as his mother approaches, he memorizes in his head some sentence from a foreign language; but he also has a foreign book in front of him; and again he produces gurglings in his throat and gratings of his teeth; he has two fingers ready to plug his ears; or he makes use of a more complex apparatus, a short-wave radio with the earplug in one ear, the other ear being plugged with a single finger, leaving the other hand free to hold the book and leaf through it. It is a combinatorial, a panoply of all possible disjunctions, but one whose particular characteristic is to be inclusive and ramified to infinity, and not limitative and exclusive. These inclusive disjunctions are characteristic of schizophrenia, and complement the stylistic schema of the impersonal and the conditional: sometimes the student will have put a finger in each ear, sometimes a finger in one ear, either the left or the right ear, with the other ear being filled sometimes by the earplug, sometimes by another object, with the free hand either holding a book, or making a noise on the table . . . It is a litany of disjunctions, in which we recognize Beckett's characters, with Wolfson among them.[5] Wolfson needs to use all these ripostes, he has to be constantly on the lookout, because his mother, for her part, is also waging a combat with language: either to cure her evil demented son, as he himself says, or for the joy of "making the eardrum of her dear son vibrate with her vocal cords," or through aggressiveness and authority, or for some more obscure reason, sometimes she shuffles about in the next room, making her American radio reverberate, and then enters noisily into the patient's room, which has neither lock nor key, while at other times she walks about with light feet, and then silently opens the door and screams out a phrase in English. But the situation is even more complex, for the student's entire disjunctive arsenal is also indispensable in the street and in public places, where he is certain to hear English being spoken, and indeed may be heckled at any moment. Moreover, in his second book he describes a more perfect apparatus that can be used while moving about: a stethoscope in his ears, plugged into a portable tape recorder, whose earplugs can be removed or inserted at will, and the sound raised or lowered, while he reads a foreign newspaper. This use of the stethoscope is especially satisfying to him in the hospitals he goes to, since he thinks medicine is a false science, far worse than any science he can imagine in language and in life. If it is true that he first used this apparatus in 1976, well before the appearance of the Walkman, we can believe him when he says that he is its true inventor, and that for the first time in history a makeshift schizophrenic object lies at the origin of an apparatus that is now spread over the entire universe, and that will in turn schizophrenize entire peoples and generations.

The mother tempts and attacks him in yet another way. Whether from good intentions, or to distract him from his studies, or in an attempt to surprise him, sometimes she noisily puts away packages of food in the kitchen, while at other times she comes in and brandishes them under his nose and then leaves, only to suddenly return a short time thereafter. Then, during her absence, the student sometimes gives himself over to an alimentary orgy, tearing open the packages, licking them, absorbing their contents indiscriminately. The danger here is multiple, because the packages have English labels that he has forbidden himself to read (except with a quick glance, in order to find easily converted inscriptions like *vegetable oil*), or because he cannot know in advance if they contain a food he likes, or because eating makes him heavy and distracts him from the study of languages, or because the morsels of food, even under the ideal conditions of the packages' sterilization, contain larva, little worms, and eggs that have been made even more harmful by air pollution, "trichinas, tapeworms, earthworms, pinworms, ankylosi, flukes, little eels." He feels as much guilt after eating as he does after hearing his mother speak English. To ward off this new form of danger, he takes great pains to "memorize" a foreign phrase he had already learned; better yet, he fixes in his mind, he invests with all his strength, a certain number of calories, or the chemical formulas that correspond to the desired food, intellectualized and purified—for example, the "long chains of unsaturated carbon atoms" of vegetable oil. He combines the force of the chemical structures with that of the foreign words, either by making a repetition of words correspond to an absorption of calories ("he would repeat the same four or five words twenty or thirty times, while he avidly ingests a sum of calories equal in hundreds to the second pair of numbers or equal in thousands to the first pair of numbers"), or by identifying the phonetic elements of the foreign words with the chemical formulas of transformation (for example, the pairs of vowels-phonemes in German, and more generally the elements of language that are changed automatically "like an unstable chemical compound or a radioactive element with an extremely short half-life").

There is therefore a profound equivalence, on the one hand, between the intolerable maternal words and the poisonous or spoiled foods, and on the other hand, between the foreign words of transformation and the formulas or unstable atomic linkages. The most general problem, as the foundation of these equivalences, is revealed at the end of the book: Life and Knowledge. Foods and maternal words are life, foreign languages and atomic formulas are knowledge. How can one justify life, which is suffering and crying? How can one justify life, an "evil and sick matter" that feeds off his own sufferings and cries? The only justification of life is knowledge, which to him is the only thing Beautiful and True. Against the maternal language, which is the cry of life, he has to unite every foreign language in a total and continuous idiom, as the knowledge of language or philology. Against the lived body, its larvae and eggs, which constitute the sufferings of life, he has to unite every atomic combination in a total formula and a periodic table, as the knowledge of the body or molecular biology. Only an "intellectual exploit" is Beautiful and True, and alone is able to justify life. But how can knowledge have this justifying continuity and totality, since it is made up of every foreign language and every unstable formula, in which an interval always subsists that menaces the Beautiful, and from which only a grotesque totality emerges that overturns the True? Is it ever possible "to represent in a continuous fashion the relative positions of diverse atoms of a fairly complicated biochemical compound . . . and to demonstrate at once, instantaneously, yet also in a continuous fashion, the logic, the proofs for the truth of the periodic table of the elements?"

Here then is the great equation of fact, as Roussel would have said:

$$\frac{\text{maternal words}}{\text{foreign languages}} = \frac{\text{foods}}{\text{molecular structures}} = \frac{\text{life}}{\text{knowledge}}$$

If we consider the numerators, we see that what they have in common is that they are all "partial objects." But this notion remains all the more obscure in that it does not refer to a lost totality. What appears as a partial object, in fact, is something that is menacing, explosive, bursting, toxic, or poisonous. Or what contains such an object. Or else the pieces into which it explodes. In short, the partial object is in a box, and bursts into pieces when we open the box, but what is called "partial" is as much the box as its contents, although there are differences between them, namely, their voids and intervals. Thus, foods are enclosed in boxes, but they nonetheless contain larvae and worms, especially when Wolfson tears open the boxes with his bare teeth. The maternal language is a box containing words that are always cutting; but letters (especially consonants) are constantly falling from these words, and must be avoided or warded off as so many thorns or splinters that are particularly harmful or harsh. And is not the body itself a box containing organs as so many parts? But are not these parts menaced by various microbes, viruses, and especially cancers, which make them explode, leaping from one part to another so as to tear apart the entire organism? The organism is as maternal as food or words: it even seems that the penis is a feminine organ par excellence, as in the case of dimorphism, where a collection of rudimentary male organs appear as organic appendices of the female body ("the female genital organ, rather than the vagina, seems to him to be a greasy rubber tube ready to be inserted by the hand of a woman into the last section of the intestine, of his intestine," which is why nurses seem to him to be professional sodomists par excellence). The beautiful mother, now one-eyed and cancerous, can thus be said to be a collection of partial objects, which are explosive boxes of different types and levels. Within each type, and at every level, these partial objects continually break apart in the void, and open up intervals between the letters of a word, the organs of a body, or mouthfuls of food (the spacing that governs them, as in Wolfson's meal). This is the clinical picture of the schizophrenic student: aphasic, hypochondriac, anorexic.

The numerators of the great equation therefore give us a first derivative equation:

$$\frac{\text{maternal words}}{\text{hurtful letters}} = \frac{\text{foods}}{\text{harmful larvae}} = \frac{\text{organism}}{\text{cancerous organs}} = \begin{array}{l}\text{an unjust,}\\ \text{sick, and}\\ \text{painful life}\end{array}$$

How can we draw up the other equation, that of the denominators? This is not unrelated to Artaud, and to Artaud's combat. In Artaud, the peyote rite also confronts *letters* and *organs*, but it makes them move in the other direction, toward inarticulate breaths, toward a nondecomposable body without organs. What it extracts from the maternal language are breath-words that belong to no language, and from the organism, a body without organs that has no generation. To the dirty writing, the disgusting organisms, the organ-letters, the microbes and parasites, there stands opposed the fluid breath or the pure body—but this opposition must be a transition that restores to us this murdered body, these stifled breaths.[6] But Wolfson is not at the same "level," because the letters still belong to the maternal words, and the breaths still have to be discovered in foreign words, so that he remains mired in the condition of resemblance between sound and meaning. He lacks a creative syntax. Nonetheless, the combat has the same nature, the same sufferings, and should also make us pass from wounding letters to animated breaths, from sick organs to the cosmic body without organs. To maternal words and harsh letters, Wolfson opposes the action that comes from the words of one or more languages, which must fuse together, enter a new phonetic writing, form a liquid totality or alliterative continuity. To poisonous foods, Wolfson opposes the continuity of a chain of atoms and the totality of a periodic table, which must be absorbed rather than divided into parts, reconstituting a pure body rather than sustaining a sick one. It will be noted that the conquest of this new dimension, which turns away from the infinite process of explosions and intervals, proceeds for its part with two circuits, one fast, the other slow. We have seen this with words, since on the one hand the maternal words must be converted as quickly as possible, and continuously, but on the other hand the foreign words can only extend their domain and form a whole thanks to multilingual dictionaries that no longer pass through the maternal language. Likewise, the speed of a chemical transformation's half-life, and the amplitude of a periodic table of the elements. Even horse races inspire in him two factors that guide him in his betting, as a minimum and a maximum: the smallest number of previous "trials" by the horse, but also the universal calendar of historical birthdays that can be linked to the name of the horse, the owner, the jockey, and so on (hence the "Jewish horses" and the great Jewish festivals).

The denominators of the great equation would thus give us a second derivative equation:

$$\frac{\text{foreign words}}{\text{tower of Babel (all languages)}} = \frac{\text{chains of atoms}}{\text{periodic table}} = \frac{\text{Knowledge, reconstitution of a pure body and its breaths}}{}$$

If the partial objects of life referred to the mother, why not refer the transformations and totalizations of knowledge to the father? Especially since the father is double, and is presented on two circuits: the first circuit, lasting a short period of time, for the stepfather-chef who is always changing jobs like a "radioactive element with a half-life of 45 days"; and the second circuit, having a great amplitude, for the nomadic father whom the young man encounters at a distance in public places. Must not Wolfson's double "failure"—the persistence of pathogenic intervals and the constitution of illegitimate totalities—be related to this Medusa-mother with a thousand penises, and to the scission of the father?[7] Psychoanalysis contains but a single error: it reduces all the adventures of psychosis to a single refrain, the eternal daddy-mommy, which is sometimes played by psychological characters, and sometimes raised to the level of symbolic functions. But the schizophrenic does not live in familial categories, he wanders among worldwide and cosmic categories—this is why he is always studying something. He is continually rewriting *De natura rerum*. He evolves in things and in words. What he terms "mother" is an organization of words that has been put in his ears and mouth, an organization of things that has been put in his body. It is not my language that is maternal, it is my mother who is a language; it is not my organism that comes from the mother, it is my mother who is a collection of organs, the collection of *my own* organs. What one calls Mother is Life. And what one calls Father is foreignness [*étrangeté*], all these words I do not know, and that cut through my own; all these atoms that constantly enter and leave my body. It is not the father that speaks foreign languages and is familiar with atoms; it is the foreign languages and atomic combinations that are my father. The father is the crowd of my atoms and the set of my glossolalias—in short, Knowledge.

And the struggle between knowledge and life is the bombardment of the body by atoms, and cancer is the riposte of the body. How can knowledge heal life, and in some way justify it? All the world's doctors—those "green bastards" who come in pairs like fathers—will never be able to cure the cancerous mother by bombarding her with atoms. But it is not a question of the father or the mother. The young man could accept his mother and father as they are, "modify at least some of his pejorative conclusions with regard to his parents," and even return to the maternal language at the end of his linguistic studies. This is how he concluded his first book—with a certain hope. The question, however, lies elsewhere, since it concerns the body in which he lives, with all the metastases that constitute the earth, and the knowledge in which he evolves, with all the languages that never stop speaking, all the atoms that never stop bombarding. It is here, in the world, in the real, that the pathogenic intervals are opened up, and the illegitimate totalities are made and unmade. It is here that the problem of existence is posed, the problem of his own existence. What makes the student sick is the world, not his father-mother. What makes him sick is the real, not symbols. The only "justification" of life would be for all the atoms to bombard the cancer-Earth once and for all, and return it to the great void: the resolution of all equations, the atomic explosion. More and more, the student will combine his readings on cancer, from which he learns how the disease progresses, with his monitoring of shortwave radio, which announces the possibility of a radioactive Apocalypse that would put an end to all cancer: "especially since one could easily claim that planet Earth as a whole has contracted the most horrible cancer possible, a portion of its own substance having run amok and started multiplying and metastasizing itself, and whose effect is the wrenching phenomena of the here-below, a fabric woven ineluctably from an infinity of lies, injustices, sufferings . . . , an evil that at present is nonetheless treatable and curable by extremely strong and persistent doses of artificial radioactivity . . . !' "

So that the primary great principal equation would now show what it hides:

$$\frac{\text{metastases of cancer}}{\text{atomic apocalypse}} = \frac{\text{cancer-Earth}}{\text{bomb-God}} = \frac{\text{life}}{\text{knowledge}}$$

For "God is the bomb, that is, quite obviously the set of nuclear bombs necessary to sterilize our extremely cancerous planet by radioactivity . . . , *Elohim hon petsita*, literally, God he bombs . . ."

Unless there is "possibly" yet another way, indicated in the fiery pages of an "additional chapter" in the first book. Wolfson seems to follow in the footsteps of Artaud, who had gone beyond the question of father-mother, and then that of the bomb and the tumor, and wanted to have done with the universe of "judgment," to discover a new continent. On the one hand, knowledge is not opposed to life, because even when it takes as its object the dullest chemical formula of inanimate matter, the atoms of this formula are still those that enter into the composition of life, and what is life if not their adventure? And on the other hand, life is not opposed to knowledge, for even the greatest pain offers a strange knowledge to those who experience it, and what is knowledge if not the adventure of the painful life in the brains of great men (which moreover look like pleated irrigators)? We impose little pains upon ourselves to persuade ourselves that life is tolerable, and even justifiable. But one day, the student of languages, familiar with masochistic behaviors (cigarette burns, voluntary asphyxias), encounters the "revelation," and encounters it precisely on the occasion of a very moderate pain he inflicts on himself: that life is absolutely unjustifiable, and all the more so in that it does not have to be justified . . . The student glimpses "the truth of truths," without being able to penetrate it further. What comes to light is an event: life and knowledge are no longer opposed, they are no longer even distinguishable from each other, once the former abandons its born organisms and the latter its acquired knowledges, and both of them engender new and extraordinary figures that are revelations of Being—perhaps those of Roussel or Brisset, and even of Artaud, the great story of humanity's "innate" breath and body.

The procedure, the linguistic procedure, is necessary for all this. All words recount a story of love, a story of life and knowledge, but this story is neither designated nor signified by words, nor translated from one word into another. Rather, the story concerns what is "impossible" in language, and thus what belongs to language alone: its *outside*. It is made possible only by means of a procedure, which testifies to madness. Moreover, psychosis is inseparable from a linguistic procedure, which must not be confused with any of the known categories of psychoanalysis, since it has another destination.[8] The procedure pushes language to its limit, yet for all that it does not cross this limit. It lays waste to designations, significations, and translations—but it does so in order that language might finally confront, on the other side of its limit, the figures of an unknown life and an esoteric knowledge. The procedure is merely the condition, however indispensable it may be. He who knows how to cross the limit accedes to new figures. Perhaps Wolfson remains on the edge, an almost reasonable prisoner of madness, without being able to extract from his procedure the figures he scarcely offers us a glimpse of. For the problem is not to go beyond the bounds of reason, it is to cross the bounds of unreason as a victor: then one can speak of "good mental health," even if everything ends badly. But the new figures of life and knowledge still remain prisoners in Wolfson's psychotic procedure. His procedure, in a certain manner, remains unproductive. And yet it is one of the greatest experiments ever made in this area. This is why Wolfson keeps saying "paradoxically" that it is sometimes more difficult to remain slumped in one's chair, immobilized, than it is to get up and and move farther on . . .

3

Lewis Carroll

In Lewis Carroll, everything begins with a horrible combat, the combat of depths: things explode or make us explode, boxes are too small for their contents, foods are toxic and poisonous, entrails are stretched, monsters grab at us. A little brother uses his little brother as bait. Bodies intermingle with one another, everything is mixed up in a kind of cannibalism that joins together food and excrement. Even words are eaten. This is the domain of the action and passion of bodies: things and words are scattered in every direction, or on the contrary are welded together into nondecomposable blocks. Everything in depth is horrible, everything is nonsense. *Alice in Wonderland* was originally to have been entitled *Alice's Adventures Underground.*

But why didn't Carroll keep this title? Because Alice progressively conquers surfaces. She rises or returns to the surface. She creates surfaces. Movements of penetration and burying give way to light lateral movements of sliding; the animals of the depths become figures on cards without thickness. All the more reason for *Through the Looking-Glass* to invest the surface of a mirror, to institute a game of chess. Pure events escape from states of affairs. We no longer penetrate in depth, but through an act of sliding pass through the looking-glass, turning everything the other way round like a left-hander. The stock market of Fortunatus described by Carroll is a Möbius strip on which a single line traverses the two sides. Mathematics is good because it brings new surfaces into existence, and brings peace to a world whose mixtures in depth would be terrible: Carroll the mathematician, or Carroll the photographer. But the world of depths still rumbles under the surface, and threatens to break through it. Even unfolded and laid out flat, the monsters still haunt us.

Carroll's third great novel, *Sylvie and Bruno*, brings about yet a further advance. The previous depth itself seems to be flattened out, and becomes a surface alongside the other surface. The two surfaces thus coexist, and two contiguous stories are written on them, the one major and the other minor; the one in a major key, the other in a minor key. Not one story within another, but one next to the other. *Sylvie and Bruno* is no doubt the first book that tells two stories at the same time, not one inside the other, but two contiguous stories, with passages that constantly shift from one to the other, sometimes owing to a fragment of a sentence that is common to both stories, sometimes by means of the couplets of an admirable song that distributes the events proper to each story, just as much as the couplets are determined by the events: the Mad Gardener's song. Carroll asks, Is it the song that determines the events, or the events, the song? With *Sylvie and Bruno*, Carroll makes a scroll book in the manner of Japanese scroll paintings. (Eisenstein thought of scroll painting as the true precursor of cinematographic montage and described it in this way: "The scroll's ribbon rolls up by forming a rectangle! It is no longer the medium that rolls up on itself; it is what is represented on it that rolls up at its surface.") The two simultaneous stories of Sylvie and Bruno form the final term of Carroll's trilogy, a masterpiece equal to the others.

It is not that surface has less nonsense than does depth. But it is not the same nonsense. Surface nonsense is like the "Radiance" of pure events, entities that never finish either happening or withdrawing. Pure events without mixture shine above the mixed bodies, above their embroiled actions and passions. They let an incorporeal rise to the surface like a mist over the earth, a pure "expressed" from the depths: not the sword, but the flash of the sword, a flash without a sword like the smile without a cat. Carroll's uniqueness is to have allowed nothing to pass through sense, but to have played out everything in nonsense, since the diversity of nonsenses is enough to give an account of the entire universe, its terrors as well as its glories: the depth, the surface, and the volume or rolled surface.

4

The Greatest Irish Film (Beckett's "Film")

The Problem

If it is true, as the Irish Bishop Berkeley said, that to be is to be perceived (*esse est percipi*), is it possible to escape perception? How does one become imperceptible?[1]

The History of the Problem

We might imagine that the whole story is that of Berkeley, who had enough of being perceived (and of perceiving). The role, which could only have been played by Buster Keaton, would be that of Bishop Berkeley. Or rather, it is the transition from one Irishman to another, from Berkeley who perceived and was perceived, to Beckett who had exhausted "all the joys of *percipere* and *percipi*."[2] We must therefore propose a cutting of the film (or a distinction of cases) that differs slightly from the one proposed by Beckett himself.

The Condition of the Problem

There must be something unbearable in the fact of being perceived. Is it the fact of being perceived by a third party? No, since possible perceiving third parties recoil once they realize they are being perceived, not simply by each other, but each one by himself. Thus there is something intrinsically terrifying in the fact of being perceived, but what?

The Givens of the Problem

As long as perception (the camera) is behind the character, it is not dangerous because it remains unconscious. It seizes the character only when it approaches him at an oblique angle and makes him conscious of being perceived. We will say, by convention, that the character becomes conscious of being perceived, that it "enters into *percipi*," when the camera exceeds an angle of forty-five degrees behind the character's back, from one side or the other.

The First Case: The Wall and the Staircase, Action

The character can limit the danger by walking quickly along a wall; in this way, he leaves only one side unprotected. To make a character walk along a wall is the first cinematographic act (all the great filmmakers have attempted it). Of course, the action is more complex when it becomes vertical and even spiral-like, as in a staircase, since the unprotected side alternates relative to the angle of view. In any case, whenever the forty-five-degree angle is surpassed, the character comes to a halt, stops the action, flattens himself against the wall, and hides the exposed side of his face with his hand, or with a handkerchief or cabbage leaf that could be drawn from his hat. Such is the first case, the perception of action, which can be neutralized by stopping the action.

The Second Case: The Room, Perception

This is the second cinematographic act: the interior, what takes place between the walls. Previously, the character was not considered to be perceiving: it was the camera that furnished him with a "blind" perception, sufficient to his action. But now the camera perceives the character in the room, and the character perceives the room: all perception becomes double. Previously, human third parties could potentially perceive the character, but they were neutralized by the camera. Now, the character perceives for himself, his perceptions become things that in turn perceive him: not only animals, mirrors, *a lithograph of the good Lord*, photos, but even utensils (as Eisenstein said after Dickens: the kettle is looking at me . . .). In this regard, things are more dangerous than humans beings: I do not perceive them without their perceiving me, all perception as such being the perception of perception. The solution to this second case consists in expelling the animals, veiling the mirror, covering the furniture, pulling down the lithograph, and tearing up the photos: the extinction of double perception. On the street, a bit earlier, the character still had a space-time at his disposal, and even fragments of a past (the photos he was carrying). In the room, he still had sufficient strength at his disposal to form images that would restore his perception. But now he has nothing but the present, in the form of a hermetically sealed room in which all ideas of space and time, all divine, human, or animal images, all images of things, have disappeared. All that remains is the Rocking Chair in the center of the room, because, more than any bed, it is the sole piece of furniture that exists before or after man, that which suspends us in the middle of nothingness (to-and-fro).

The Third Case: The Rocking Chair, Affection

The character was able to sit in the rocking chair and doze off only to the degree that the perceptions were extinguished. But perception still lies in wait behind the rocking chair, where it has both sides at its disposal simultaneously. And it seems to have lost the goodwill it manifested earlier, when it hurried to close off the angle it had inadvertently surpassed, protecting the character from potential third parties. Now it surpasses the angle deliberately, trying to surprise the dozing character. The character defends himself and curls up, ever more feebly. The camera perception takes advantage of this; it surpasses the angle definitively, turns around, faces the sleeping character, and draws near to him. It then reveals what it is: the perception of affection, that is, the perception of the self by itself, or pure Affect. It is the reflexive double of the convulsive man in the rocking chair. It is the one-eyed person who looks at the one-eyed character. It was waiting for the right moment. This, then, is what was so terrifying: that perception was the perception of the self by itself, "insuppressible" in this sense. This is the third cinematographic act, the close-up, the affect or the perception of affection, the perception of oneself. It too will be extinguished, but at the same time as the movement of the rocking chair stops and the character dies. Is this not precisely what is needed, to cease to be in order to become imperceptible, according to the conditions set forth by Bishop Berkeley?

The General Solution

Beckett's film traversed the three great elementary images of the cinema, those of action, perception, and affection. But nothing is ever finished in Beckett, nothing ever dies. When the rocking chair is immobilized, what is set in motion is the Platonic idea of the Rocking Chair, the rocking chair of the spirit. When the character dies, as Murphy said, it is because he has already begun to move in spirit. He is like a cork floating on a tempestuous ocean: he no longer moves, but is in an element that moves. Even the present has disappeared in its turn, in a void that no longer involves obscurity, in a becoming that no longer includes any conceivable change. The room has lost its partitions, and releases an atom into the luminous void, an impersonal yet singular atom that no longer has a Self by which it might distinguish itself from or merge with others. Becoming imperceptible is Life, "without cessation or condition" . . . attaining to a cosmic and spiritual lapping.

5

On Four Poetic Formulas That Might Summarize the Kantian Philosophy

"The time is out of joint."
—Shakespeare[1]

Time is out of joint, time is unhinged.[2] The hinges are the axis on which the door turns. The hinge, *Cardo,* indicates the subordination of time to precise cardinal points, through which the periodic movements it measures pass. As long as time remains on its hinges, it is subordinated to extensive movement; it is the measure of movement, its interval or number. This characteristic of ancient philosophy has often been emphasized: the subordination of time to the circular movement of the world as the turning Door, a revolving door, a labyrinth opening onto its eternal origin. It will entail an entire hierarchization of movements according to their proximity to the Eternal, according to their necessity, their perfection, their uniformity, their rotation, their composite spirals, their particular axes and doors, and the numbers of Time that correspond to them. Time no doubt tends to free itself when the movement it measures itself becomes increasingly *aberrant* or *derived* [*dérivé*], marked by material, meteorological, and terrestrial contingencies; but this is a downward tendency that still depends on the adventures of movement.[3] Time thus remains subordinate to what, in movement, is both originary *and* derived.

Time *out of joint,* the door off its hinges, signifies the first great Kantian reversal: movement is now subordinated to time. Time is no longer related to the movement it measures, but rather movement to the time that conditions it. Moreover, movement is no longer the determination of objects, but the description of a space, a space we must set aside in order to discover time as the condition of action. Time thus becomes unilinear and rectilinear, no longer in the sense that it would measure a derived movement, but in and through itself, insofar as it imposes the succession of its determination on every possible movement. This is a rectification of time. Time ceases to be curved by a God who makes it depend on movement. It ceases to be cardinal and becomes ordinal, the order of an empty time. In time, there is no longer anything either originary or devived that depends on movement. The labyrinth takes on a new look—neither a circle nor a spiral, but a thread, a pure straight line, all the more mysterious in that it is simple, inexorable, terrible—"the labyrinth made of a single straight line which is indivisible, incessant."[4] Hölderlin portrayed Oedipus as having already entered into this strict march of the slow death, following an order of time that had ceased to "rhyme."[5] Nietzsche, in a similar sense, considered it to be the most Semitic of the Greek tragedies. Yet Oedipus is still urged on by his wandering as a derived movement. It is Hamlet, rather, who completes the emancipation of time. He truly brings about the reversal because his own movement results from nothing other than the succession of the determination. Hamlet is the first hero who truly needed time in order to act, whereas earlier heroes were subject to time as the consequence of an original movement (Aeschylus) or an aberrant action (Sophocles). The *Critique of Pure Reason* is the book of Hamlet, the prince of the north. Kant's historical situation allowed him to grasp the implications of this reversal. Time is no longer the cosmic time of an original celestial movement, nor is it the rural time of derived meteorological movements. It has become the time of the city and nothing other, the pure order of time.

It is not succession that defines time, but time that defines the parts of movement as successive inasmuch as they are determined within it. If time itself were succession, it would have to succeed in another time, to infinity. Things succeed each other in diverse times, but they are also simultaneous in the same time, and they subsist in an indeterminate time [*un temps quelconque*]. It is no longer a question of defining time by succession, nor space by simultaneity, nor permanence by eternity. Permanence, succession, and simultaneity are modes or relations of time (*duration, series, set*). They are the fragments [*éclats*] of time.

Consequently, just as time can no longer be defined by succession, space can no longer be defined by coexistence or simultaneity. Each of them, space and time, will have to find completely new determinations. Everything that moves and changes is in time, but time itself does not change or move, any more than it is eternal. It is the form of everything that changes and moves, but it is an immutable form that does not change—not an eternal form, but precisely the form of what is *not* eternal, the immutable form of change and movement. Such an autonomous form seems to point to a profound mystery: it requires a new definition of time (and space).

> *"I is an other."*
> —Rimbaud[6]

The ancients also conceived of time in another way, as a mode of thought or an intensive movement of the soul, a kind of spiritual or monastic time. Descartes brought about its secularization or laïcization with the *cogito*: the *I think* is an act of instantaneous determination, which implies an undetermined existence (*I am*) and determines this existence as that of a thinking substance (I am *a thing that thinks*). But how can the determination apply to the undetermined if we cannot say under what form it is "determinable"? This Kantian objection could lead to no other result than the following: our undetermined existence is determinable only in time, under the form of time. Hence the "I think" affects time, and only determines the existence of a "self" [*moi*] that changes in time and presents a certain degree of consciousness at every moment. Time as the form of determinability therefore does not depend upon the intensive movement of the soul; on the contrary, the intensive production of a degree of consciousness at every moment depends on time. Kant brings about a second emancipation of time, and completes its laïcization.

The Self is in time and is constantly changing: it is a passive, or rather receptive, "self" that experiences changes in time. The *I* is an act (I think) that actively determines my existence (I am), but can only determine it in time, as the existence of a passive, receptive, and changing *self*, which only represents to itself the activity of *its own* thought. The I and the Self are thus separated by the line of time, which relates them to each other only under the condition of a fundamental difference. My existence can never be determined as that of an active and sponta-

neous being, but as a passive "self" that represents to itself the "I"—
that is, the spontaneity of the determination—as an Other that affects
it ("the paradox of inner sense"). Oedipus, according to Nietzsche, is
defined by a purely passive attitude, but one that is related to an activity that continues after his death.[7] For all the more reason, Hamlet displays his eminently Kantian character whenever he appears as a passive existence, who, like an actor or sleeper, receives the activity of his
own thought as an Other, which is nonetheless capable of giving him a
dangerous power that defies pure reason. In Beckett, it is Murphy's
"metabulia."[8] Hamlet is not a man of skepticism or doubt, but the
man of the Critique. I am separated from myself by the form of time
and yet I am one, because the I necessarily affects this form by bringing
about its synthesis—not only of successive parts to each other, but
at every moment—and because the Self is necessarily affected by the I
as the content of this form. The form of the determinable makes the
determined Self represent the determination to itself as an Other. In
short, the madness of the subject corresponds to the time out of joint.
There is, as it were, a double derivation of the I and the Self in time,
and it is this derivation that links or stitches them together. Such is the
thread of time.

In a certain sense, Kant goes further than Rimbaud. For Rimbaud's
great formula takes on its full force only by appealing to recollections
from school. Rimbaud gives his formula an Aristotelian interpretation:
"So much the worse for the wood that finds itself a violin! . . . If the
copper wakes up a bugle, that is not its fault . . ." This is like a concept-
object relation in which the concept is an active form, and the object a
merely potential matter. It is a mold, a process of molding. For Kant, by
contrast, the I is no longer a concept but the representation that accompanies every concept; and the Self is not an object, but that to which all
objects are related as to the continuous variation of its own successive
states, and to the infinite modulation of its degrees at each instant. The
concept-object relation subsists in Kant, but it is doubled by the I-Self
relation, which constitutes *a modulation, and no longer a mold*. In this
sense, the compartmentalized distinction between forms as concepts
(violin-bugle) and matters as objects (wood-copper) gives way to the
continuity of a one-way linear development that requires the establish-
ment of new formal relations (time) and the disposition of a new type
of matter (phenomenon). It is as if, in Kant, one could already hear
Beethoven, and soon Wagner's continuous variation.

If the I determines our existence as a passive self changing in time, time is the formal relation through which the mind affects itself, or the way we are internally affected by ourselves. Time can thus be defined as the Affect of the self by itself, or at least as the formal possibility of being affected by oneself. It is in this sense that time as an immutable form, which can no longer be defined by simple succession, appears as the *form of interiority* (inner sense), whereas space, which can no longer be defined by coexistence or simultaneity, appears for its part as the form of exteriority, the formal possibility of being affected by something else as an exterior object. "Form of interiority" does not simply mean that time is interior to the mind, because space is no less so. Nor does "form of exteriority" mean that space presupposes "something else," since it is space, on the contrary, that makes possible every representation of objects as other or exterior. But this amounts to saying that exteriority entails as much immanence (because space remains interior to my mind) as interiority entails transcendence (because in relation to time my mind is represented as other than myself). It is not time that is interior to us, or at least it is not specifically interior to us; it is we who are interior to time, and for this reason time always separates us from what determines us by affecting it. Interiority constantly hollows us out, splits us in two, doubles us, even though our unity subsists. But because time has no end, this doubling never reaches its limit: *time is constituted by a vertigo or oscillation,* just as unlimited space is constituted by a sliding or floating.

> *"It is an extremely painful thing to be ruled by laws*
> *that one does not know! . . . For the essence of*
> *such laws in this way necessitates the secret of their*
> *content."*   —Kafka[9]

Which amounts to saying *the* Law, since one can hardly distinguish between laws one does not know. The conscience of antiquity speaks of laws because, under certain conditions, they give us knowledge of the Good or the Best: laws express the Good from which they are derived. Laws are a "second resort," a representative of the Good in a world deserted by the gods. When the true Politics is absent, it leaves behind general directives that men need to know in order to act correctly. From the point of view of knowledge, laws are like the imitation of the Good in a given case.

In the *Critique of Practical Reason,* by contrast, Kant reverses the relationship between the law and the Good, and thereby raises the law to the level of a pure and empty uniqueness. The good is what the Law says it is—it is the good that depends on the law, and not vice versa. As first principle, the law has neither interiority nor content, since any content would refer it back to a Good of which it would be the imitation. It is a pure form that has no object, whether sensible or intelligible. It does not tell us what we must do, but what subjective rule we must obey no matter what our action. Any action whose maxim can be *thought* without contradiction as universal, and whose motive has no object other than this maxim, will be moral (lying, for example, cannot be thought as universal, since it at least implies people who believe it and who, in believing it, are not lying). The law is thus defined as the pure form of universality. It does not tell us what aim the will must pursue to be good, but what form it must take to be moral. It does not tell us what we must do, it simply tells us "You must!," leaving us to deduce from it the good, that is, the aims of this pure imperative. The law is not known because there is nothing in it to know: it is the object of a purely *practical* determination, and not a theoretical or speculative one.

The law is indistinguishable from its sentence, and the sentence is indistinguishable from its implementation or execution. If the law is primary, it no longer has any way of distinguishing between the "accusation," the "defense," and the "verdict."[10] The law coincides with its imprint on our heart and in our flesh. But it does not thereby even give us a final knowledge of our faults, for what its needle writes on us is *Act through duty* (and not merely in conformity with duty) . . . It writes nothing else. Freud showed that, if duty in this sense presupposes a renunciation of interests and inclinations, the law will exert itself all the more strongly and rigorously the deeper our renunciation. Thus, the more we observe the law with exactitude, the more severe it becomes. Even the most holy are not spared.[11] *It never acquits us,* neither of our virtues nor of our vices or our faults: at every moment there is only an apparent acquittal, and the moral conscience, far from appeasing itself, is intensified by all our renunciations and pricks us even more strongly. This is not Hamlet, but Brutus. How could the law reveal its secret without making the renunciation on which it feeds impossible? An acquittal can only be hoped for, "which makes up for the impotence of speculative reason," no longer at a given moment, but from the viewpoint of a progress that continues to infinity in its ever increasing conformity with the law (sanctification as the consciousness of perseverance in moral progress). This path, which exceeds the limits of our life and requires the soul's immortality, follows the straight line of time, inexorable and incessant, upon which we remain in constant contact with the law. But this indefinite prolongation, rather than leading us to a paradise above, already installs us in a hell here below. Rather than announcing immortality, it distills a "slow death," and continuously *defers the judgment of the law.* When time is out of joint, we have to renounce the ancient cycle of faults and expiations in order to follow the infinite route of the slow death, the deferred judgment, or the infinite debt. Time leaves us no other juridical options than those of Kafka in *The Trial*: either an "apparent acquittal" or an "unlimited postponement."

> *"To attain the unknown by disorganizing* all the senses . . . *a long, boundless, and systematized* disorganization of all the senses."   —Rimbaud[12]

Or rather, an unregulated exercise of all the faculties. This would be the fourth formula of a profoundly romantic Kant in the *Critique of Judgment*. This is because, in the first two Critiques, the various subjective faculties entered into relationships with each other, but these relationships were rigorously regulated, since there was always a dominant or determining fundamental faculty that imposed its rule upon the others. There were numerous faculties: outer sense, inner sense, the imagination, the understanding, reason, each of which was well defined. But in the *Critique of Pure Reason,* it was the understanding that dominated, because it determined inner sense through the intermediary of a synthesis of the imagination, and even reason submitted to the role the understanding assigned to it. In the *Critique of Practical Reason,* the fundamental faculty was reason, because reason constitutes the pure form of the universality of law, the other faculties following as they might (the understanding applied the law, the imagination received the sentence, inner sense experienced the consequences or the sanction). But now we see Kant, at an age when great authors rarely have anything new to say, confronting a problem that will lead him into an extraordinary undertaking: if the faculties can thus enter into variable relationships in which each faculty is in turn regulated by one of the others, it must follow that, taken together, they are capable of free and unregulated relationships in which each faculty goes to its own limit, and yet in this way shows the possibility of its entering into an *indeterminate* [*quelconque*] harmony with the others. This will be the *Critique of Judgment* as the foundation of romanticism.

This is no longer the aesthetic of the *Critique of Pure Reason*, which considered the sensible as a quality that could be related to an object in space and time; nor is it a logic of the sensible, nor even a new logos that would be time. It is an aesthetic of the Beautiful and the Sublime, in which the sensible takes on an autonomous value for itself and is deployed in a pathos beyond all logic, and which will grasp time as it bursts forth [*dans son jaillissement*], at the very origin of its thread and its vertigo. This is no longer the Affect of the *Critique of Pure Reason*, which linked the Self to the I in a relationship that was still regulated by the order of time; it is a Pathos that lets them evolve freely in order to form strange combinations as sources of time, "arbitrary forms of possible intuitions." It is no longer the determination of an I, which must be joined to the determinability of the Self in order to constitute knowledge; it is now the undetermined unity of all the faculties (the Soul), which makes us enter the unknown.

What is in question in the *Critique of Judgment* is how certain phenomena, which will define the Beautiful, give to the inner sense of time an autonomous supplementary dimension; to the imagination, a power [*pouvoir*] of free reflection; and to the understanding, an infinite conceptual capacity [*puissance*]. The various faculties enter into a spontaneous accord that is no longer determined by any one of them, which is all the more profound in that it no longer has any rule, and which demonstrates a spontaneous accord of the Self and the I under the conditions of a beautiful Nature. The Sublime goes even further in this direction: it brings the various faculties into play in such a manner that they struggle against each other like wrestlers, with one faculty pushing another to its maximum or limit, to which the second faculty reacts by pushing the first toward an inspiration it would not have had on its own. One faculty pushes another to a limit, but they each make the one go beyond the limits of the other. The faculties enter into relationship at their deepest level, where they are most foreign to each other. They interact at the point where the distance between them is at its greatest. There is a terrible struggle between the imagination and reason, but also between the understanding and inner sense, a battle whose episodes will be the two forms of the Sublime, and then Genius. There is a tempest in the chasm opened up inside the subject. In the first two Critiques, the dominant or fundamental faculty was able to make the other faculties enter into the closest possible harmonics with itself. But now, in an exercise of limits, the various faculties mutually produce the most remote harmonics in each other, so that they form essentially dissonant accords. The emancipation of dissonance, the discordant accord, is the great discovery of the *Critique of Judgment,* the final Kantian reversal. The separation that joins was the first of Kant's themes in the *Critique of Pure Reason.* But in the end, he discovers the discord that produces an accord. An unregulated exercise of all the faculties, which was to define future philosophy, just as for Rimbaud the disorder of all the senses would define the poetry of the future. A new music as discord, and as discordant accord, the source of time.

This is why we have proposed four formulas, which are obviously arbitrary in relation to Kant, but not arbitrary in relation to what Kant has left us for the present and the future. De Quincey's admirable text *The Last Days of Immanuel Kant* said everything, but only the reverse side of things that will find their full development in the four poetic formulas of Kantianism. This is the Shakespearean aspect of Kant, who begins as Hamlet and winds up as Lear, whose daughters would be the post-Kantians.

6

Nietzsche and Saint Paul, Lawrence and John of Patmos

It's not the same, it can't be the same . . .[1] D. H. Lawrence intervenes in the scholarly debates of those who ask if the same John wrote both the gospel and the Apocalypse.[2] Lawrence intervenes with very passionate arguments, which have all the more force in that they imply a method of evaluation, a typology: the same type of man could not have written the gospel and the Apocalypse. It matters little that each of the two texts is complex or composite, and includes so many different things. The question does not concern two individuals or two authors, but two types of man, two regions of the soul, two completely different ensembles. The gospel is aristocratic, individual, soft, amorous, decadent, always rather cultivated. The Apocalypse is collective, popular, uncultivated, hateful, and savage. Each of these words would have to be explained in order to avoid misunderstandings. But already the evangelist and the apocalypst cannot be the same. John of Patmos does not even assume the mask of the evangelist, nor that of Christ; he invents another mask, he fabricates another mask that unmasks Christ or, if you prefer, that is superimposed on Christ's mask. John of Patmos deals with cosmic terror and death, whereas the gospel and Christ dealt with human and spiritual love. Christ invented a religion of love (a practice, a way of living and not a belief), whereas the Apocalypse brings a religion of Power [*Pouvoir*]—a belief, a terrible manner of *judging*. Instead of the gift of Christ, an infinite debt.

It goes without saying that Lawrence's text is best read after having read or reread the text of the Apocalypse. We can immediately sense the topicality of both the Apocalypse and Lawrence's denunciation of it. This topicality does not consist in historical correspondences of the type "Nero = Hitler = Antichrist," nor in the suprahistorical sentiment of the end of the world, nor in the atomic, economic, ecologic, and science fiction panic of the millenarians. If we are steeped in the Apocalypse, it is rather because it inspires ways of living, surviving, and judging in each of us. It is a book for all those who think of themselves as survivors. It is the book of Zombies.

Lawrence is closely related to Nietzsche. We can assume that Lawrence would not have written his text without Nietzsche's *Antichrist*. Nietzsche himself was not the first. Nor even Spinoza. A certain number of "visionaries" have opposed Christ as an amorous person to Christianity as a mortuary enterprise. Not that they have an overly accommodating attitude toward Christ, but they do feel the need to avoid confusing him with Christianity. In Nietzsche, there is the great opposition between Christ and Saint Paul: Christ, the softest, most amorous of the decadents, a kind of Buddha who frees us from the domination of priests and the ideas of fault, punishment, reward, judgment, death, and what follows death—this bearer of glad tidings is doubled by the black Saint Paul, who keeps Christ on the cross, ceaselessly leading him back to it, making him rise from the dead, displacing the center of gravity toward eternal life, and inventing a new type of priest even more terrible than its predecessors. "Paul's invention, his means to priestly tyranny, to herd formation: the belief in immortality—*that is, the doctrine of 'judgment.*'"[3] Lawrence takes up the opposition once again, but this time he opposes Christ to the red John of Patmos, the author of the Apocalypse. This was Lawrence's mortal book, since it only slightly preceded his red hemoptysical death, just as the *Antichrist* preceded Nietzsche's collapse. Before dying, one last "joyful message," one last glad tiding. It is not that Lawrence simply imitates Nietzsche. Rather, he picks up an arrow, Nietzsche's arrow, and shoots it elsewhere, aims it in a different direction, on another comet, to another audience: "Nature propels the philosopher into mankind like an arrow; it takes no aim, but hopes the arrow will stick somewhere."[4] Lawrence takes up Nietzsche's initiative by taking John of Patmos as his target, and no longer Saint Paul. Many things change or are supplemented from one initiative to another, and even what they have in common gains in strength and novelty.

Christ's enterprise is individual. In itself, the individual is not necessarily opposed to the collectivity; individual and collective stand opposed in each of us like two different parts of the soul. Now Christ rarely addressed himself to what is collective in us. His problem

> was rather to undo the collective system of the Old Testament priesthood, of the Jewish priesthood and its power, but only to liberate the individual soul from this morass. As for Caesar, he would give him his due. That is why he is aristocratic. He thought a culture of the individual soul would be enough to chase off the monsters buried in the collective soul. A political error. He left us to manage with the collective soul, with Caesar, outside us and inside us. On this score, he constantly deceived his apostles and disciples. We might even imagine that he did so on purpose.
>
> He did not want to be a master or to help his disciples (only to love them, he said, but what did that hide?).
>
> He did not *really* mix with them, or even really work or act with them. *He was alone all the time.* He puzzled them utterly, and in some part of them, he let them down. He refused to be their physical power-lord. The power-homage in a man like Judas found itself betrayed. So it betrayed back again.[5]

The apostles and disciples made Christ pay for it: denial, betrayal, falsification, the shameless doctoring of the Good News. Lawrence says that the principal character of Christianity is Judas.[6] And then John of Patmos, and then Saint Paul. Each of them took advantage of the protest of the collective soul, the part neglected by Christ. The Apocalypse takes advantage of the claims of the "poor" or the "weak," for they are not who we think they are: they are not the humble or the unfortunate, but those extremely fearsome men who have nothing but a collective soul. Among Lawrence's most beautiful passages are those on the Lamb. John of Patmos foretells the lion of Judah, but instead a lamb appears, a horned lamb who roars like a lion and has become particularly cunning, and who is made all the more cruel and terrifying by being presented as a sacrificial victim and no longer as a sacrificer or an executioner. But the lamb is a more dreadful executioner than the others. "John insists on a lamb 'as it were slain': but we never see it slain, we only see it slaying mankind by the million. Even when it comes on in a victorious bloody shirt at the end, the blood is not its *own* blood . . ."[7] In truth, it is Christianity that becomes the Antichrist; it betrays Christ, it forces a collective soul on him behind his back, and in return it gives the collective soul a superficial individual figure, the little lamb. Christianity, and above all John of Patmos, founded a new type of man, and a type of thinker that still exists today, enjoying a new reign: the carnivorous lamb, the lamb that bites and then cries, "Help! What did I ever do to you? It was for your own good and our common cause." What a curious figure, the modern thinker. These lambs in lion's skin, with oversized teeth, no longer need either the priests' habit or, as Lawrence said, the Salvation Army: they have conquered many other means of expression, many other popular forces.

What the collective soul wants is Power [*Pouvoir*]. Lawrence does not say simple things, and it would be wrong here to think we have understood him immediately. The collective soul does not simply want to seize power or to replace the despot. On the one hand, it wants to destroy power, it hates power and strength [*puissance*], John of Patmos hates Caesar or the Roman Empire with all his heart. On the other hand, however, it also wants to penetrate into every pore of power, to swarm in its centers, to multiply them throughout the universe. It wants a cosmopolitan power, not in full view like the Empire, but rather in every nook and cranny, in every dark corner, in every fold of the collective soul.[8] Finally and above all, it wants an ultimate power that makes no appeal to the gods, but is itself the power of a God without appeal who judges all other powers. Christianity does not form a pact with the Roman Empire, but transmutes it. With the Apocalypse, Christianity invents *a completely new image of power*: the system of Judgment. The painter Gustave Courbet (there are numerous resemblances between Lawrence and Courbet) spoke of people who woke up at night crying, "I want to judge! I have to judge!" The will to destroy, the will to infiltrate every corner, the will to forever have the last word—a triple will that is unified and obstinate: Father, Son, and Holy Spirit. Power singularly changes its nature, its extension, its distribution, its intensity, its means, and its end. A counterpower, which is both a power of nooks and crannies and a power of the last men. Power no longer exists except as the long politics of vengeance, the long enterprise of the collective soul's narcissism. The revenge and self-glorification of the weak, says Lawrence-Nietzsche. Even the Greek asphodel will become the Christian narcissus.[9] And what details are provided in the list of vengeances and glories . . . The weak can be reproached for only one thing, and that is for not being hard enough, for not being puffed up enough with their own glory and certainty.

Now for this enterprise of the collective soul, a new race of priests, a new type, would have to be invented, even if this meant turning against the Jewish priest. The latter had not yet attained universality or finality, he was still too local, he was still waiting for something. The Christian priest would have to take over from the Jewish priest, even if both would have to turn against Christ. Christ will be made to submit to the worst of prostheses: he will be turned into the hero of the collective soul, he will be made to give the collective soul something he never wanted to give. Or rather, Christianity will give him what he always hated, a collective Ego, a collective soul. The Apocalypse is a monstrous ego grafted onto Christ. John of Patmos's efforts are all directed toward this aim: "Always the titles of power, and never the titles of love. Always Christ the omnipotent conqueror flashing his great sword and destroying, destroying vast masses of men, till blood runs up to the horses' bridles. Never Christ the Savior: never. In the Apocalypse, the Son of Man comes to bring a new and terrible *power* on to the earth, power greater than that of any Pompey or Alexander or Cyrus. Power, terrific, smiting power. . . . So that we are left puzzled."[10] For this, Christ will be forced to rise from the dead, he will be given injections. He who did not judge, who did not want to judge, will be made into an essential cog in the system of Judgment. For the vengeance of the weak, or the new power, achieves its utmost precision when judgment—the abominable faculty—becomes the master faculty of the soul. (On the minor question of a Christian philosophy: yes, there is a Christian philosophy, not so much as a function of belief, but as soon as judgment is considered to be an autonomous faculty, and for this reason needs both the system and the guarantee of God.) The Apocalypse won: we have never left the system of judgment. "Then I saw thrones, and seated upon them were those to whom judgment was committed."[11]

In this regard, the working method of the Apocalypse is fascinating. The Jews had invented something very important in the order of time, which was *postponed destiny*. Having failed in their imperial ambition, the chosen people had been put on hold, they were left waiting, they had become "a people of postponed destiny."[12] This situation remains essential throughout all of Jewish prophetism, and already explains the presence of certain apocalyptic elements in the prophets. But what is new in the Apocalypse is that this waiting now becomes the object of an unprecedented and maniacal programming. The Apocalypse is undoubtedly the first great program book, a great spectacle. The small and large death, the seven seals, the seven trumpets, the seven vials, the first resurrection, the millennium, the second resurrection, the last judgment—this is what fills up and occupies the wait. A kind of Folies-Bergère with a celestial city and an infernal lake of sulfur. All the details of the sufferings, the scourges and plagues reserved for the enemies in the lake, the glory of the elect in the city, the need of the latter to measure their self-glory through the suffering of others—all this will be programmed down to the minute in the long revenge of the weak. It is the spirit of revenge that introduces the program into the wait ("revenge is a dish that . . .").[13] Those who wait must be given something to do. The wait has to be organized from start to finish: the martyred souls have to wait until there is a sufficient number of martyrs for the show to begin.[14] And then there is the short wait of half an hour before the opening of the seventh seal, the long wait lasting a millennium . . . Above all, the End must be programmed. "They needed to know the end as well as the beginning, never before had men wanted to know the end of creation. . . . Flamboyant hate and a simple lust . . . for the end of the world."[15] There is an element here that does not appear as such in the Old Testament but only in the collective Christian soul, which opposes the apocalyptic vision to the prophetic word, the apocalyptic program to the prophetic project. For if the prophet waits, already filled with *ressentiment*, he nonetheless does so in time, in life—he is waiting for an advent. And he waits for this advent as something new and unforeseen, something of which he can merely sense the presence or gestation in God's plan. Whereas Christianity can no longer wait for anything but a return, and the return of something programmed down to the smallest detail. If Christ is dead, then the center of gravity is effectively displaced—it is no longer in life but has passed beyond life into an afterlife. Postponed destiny changes meaning with Christianity, since it is no longer simply deferred but "postferred," placed *after* death, after the death of Christ and the death of each and every person.[16] One is now faced with the task of filling up a monstrous and drawn-out time between Death and the End, between Death and Eternity. It can only be filled with visions: "I looked, and behold . . . ," "and I saw . . ." Apocalyptic *vision* replaces the prophetic *word*, programming replaces project and action, an entire theater of phantasms supplants both the action of the prophets and the passion of Christ. Phantasms, phantasms, the expression of the instinct for vengeance, the weapon of the weak's vengeance. The Apocalypse breaks not only with prophetism, but above all with the elegant immanence of Christ, for whom eternity was first experienced in life and could only be experienced in life ("to feel oneself in heaven").

And yet it is not difficult to demonstrate the Jewish sources of the Apocalypse at every point: not only in the postponed destiny, but in the entire system of reward-punishment, sin-redemption, the need for the enemy to suffer a long time, in his spirit as much as in his flesh—in short, the birth of morality, and allegory as the expression of morality, as the means of moralization . . . But what is even more interesting in the Apocalypse is the presence and reactivation of a diverted pagan source. That the Apocalypse is a composite book is not extraordinary; it would rather have been surprising in this period if a book were not composite. Lawrence, however, distinguishes between two kinds of composite books, or rather two poles: in extension, when the book includes several other books, by different authors, from different places, traditions, and so on; or in depth, when it straddles several strata, traverses them, mixes them up if need be, making one substratum show through the surface of the most recent stratum, a probe book [*livre-sondage*] and no longer a syncretic book. A pagan, a Jewish, and a Christian stratum: these are what mark the great parts of the Apocalypse, even if a pagan sediment slides into a fault line in the Christian stratum, filling up a Christian void (Lawrence analyzes the example of the famous chapter 12 of the Apocalypse, in which the pagan myth of a divine birth, with the astral Mother and the great red dragon, fills the emptiness of Christ's birth).[17] Such a reactivation of paganism is not frequent in the Bible. One can assume that the prophets, the evangelists, and Saint Paul himself were well aware of the heavenly bodies, the stars, and the pagan cults; but they chose to suppress them to the maximum, to cover up this stratum. There is but one case in which the Jews had an absolute need to return to this stratum, namely, when it was a matter of *seeing*, when they needed to see, when Vision assumed a certain autonomy in relation to the Word. "The Jews of the post-David period had no eyes of their own to see with. They peered inward at their Jehovah till they were blind: then they looked at the world with the eyes of their neighbors. When the prophets had to see visions, they had to see Assyrian or Chaldean visions. They borrowed other gods to see their own invisible God by."[18] The men of the new Word have need of the old pagan eye. This was already true of the apocalyptic elements that appear in the prophets: Ezekiel needed Anaximander's perforated wheels ("it is a great relief to find Anaximander's wheels in Ezekiel").[19]

But it is John of Patmos, the author of the Apocalypse, the book of Visions, who most needs to reactivate the pagan source, and who is in the best situation to do so. John knew very little about Jesus and the evangelists, and what he knew he knew poorly; but "it seems to me he knew a good deal about the pagan value of symbols, as contrasted with the Jewish or Christian values."[20]

Here we see Lawrence, with all his horror of the Apocalypse, through this horror, experiencing an obscure sympathy, even a kind of admiration, for this book, precisely because it is sedimented and stratified. Nietzsche also experienced this peculiar fascination for what he found horrible and disgusting: "How interesting it is," he said. Lawrence no doubt has a certain sympathy for John of Patmos, he finds him interesting, perhaps the most interesting of men, he sees an excessiveness and presumptuousness in him that are not without their charm. This is because the "weak," these men of *ressentiment* who are waiting to wreak their vengeance, enjoy a hardness that they use to their own advantage, to their own glory, but that comes to them from elsewhere. Their profound lack of culture, and the exclusivity of a book that for them assumes the figure of THE book—THE BOOK, the Bible and especially the Apocalypse—allows them to remain open to the thrust of a very old stratum, a secret sediment that others no longer cared to know about. Saint Paul, for example, is still an aristocrat: not an aristocrat like Jesus, but a different type of aristocrat who is too cultivated not to be able to recognize, and thus to efface or repress, the sediments that would betray his program. What censorious treatment Saint Paul is able to apply to the pagan stratum, and what selection to the Jewish stratum! He needs a Jewish stratum that has been revised and corrected, converted, but he needs the pagan source to be and to remain buried—and he has enough culture to do so himself. John of Patmos, however, is a man of the people. He is a kind of uneducated Welsh miner. Lawrence opens his commentary on the Apocalypse with a portrait of these English miners, whom he knows well and marvels at: hard, very hard, endowed with "a rough and rather wild, somewhat 'special' sense of power," religious men par excellence, brandishing the Apocalypse with vengeance and self-glorification, organizing dark Tuesday-evening meetings in their primitive Methodist chapels.[21] Their natural leader is neither the apostle John nor Saint Paul but John of Patmos. They are the collective and popular soul of Christianity, whereas Saint Paul (and also Lenin, Lawrence adds) was still an aristocrat who went to the people. Miners know all about strata. They have no need to be well read, for the pagan depth rumbles deep within them. They are open to a pagan stratum, they set it loose, they make it come to them, saying only: it's coal, it's Christ. They bring about the most fearsome diversion of a stratum so that it can be used by the Christian, mechanical, and technical world. The Apocalypse is a great machinery, an *already industrialized organization*, a Metropolis. By drawing on his own lived experience, Lawrence thinks of John of Patmos as an English miner, and the Apocalypse as a series of engravings hung in the miner's house—the mirror of a popular, hard, pitiless, and pious face. It is the same cause as Saint Paul's, the same enterprise, but it is by no means the same type of man, or the same process, or the same function. Saint Paul is the ultimate manager, while John of Patmos is a laborer, the terrible laborer of the last hour. The director of the enterprise must prohibit, censure, and select, whereas the laborer must hammer, extend, compress, and forge a material . . . This is why, in the Nietzsche-Lawrence alliance, it would be wrong to think that the difference between their targets—Saint Paul for one, John of Patmos for the other—is merely anecdotal or secondary. It marks a radical difference between the two books. Lawrence knows Nietzsche's arrow well, but in turn he shoots it in a completely different direction, even if they both wind up in the same hell, dementia and hemoptysis, with Saint Paul and John of Patmos occupying all of heaven.

But Lawrence soon recovers all his distrust and horror for John of Patmos. For this reactivation of the pagan world, sometimes moving and even grandiose in the first part of the Apocalypse—what is it used for, what is it made to serve in the second part? It would be wrong to say that John hates paganism. "He accepts it almost as naturally as his own Hebrew culture, and far more naturally than the new Christian spirit, which is alien to him."[22] His enemy is not the pagans but the Roman Empire. Now the pagans are not the Romans, but rather the Etruscans; they are not even the Greeks, but the Aegean peoples, the Aegean civilization. But to ensure the fall of the Roman Empire in a vision, the entire Cosmos must be gathered together, convoked, brought back to life—and then it must all be destroyed, so that the Roman Empire will itself be brought down and buried under its debris. Such is the strange diversion, the strange expedient through which one avoids attacking the enemy directly: to establish its ultimate power and its celestial city, the Apocalypse needs to destroy the world, and only paganism furnishes it with a world, a cosmos. It therefore calls up the pagan cosmos only in order to finish it off, to bring about its hallucinatory destruction. Lawrence defines the cosmos in a very simple manner: *it is the locus of great vital symbols and living connections,* the more-than-personal life. For cosmic connections, the Jews will substitute the alliance of God with the chosen people; for the supra—or infra—personal life, the Christians will substitute the small, personal link of the soul with Christ; for symbols, the Jews and the Christians will substitute allegory. And this pagan world, which, despite everything, remained alive and continued to live deep in us with all its strength, is flattered, invoked, and made to reappear by the Apocalypse—but only to make sure that it is definitively murdered, not even out of direct hatred, but because it is needed as a means. The cosmos had already been subjected to many blows, but it is with the Apocalypse that it dies.

When the pagans spoke about the world, what interested them was always its beginnings, and its leaps from one cycle to another; but now there is nothing but an End lying at the limit of a long flat line. Necrophiliacs, we are no longer interested in anything but this end, since it is definitive. When the pagans, the pre-Socratics, spoke of destruction, they always saw it as an injustice that resulted from the excess of one element over another, and the unjust one was above all else the destroyer. But now, *it is destruction that is called just,* it is the will to destroy that is called Justice and Holiness. This is the innovation of the Apocalypse. It does not criticize the Romans for being destroyers, nor does it want to, for this is a good thing; Rome-Babylon is criticized for being an insurgent, a rebel, for sheltering rebels, great or small, rich or poor. To destroy, to destroy an anonymous and interchangeable enemy, an *unspecified* enemy, has become the most essential act of the new justice. The unspecified enemy is designated as anyone who does not conform to God's order. It is curious to note how, in the Apocalypse, everyone will have to be marked, will bear a mark on forehead or hand, the mark of the Beast or of Christ; and the Lamb will mark 144,000 persons, and the Beast . . . Whenever a radiant city is programmed, we can be assured that it is a way to destroy the world, to render it "uninhabitable," and to begin the hunt for the unspecified enemy.[23] There are not many resemblances, perhaps, between Hitler and the Antichrist, but there is a great resemblance between the New Jerusalem and the future that we are now being promised, not only in science fiction, but in the military-industrial plans of an absolute worldwide State. The Apocalypse is not a concentration camp (Antichrist); it is the great military, police, and civil security of the new State (the Heavenly Jerusalem). The modernity of the Apocalypse lies not in its predicted catastrophes, but in its programmed self-glorification, the institution of glory in the New Jerusalem, the demented installation of an ultimate judiciary and moral power. The New Jerusalem, with its wall and its great street of glass, is an architectural terror: "And the city had no need of the sun, neither of the moon, to shine in it. . . . And nothing unclean shall enter it . . . but only those who are written in the Lamb's book of life."[24] Involuntarily, the Apocalypse at least persuades us that what is most terrifying is not the Antichrist, but this new city descended from heaven, the holy city "prepared like a bride adorned for her husband."[25] All relatively healthy readers of the Apocalypse will feel they are already in the lake of sulfur.

Among Lawrence's most beautiful pages are thus those concerning this reactivation of the pagan world, but under such conditions that the vital symbols are in complete decline, and all their living connections are severed. "The greatest literary falsification," said Nietzsche. Lawrence is at his best when he analyzes the precise themes of this decadence and falsification in the Apocalypse (we limit ourselves to indicating certain points):

1. *The transformation of hell.* With the pagans, hell is not separated off, but depends on the transformation of elements in a cycle: when the fire becomes too strong for the soft waters, it burns them, and the water produces salt like the child of injustice who corrupts it and makes it bitter. Hell is the bad aspect of the subterranean water. If the unjust are gathered there, it is because hell is itself the effect of an elementary injustice, an avatar of elements. But the idea that hell is itself separate, that it exists for itself, that it is one of two expressions of the final justice—these are ideas that would have to wait for Christianity. "The old Jewish hells of Sheol and Gehenna were fairly mild, uncomfortable, abysmal places like Hades, and when a New Jerusalem was created from heaven, they disappeared" *in principle* in favor of a "brilliant sulfureous torture-lake" where souls burn forever and ever.[26] Even the sea will be poured into the pond of sulfur for good measure. That way there will no longer be any connections at all.

2. *The transformation of the riders.* To try to rediscover what a truly pagan horse is—what connections it establishes between colors, tem-

peraments, astral natures, and the parts of the soul as riders—it is necessary to examine not the horse as seen, but rather the lived symbiosis of the man-horse. White, for example, is also blood, which acts as a pure white light, whereas red is merely the clothing of blood furnished by the bile. A vast interlinking of lines, planes, and relations.[27] But with Christianity, the horse is nothing but a beast of burden to which one says "Come!" and what it bears are abstractions.

3. *The transformation of colors and of the dragon.* Lawrence develops a very beautiful becoming of colors. For the oldest dragon is red, golden-red, extending through the cosmos in a spiral or coiled around man's vertebral column. But when the moment of his ambiguity arrives (Is he good? Is he bad?), he still remains red for man, whereas the good cosmic dragon becomes a translucent green in the midst of the stars, like a spring breeze. Red has become dangerous for man (Lawrence, let us not forget, is writing in the midst of his fits of spitting blood). But finally the dragon turns white, a white without color, the dirty white of our logos, a kind of large gray worm. When does gold change into currency? Precisely when it ceases to be the reddish gold of the first dragon, when the dragon takes on the papier-mâché color of pale Europe.[28]

4. *The transformation of woman.* The Apocalypse again renders a fugitive homage to the great cosmic Mother, enveloped in the sun, with the moon under her feet. But she is planted there, severed from any connection. And her child is taken away from her, "caught up unto God"; she is sent out into the desert, which she will never leave.[29] She only returns in the inverted form of the whore of Babylon: still splendid, seated on the red dragon, promising destruction. This seems to be the woman's only choice: either to be the dragon's whore, or to make herself prey to "all the grey little snakes of modern shame and pain" (today's women, as Lawrence says, are told to "make something worth while" of their lives, to make the best of the worst, without ever thinking that this is even worse; this is why women assume a strangely policelike role, the modern "police-woman").[30] But it was the Apocalypse that had already transformed the angelic powers into odd police agents.

5. *The transformation of the twins.* The pagan world was not only made up of living conjunctions; it also included borders, thresholds and doors, disjunctions, so that something passes between two things,

or a substance passes from one state to another, or alternates with another while avoiding dangerous mixes. The twins have precisely this role as disjunctors: masters of wind and rain, because they open the doors of heaven; sons of thunder, because they part the clouds; guardians of sexuality, because they maintain the opening in which birth insinuates itself, and make blood and water alternate, while outlining the mortal point in which everything would be mixed without measure. The twins are thus the masters of flows, their passage, their alternation, and their disjunction.[31] This is why the Apocalypse needs to have them killed and rise to heaven—not for the pagan world to reach its periodic excess [démesure], but for its measure to come from elsewhere, like a death sentence.

6. *The transformation of symbols into metaphors and allegories.* The symbol is a concrete cosmic force [puissance]. Popular consciousness, even in the Apocalypse, retains a certain sense of the symbol while adoring brute Power [pouvoir]. And yet what differences there are between a cosmic force and the idea of an ultimate power . . . One by one, Lawrence sketches out certain characteristic features of the symbol. It is a dynamic process that enlarges, deepens, and expands sensible consciousness; it is an ever increasing becoming-conscious, as opposed to the closing of the moral consciousness upon a fixed allegorical idea. It is a method of the Affect, intensive, a cumulative intensity, which merely marks the threshold of a sensation, the awakening of a state of consciousness: the symbol means nothing, and has neither to be explained nor interpreted, as opposed to the intellectual consciousness of allegory. It is a *rotative thought,* in which a group of images turn ever more quickly around a mysterious point, as opposed to the linear allegorical chain. Consider the Sphinx's riddle: "What is it that goes first on four legs, then on two, and then on three?" It would be rather foolish to see this as three linked parts whose final response would be Man. It comes to life, on the contrary, only if one feels the three groups of images in the process of whirling around the most mysterious point of man: images of the animal-child; then those of the creature on two paws, a monkey, bird, or frog; and then those of the unknown beast on three paws, from beyond the seas and deserts. This is precisely what the rotative symbol is. It has neither beginning nor end, it does not lead us anywhere, and above all it has no final point, nor even stages. It is always in the middle [au milieu], in the

midst of things, between things. It has only a milieu, milieus that are ever more profound. The symbol is a maelstrom, it makes us whirl about until it produces that intense state out of which the solution, the decision, emerges. The symbol is a *process of action and decision;* in this sense, it is linked to the oracle that furnished it with these whirling images. For this is how we make a true decision: we turn into our-selves, upon ourselves, ever more rapidly, "until a center is formed and we know what to do." Just the opposite occurs in allegorical thought, which is no longer an active thought but a thought that ceaselessly postpones or defers. *It replaced the force [puissance] of decision with the power [pouvoir] of judgment.* Furthermore, it wants a final point as the last judgment. And it places these provisional points between each sentence, between each segment, as so many stages in a path pre-paring for the second coming. No doubt it is the sense of sight, books, and reading that have given us this taste for points, segmentary lines, beginnings, ends, and stages. The eye is the sense organ that separates us: allegory is visual, whereas the symbol evokes and unites all the other senses. When the book was still scrolled, it perhaps retained its power as a symbol. But how, precisely, can we explain the strange fact that the book of the seven seals is supposed to be a scroll, and yet that the seals are broken successively, in stages—apart from the fact that the Apocalypse needs to put points everywhere, to install segments everywhere? The symbol is made up of physical connections and dis-junctions, and even when we find ourselves before a disjunction, some-thing nonetheless happens in the interval, a substance or flow. For the symbol is the thought of flows, in contrast to the intellectual and linear process of allegorical thought. "The modern mind apprehends parts, bribes, and pieces, and puts a point after each sentence, whereas the sensible consciousness apprehends the whole as a flow or flux." The Apocalypse reveals its own aim: to disconnect us from the world and from ourselves.[32]

Exeunt the pagan world. The Apocalypse made it rise again for one last time in order to destroy it forever. We must therefore return to the other axis: no longer the opposition between the Apocalypse and the pagan world, but the completely different opposition between the Apocalypse and Christ as a person. Christ had invented a religion of love, that is, an aristocratic culture of the individual part of the soul; the Apocalypse invents a religion of Power, that is, a terrible popular cult of the collective part of the soul. The Apocalypse turns Christ into a collective ego, it gives him a collective soul—and then everything changes. The vitality of love is transmuted into an enterprise of revenge, and the evangelical Christ is transmuted into the apocalyptic Christ (the man with the sword between his teeth). Hence the importance of Lawrence's admonition: the John who wrote the gospel is not the same John who wrote the Apocalypse. And yet *perhaps they are more united than if they were the same*. And the two Christs are more united than if they were the same, "two sides of the same medal."[33]

To explain this complementarity, is it enough to say that Christ had "personally" neglected the collective soul, thereby leaving it a wide-open field? Or is there indeed a more profound, a more abominable reason? Lawrence here throws himself into a complex affair: it seems to him that the reason for the deviation, for the disfiguration, was not simple negligence, but instead has to be sought in Christ's love, in the manner in which he loved. For this is what was already horrible—the manner in which Christ loved. This is what would permit a religion of Power to be substituted for the religion of love. In Christ's love, there was a kind of abstract identification, or worse, *an ardor to give without taking anything*. Christ did not want to meet his disciples' expectations, and yet he did not want to keep anything, not even the inviolable part of himself. There was something suicidal about him. Shortly before his text on the Apocalypse, Lawrence wrote a novel entitled *The Man Who Died*: he imagines Christ resuscitated ("they took me down too soon"), but also nauseated, telling himself "never again." Found by Mary Magdalene, who wants to give up everything for him, he perceives a small glimmer of triumph in the woman's eye, an accent of triumph in her voice—and he recognizes himself in it. Now this is the same glimmer, the same accent, of *those who take without giving*. There is the same fatality in Christ's ardor and in Christian cupidity, in the religion of love and in the religion of power: "I gave more than I took, and *that also* is woe and vanity. . . . It only means another death. . . . Now he knew . . . that the body rises again to give and to take, to take and to give, ungreedily." Throughout his work, Lawrence tended toward this task: to track down and diagnose the small and evil glimmer wherever it may be found, whether in those who take without giving *or* in those who give without taking—John of Patmos and Christ.[34] Between Christ, Saint Paul, and John of Patmos, the chain closes in on itself: Christ the aristocrat, the artist of the individual soul, who wants to give this soul; John of Patmos, the worker, the miner, who lays claim to the collective soul and wants to take everything; and Saint Paul, who closes the link, a kind of aristocrat going to the people, a kind of Lenin who will organize the collective soul, who will make it "an oligarchy of martyrs"—he gives Christ the aims, and the Apocalypse the means. Was not all this essential to the formation of the system of judgment? Individual suicide and mass suicide, with self-glorification on all sides. Death, death, this is the only judgment.

Save the individual soul, then, as well as the collective soul, but how? Nietzsche ended the *Antichrist* with his famous Law against Christianity. Lawrence ends his commentary on the Apocalypse with a kind of manifesto—what he elsewhere calls a "litany of exhortations":[35] Stop loving. Oppose to the judgment of love "a *decision* that love can never vanquish." Arrive at the point where you can no longer give any more than you can take, where you know you will no longer "give" anything, the point of Aaron or *The Man Who Died,* for the problem has passed elsewhere: to construct banks between which a flow can run, break apart or come together.[36] Do not love anymore, do not give of yourself, do not take: in this way you will save the individual part of yourself. For love is not the individual part, it is not the individual soul, it is rather what makes the individual soul an *Ego* [*Moi*]. Now an ego is something to be given or taken, which wants to love or be loved, it is an allegory, an image, a Subject, it is not a true relation. The ego is not a relation but a reflection, it is the small glimmer that makes a subject, the glimmer of triumph in an eye ("the dirty little secret," as Lawrence sometimes said). A worshipper of the sun, Lawrence nonetheless said that the sun's glimmer on the grass is not enough to make a relation. He derived an entire conception of painting and music from this. What is individual is the relation, it is the soul and not the ego. The ego has a tendency to identify itself with the world, but it is already dead, whereas the soul extends the thread of its living "sympathies" and "antipathies."[37] Stop thinking of yourself as an ego in order to live as a flow, a set of flows in relation with other flows, outside of oneself and within oneself. Even scarcity is a flow, even drying up, even death can become one. *Sexual* and *symbolic:* in effect they amount to the same thing, and have never meant anything else—the life of forces or flows.[38] There is a tendency in the ego to annihilate itself, which finds a certain propensity in Christ and its full realization in Buddhism: hence Lawrence's (and Nietzsche's) distrust of the East. The soul as the life of flows is the will to live, struggle and combat. It is not only the disjunction, but also the conjunction of flows that is struggle and combat, like wrestlers engaging each other. Every accord is dissonant. War is just the opposite. War is the general annihilation that requires the participation of the ego, but combat rejects war, it is the conquest of the soul. The soul refuses those who want war, because they confuse it with struggle, but also those who renounce struggle, because they confuse it with war: militant Christianity and pacifist Christ. The inalienable part of the soul appears when one has ceased to be an ego; it is this eminently flowing, vibrating, struggling part that has to be conquered.

The collective problem, then, is to institute, find, or recover a maximum of connections. For connections (and disjunctions) are nothing other than the physics of relations, the cosmos. Even disjunction is physical, like two banks that permit the passage of flows, or their alternation. But we, we live at the very most in a "logic" of relations (Lawrence and Russell did not like each other at all). We turn disjunction into an "either/or." We turn connection into a relation of cause and effect or a principle of consequence. We abstract a reflection from the physical world of flows, a bloodless double made up of subjects, objects, predicates, and logical relations. In this way we extract the system of judgment. It is not a question of opposing society and nature, the artificial and the natural. Artifices matter little. But whenever a physical relation is translated into logical relations, a symbol into images, flows into segments, exchanged, cut up into subjects and objects, each for the other, we have to say that the world is dead, and that the collective soul is in turn enclosed in an ego, whether that of the people or a despot. These are the "false connections" that Lawrence opposed to Physis. According to Lawrence's critique, money, like love, must be reproached not for being a flow, but for being a false connection that mints subjects and objects: when gold is turned into loose change . . .[39] There is no return to nature, but only a political problem of the collective soul, the connections of which a society is capable, the flows it supports, invents, leaves alone, or does away with. Pure and simple sexuality, yes, if what one means by that is the individual and social physics of relations as opposed to asexual logic. Like other people of genius, Lawrence died while carefully refolding his bandages, carefully arranging them (he presumed that Christ had done the same), and by turning around this idea, in this idea . . .

7

Re-presentation of Masoch

Masoch is neither a pretext for psychiatry or psychoanalysis, nor even a particularly striking figure of masochism.[1] This is because his work keeps all extrinsic interpretation at a distance. More a physician than a patient, the writer makes a diagnosis, but what he diagnoses is the world; he follows the illness step by step, but it is the generic illness of man; he assesses the chances of health, but it is the possible birth of a new man: "the legacy of Cain," "the Sign of Cain" as the total work. If the characters, situations, and objects of masochism receive this name, it is because they assume, in Masoch's novels, an unknown, immeasurable dimension that surpasses the unconscious no less than individual consciousnesses. In his novels, the hero is swollen with powers that exceed his soul as much as his milieu. What we must consider in Masoch, therefore, are his contributions to the art of the novel.

In the first place, Masoch displaces the question of suffering. The sufferings that the masochistic hero has inflicted on himself, though acute, depend upon a contract. It is this contract of submission, made with the woman, that constitutes the essential element of masochism. But the manner in which the contract is rooted in masochism remains a mystery. It seems to have something to do with breaking the link between desire and pleasure: pleasure interrupts desire, so that the constitution of desire as a process must ward off pleasure, repress it to infinity. The woman-torturer sends a delayed wave of pain over the masochist, who makes use of it, obviously not as a source of pleasure, but as a flow to be followed in the constitution of an uninterrupted process of desire. What becomes essential is waiting or suspense as a plenitude, as a physical and spiritual intensity. The rituals of suspension become the novelistic figures par excellence, with regard to both the woman-torturer who suspends her gesture, and the hero-victim whose suspended body awaits the whip. Masoch is the writer who makes suspense, in its pure and almost unbearable state, the motivating force of the novel. In Masoch, the complementarity between the contract and infinite suspense plays a role analogous to that between the tribunal and its "unlimited postponement" in Kafka: a postponed destiny, a juridicism, an extreme juridicism, a Justice that should by no means be confused with the law.

In the second place, there is the role of the animal, as much for the woman in furs as for the victim (a riding or draft animal, a horse or an ox). The relationship between man and animal is without doubt something that has been constantly misunderstood by psychoanalysis, because psychoanalysis is unable to see in it anything but all-too-human Oedipal figures. The so-called masochist postcards, where old men beg like dogs before a severe mistress, tend to lead us astray as well. Masochistic characters do not imitate the animals; they enter zones of indetermination or proximity in which woman and animal, animal and man, have become indiscernible. The novel in its entirety has become a training novel [roman de dressage], the last avatar of the bildungs-roman [roman de formation]. It is a cycle of forces. Masoch's hero trains the woman who has to train him. Instead of the man transmitting his aquired forces to the innate forces of the animal, the woman transmits aquired animal forces to the innate forces of the man. Here again, the world of suspense is traversed by waves.

Delirious formations are, as it were, the kernels of art. But a delirious formation is neither familial nor private, it is world-historical: "I am a beast, a Negro. . . ," following Rimbaud's formula. The important thing, then, is to determine which regions of History and the Universe are invested by a given formation. One could draw up a map for each case: the Christian martyrs, for example, in whom Renan saw the birth of a new aesthetic. One could even imagine that it is the Virgin who puts Christ on the cross to give birth to the new man, and that it is the Christian woman who drives men to sacrifice themselves. But also courtly love, with its ordeals and procedures. Or again, the agricultural communes of the steppe, religious sects, the minorities of the Austro-Hungarian Empire, the role of women in these communes and minorities, and in panslavism. *Every delirious formation appropriates extremely varied milieus and moments, with which it links up in its own manner.* Masoch's work, which is inseparable from a literature of minorities, haunts the glacial zones of the Universe and the feminine zones of History. A great wave, the wave of Cain the wanderer, whose destiny is forever suspended, mixes times and places. The hand of a severe woman cuts across the wave and offers itself to the wanderer. For Masoch, the novel is Cainian, just as it was Ishmaelite for Thomas Hardy (the steppe and the heather). It is the broken line of Cain.

The literature of a minority is not defined by a local language that would be its defining feature, but by a treatment to which it subjects the major language. The problem is analogous in both Kafka and Masoch.[2] Masoch's language is a very pure German, but a German that is nonetheless affected, as Wanda says, by a certain trembling. This trembling need not be actualized at the level of the characters, and one must even avoid miming it; it is enough to ceaselessly indicate it, since it is no longer merely a trait of speech but a superior characteristic of the language, which depends on the legends, situations, and contents on which it feeds. A trembling that is no longer psychological but linguistic. To make the language itself stutter in this manner, at the deepest level of style, is a creative process that runs through all great works. It is as if the language were becoming animal. Pascal Quignard has shown how Masoch makes language "stammer": "stammering" is a putting into suspense, whereas "stuttering" is a repetition, a proliferation, a bifurcation, a deviation.[3] But this is not the essential difference. There are many diverse indications and procedures that the writer can apply to language in order to create a style. And whenever a language is submitted to such creative treatments, it is language in its entirety that is pushed to its limit, to music or silence. This is what Quignard shows: Masoch makes language stammer, and in this way he pushes language to its point of suspension, a song, a cry or silence—a song of the woods, a cry of the village, the silence of the steppe. The suspension of bodies and the stammering of language constitute the body-language, or the oeuvre, of Masoch.

8

Whitman

With much confidence and tranquility, Whitman states that writing is fragmentary, and that the *American* writer has to devote himself to writing in fragments. This is precisely what disturbs us—assigning this task to America, as if Europe had not progressed along this same path. But perhaps we should recall the difference Hölderlin discovered between the Greeks and the Europeans: what is natal or innate in the first must be acquired or conquered by the second, and vice-versa.[1] In a different manner, this is how things stand with the Europeans and the Americans. Europeans have an innate sense of organic totality, or composition, but they have to acquire the sense of the fragment, and can do so only through a tragic reflection or an experience of disaster. Americans, on the contrary, have a natural sense for the fragment, and what they have to conquer is the feel for the totality, for beautiful composition. The fragment already exists in a nonreflective manner, preceding any effort: we make plans, but when the time comes to act, we "tumble the thing together, letting hurry and crudeness tell the story better than fine work."[2] What is characteristic of America is therefore not the fragmentary, but the spontaneity of the fragmentary: "Spontaneous, fragmentary," says Whitman.[3] In America, literature is naturally *convulsive*: "they are but parts of the actual distraction, heat, smoke, and excitement of those times." But "convulsiveness," as Whitman makes clear, characterizes the epoch and the country as much as the writing.[4] If the fragment is innately American, it is because America itself is made up of federated states and various immigrant peoples (minorities)—everywhere a collection of fragments, haunted by the menace of secession, that is to say, by war. The experience of the American writer is inseparable from the American experience, even when the writer does not speak of America.

This is what gives the fragmentary work the immediate value of a collective statement. Kafka said that in a minor literature, that is, in the literature of a minority, there is no private history that is not immediately public, political, and popular: all literature becomes an "affair of the people," and not of exceptional individuals.[5] Is not American literature the minor literature par excellence, insofar as America claims to federate the most diverse minorities, "a Nation swarming with nations"? America brings together extracts, it presents samples from all ages, all lands, and all nations.[6] The simplest love story brings into play states, peoples, and tribes; the most personal autobiography is necessarily collective, as can still be seen in Wolfe or Miller. It is a popular literature created by the people, by the "average bulk," like the creation of America, and not by "great individuals."[7] And from this point of view, the Self [*Moi*] of the Anglo-Saxons, always splintered, fragmentary, and relative, is opposed to the substantial, total, and solipsistic I [*Je*] of the Europeans.

The world as a collection of heterogenous parts: an infinite patchwork, or an endless wall of dry stones (a cemented wall, or the pieces of a puzzle, would reconstitute a totality). The world as a *sampling:* the samples ("specimens") are singularities, remarkable and nontotalizable parts extracted from a series of ordinary parts. Samples of days, *specimen days,* says Whitman. Specimens of cases, specimens of scenes or views (*scenes, shows,* or *sights*). Sometimes the specimens are cases, in which coexistent parts are separated by intervals of space (the wounded in the hospitals), and sometimes they are specimens of views, in which the successive phases of a movement are separated by intervals of time (the moments of an uncertain battle). In both instances, the law is that of fragmentation. The fragments are grains, "granulations." Selecting singular cases and minor scenes is more important than any consideration of the whole. It is in the fragments that the hidden background appears, be it celestial or demonic. The fragment is "a reflection afar off" of a bloody or peaceful reality.[8] But the fragments—the remarkable parts, cases, or views—must still be extracted by means of a special act, an act that consists, precisely, in writing. For Whitman, fragmentary writing is not defined by the aphorism or through separation, but by a particular type of sentence that modulates the interval. It is as if the syntax that composes the sentence, which makes it a totality capable of referring back to itself, tends to disappear by setting free an infinite *asyntactic* sentence, which prolongs itself or sprouts dashes in order to create spatiotemporal intervals. Sometimes it appears as an occasional enumerative sentence, an enumeration of cases as in a catalog (the wounded in the hospital, the trees in a certain locale), sometimes it is a processionary sentence, like a protocol of phases or moments (a battle, convoys of cattle, successive swarms of bumblebees). It is an almost mad sentence, with its changes in direction, its bifurcations, its ruptures and leaps, its prolongations, its sproutings, its parentheses. Melville notes that "no American writer should write like an Englishman."[9] They have to dismantle the English language and send it racing along a line of flight, thereby rendering the language convulsive.

The law of the fragment is as valid for Nature as it is for History, for the Earth as for War, for good as for evil. For War and Nature indeed share a common cause: Nature moves forward in procession, by sections, like the corps of an army.[10] A "procession" of crows or bumblebees. But if it is true that the fragment is given everywhere, in the most spontaneous manner, we have seen that the whole, or an analogue of the whole, nonetheless has to be conquered and even invented. Yet Whitman sometimes places the Idea of the Whole *beforehand*, invoking a cosmos that beckons us to a kind of fusion; in a particularly "convulsive" meditation, he calls himself a "Hegelian," he asserts that only America "realizes" Hegel, and posits the primary rights of an organic totality.[11] He is then expressing himself like a European, who finds in pantheism a reason to inflate his own ego. But when Whitman speaks in his own manner and his own style, it turns out that a kind of whole must be constructed, a whole that is all the more paradoxical in that it only comes *after* the fragments and leaves them intact, making no attempt to totalize them.[12]

This complex idea depends on a principle dear to English philosophy, to which the Americans would give a new meaning and new developments: *relations are external to their terms*. Relations will consequently be posited as something that can and must be instituted or invented. Parts are fragments that cannot be totalized, but we can at least invent nonpreexisting relations between them, which testify to a progress in History as much as to an evolution in Nature. Whitman's poetry offers as many meanings as there are relations with its various

interlocutors: the masses, the reader, States, the Ocean . . .[13] The object
of American literature is to establish relations between the most diverse
aspects of the United States' geography—the Mississippi, the Rockies,
the Prairies—as well as its history, struggles, loves, and evolution.[14]
Relations in ever greater numbers and of increasingly subtle quality:
this is, as it were, the motor that drives both Nature and History. War
is just the opposite: its acts of destruction affect every relation, and
have as their consequence the Hospital, the generalized hospital, that
is, the place where brothers are strangers to each other, and where the
dying parts, fragments of mutilated men, coexist absolutely solitary
and without relation.[15]

The relations between colors are made up of contrasts and com-
plementarities, never given but always new, and Whitman no doubt
fabricated one of the most coloristic of literatures that could ever have
existed. The relations between sounds or bird songs, which Whitman
describes in marvelous ways, are made up of counterpoints and re-
sponses, constantly renewed and invented. Nature is not a form, but
rather the process of establishing relations. It invents a polyphony: it is
not a totality but an assembly, a "conclave," a "plenary session." Nature is inseparable from processes of companionship and conviviality,
which are not preexistent givens but are elaborated between heterogenous living beings in such a way that they create a tissue of shifting relations, in which the melody of one part intervenes as a motif in the
melody of another (the bee and the flower). Relations are not internal
to a Whole; rather, the Whole is derived from the external relations of
a given moment, and varies with them. Relations of counterpoint must
be invented everywhere, and are the very condition of evolution.

It is the same with the relationship between man and Nature.
Whitman enters into a gymnastic relationship with young oak trees, a
kind of hand-to-hand combat. He neither grounds himself in them
nor merges with them; rather, he makes something pass between the
human body and the tree, in both directions, the body receiving "some
of its elastic fibre and clear sap," but the tree for its part receiving a
little consciousness ("may-be we interchange").[16] It is the same, finally,
in the relationships between man and man. Here again, man must
invent his relation with the other. "Camaraderie" is the great word
Whitman uses to designate the highest human relation, not by virtue of
the totality of a situation but as a function of particular traits, emo-
tional circumstances, and the "interiority" of the relevant fragments

(in the hospital, for example, a relation of camaraderie must be established with each isolated dying man).[17] In this way is woven a web of variable relations, which are not merged into a whole, but produce the only whole that man is capable of conquering in a given situation. Camaraderie is the variability that implies an encounter with the Outside, a march of souls in the open air, on the "Open Road." It is in America that the relation of camaraderie is supposed to achieve its maximum extension and density, leading to virile and popular loves, all the while acquiring a political and national character—not a totalism or a totalitarianism but, as Whitman says, a "Unionism."[18] Democracy and Art themselves form a whole only in their relationship with Nature (the open air, light, colors, sounds, the night . . .); lacking these, art collapses into morbidity, and democracy, into deception.[19]

The society of comrades is the revolutionary American dream—a dream to which Whitman made a powerful contribution, and which was disappointed and betrayed long before the dream of the Soviet society. But it is also the reality of American literature, under these two aspects: spontaneity or the innate feeling for the fragmentary, and the reflection on living relations that must constantly be acquired and created. Spontaneous fragments constitute the element through which, or in the intervals of which, we attain the great and carefully considered visions and sounds of both Nature and History.

9
What Children Say

Children never stop talking about what they are doing or trying to do: exploring milieus, by means of dynamic trajectories,[1] and drawing up maps of them. The maps of these trajectories are essential to psychic activity. Little Hans wants to leave his family's apartment to spend the night at the little girl's downstairs and return in the morning—the apartment building as milieu. Or again: he wants to leave the building and go to the restaurant to meet with the little rich girl, passing by the horses at the warehouse—the street as milieu. Even Freud deems the intervention of a map to be necessary.[2]

As usual, however, Freud refers everything back to the father-mother: oddly enough, he sees the demand to explore the building as a desire to sleep with the mother. It is as if parents had primary places or functions that exist independently of milieus. But a milieu is made up of qualities, substances, powers, and events: the street, for example, with its materials (paving stones), its noises (the cries of merchants), its animals (harnessed horses) or its dramas (a horse slips, a horse falls down, a horse is beaten . . .). The trajectory merges not only with the subjectivity of those who travel through a milieu, but also with the subjectivity of the milieu itself, insofar as it is reflected in those who travel through it. The map expresses the identity of the journey and what one journeys through. It merges with its object, when the object itself is movement. Nothing is more instructive than the paths of autistic children, such as those whose maps Deligny has revealed and super-imposed, with their customary lines, wandering lines, loops, corrections, and turnings back—all their singularities.[3] Parents are themselves a milieu that children travel through: they pass through its qualities and powers and make a map of them. They take on a personal and parental form only as the representatives of one milieu within another. But it is wrong to think that children are limited before all else to their parents, and only had access to milieus *afterward,* by extention or derivation. The father and mother are not the coordinates of everything that is invested by the unconscious. There is never a moment when children are not already plunged into an actual milieu in which they are moving about, and in which the parents as persons simply play the roles of openers or closers of doors, guardians of thresholds, connectors or disconnectors of zones. The parents always occupy a position in a world that is not derived from them. Even with an infant, the parents are defined in relation to a continent-bed, as agents along the child's route. Lewin's hodological spaces, with their routes, their detours, their barriers, their agents, form a dynamic cartography.[4]

Little Richard was studied by Melanie Klein during the war. He lived and thought the world in the form of maps. He colored them in, inverted them, superimposed them, populated them with their leaders: England and Churchill, Germany and Hitler. It is the libido's business to haunt history and geography, to organize formations of worlds and constellations of universes, to make continents drift and to populate them with races, tribes, and nations. What beloved being does not envelope landscapes, continents, and populations that are more or less known, more or less imaginary? But Melanie Klein—who nonetheless went a long way in determining the milieus of the unconscious, from the point of view of substances or qualities as much as events—seems to misunderstand the cartographic activity of Little Richard. She can only see it as an *afterward,* a simple extension of parental personages, the good father, the bad mother . . . Children resist psychoanalytic forcing[5] and intoxication more than do adults: Hans and Richard inject all of their humor into the analysis. But they cannot resist for very long. They have to put away their maps, underneath which there is no longer anything but yellowed photos of the father-mother. "Mrs. K. interpreted, *interpreted,* INTERPRETED . . ." [6]

The libido does not undergo metamorphoses, but follows world-historical trajectories. From this point of view, it does not seem that the real and the imaginary form a pertinent distinction. A real voyage, by itself, lacks the force necessary to be reflected in the imagination; the imaginary voyage, by itself, does not have the force, as Proust says, to be verified in the real. This is why the imaginary and the real must be, rather, like two juxtaposable or superimposable parts of a single trajectory, two faces that ceaselessly interchange with one another, a mobile mirror. Thus the Australian Aborigines link nomadic itineraries to dream voyages, which together compose "an interstitching of routes," " in an immense cut-out [*découpe*] of space and time that must be read like a map."[7] At the limit, the imaginary is a virtual image that is interfused with the real object, and vice versa, thereby constituting a crystal of the unconscious. It is not enough for the real object or the real landscape to evoke similar or related images; it must disengage *its own* virtual image at the same time that the latter, as an imaginary landscape, makes its entry into the real, following a circuit where each of the two terms pursues the other, is interchanged with the other. "Vision" is the product of this doubling or splitting in two [*doublement ou dédoublement*], this coalescence. It is in such crystals of the unconscious that the trajectories of the libido are made visible.

A cartographic conception is very distinct from the archaeological conception of psychoanalysis. The latter establishes a profound link between the unconscious and memory: it is a memorial, commemorative, or monumental conception that pertains to persons or objects, the milieus being nothing more than terrains capable of conserving, identifying, or authenticating them. From such a point of view, the superposition of layers is necessarily traversed by a shaft that goes from top to bottom, and it is always a question of penetration. Maps, on the contrary, are superimposed in such a way that each map finds itself modified in the following map, rather than finding its origin in the preceding one: from one map to the next, it is not a matter of searching for an origin, but of evaluating *displacements*. Every map is a redistribution of impasses and breakthroughs, of thresholds and enclosures, which necessarily go from bottom to top. There is not only a reversal of directions, but also a difference in nature: the unconscious no longer deals with persons and objects, but with trajectories and becomings; it is no longer an unconscious of commemoration but one of mobilization, an unconscious whose objects take flight rather than remaining buried in the ground. In this regard, Félix Guattari has defined a schizoanalysis that opposes itself to psychoanalysis. "Lapses, parapraxes and symptoms are like birds that strike their beaks against the window. It is not a question of interpreting them. It is a question instead of identifying their trajectory to see if they can serve as indicators of new universes of reference capable of acquiring a consistency sufficient for turning a situation upside down."[8] The pharaoh's tomb, with its inert central chamber at the base of the pyramid, gives way to more dynamic models: from the drifting of continents to the migration of peoples, these are all means through which the unconscious maps the universe. *The Indian model replaces the Egyptian:* the Indians pass into the thickness of the rocks themselves, where aesthetic form is no longer identified with the commemoration of a departure or an arrival, but with the creation of paths without memory, all the memory of the world remaining in the material.[9]

Maps should not be understood only in extension, in relation to a space constituted by trajectories. There are also maps of intensity, of density, that are concerned with what fills space, what subtends the trajectory. Little Hans defines a horse by making out a list of its affects, both active and passive: having a big widdler, hauling heavy loads, having blinkers, biting, falling down, being whipped, making a row with its feet. It is this distribution of affects (with the widdler playing the role of a transformer or converter) that constitutes a map of intensity. It is always an affective constellation. Here again, it would be abusive to see this as a simple derivation from the father-mother, as does Freud—as if the "vision" of the street, so frequent at the time (a horse falls down, is whipped, struggles) were incapable of affecting the libido directly, and had to recall a lovemaking scene between the parents . . . Identifying the horse with the father borders on the grotesque and entails a misunderstanding of all the unconscious's relations with animal forces. And just as the map of movements or intensities was not a derivation from or an extension of the father-mother, the map of forces or intensities is not a derivation from the body, an extension of a prior image, or a supplement or afterword. Pollack and Sivadon have made a profound analysis of the cartographic activity of the unconscious; perhaps their sole ambiguity lies in seeing it as a continuation of the image of the body.[10] On the contrary, it is the map of intensity that distributes the affects, and it is their links and valences that constitute the image of the body in each case—an image that can always be modified or transformed depending on the affective constellations that determine it.

A list or constellation of affects, an intensive map, is a becoming: Little Hans does not form an unconscious representation of the father with the horse, but is drawn into a becoming-horse to which his parents are opposed. It is the same with little Arpad and his becoming-cock: in each case, psychoanalysis misconstrues the relationship of the unconscious with forces.[11] The image is not only a trajectory, but also a becoming. Becoming is what subtends the trajectory, just as intensive forces subtend motor forces. Hans's becoming-horse refers to a trajectory, from the apartment house to the warehouse. The passage alongside the warehouse, or even the visit to the henhouse, may be customary trajectories, but they are not innocent promenades. We see clearly why the real and the imaginary were led to exceed themselves, or even to interchange with each other: a becoming is not imaginary, any more than a voyage is real. It is becoming that turns the most negligible of trajectories, or even a fixed immobility, into a voyage; and it is the trajectory that turns the imaginary into a becoming. Each of the two types of maps, those of trajectories and those of affects, refers to the other.

What concerns the libido, what the libido invests, presents itself with an indefinite article, or rather is presented by the indefinite article: *an* animal as the qualification of a becoming or the specification of a trajectory (*a* horse, *a* chicken); a body or an organ as the power to affect and to be affected (*a* stomach, *some* eyes . . .); and even the characters that obstruct a pathway and inhibit affects, or on the contrary that further them (*a* father, *some* people . . .). Children express themselves in this manner—a father, a body, a horse. These indefinites often seem to result from a lack of determination due to the defenses of consciousness. For psychoanalysis, it is always a question of *my* father, *me*, *my* body. It has a mania for the possessive and the personal, and interpretation consists in recovering persons and possessions. "A child is being beaten" must signify "I am being beaten by my father," even if this transformation remains abstract; and "a horse falls down and kicks about with its legs" means that my father makes love with my mother. Yet the indefinite lacks nothing; above all, it does not lack determination. It is the determination of a becoming, its characteristic power, the power of an impersonal that is not a generality but a singularity at its highest point. For example, I do not play *the* horse, any more than I imitate *this or that* horse, but I become *a* horse, by reaching a zone of proximity where I can no longer be distinguished from what I am becoming.

Art also attains this celestial state that no longer retains anything of the personal or rational. In its own way, art says what children say. It is made up of trajectories and becomings, and it too makes maps, both extensive and intensive. There is always a trajectory in the work of art, and Stevenson, for example, shows the decisive importance of a colored map in his conception of *Treasure Island*.[12] This is not to say that a milieu necessarily determines the existence of characters, but rather that the latter are defined by the trajectories they make in reality or in spirit, without which they would not become. A colored map can be present in painting insofar as a painting is less a window on the world, *à l'italienne,* than an arrangement [*agencement*] on a surface.[13] In Vermeer, for example, the most intimate, most immobile becomings (the girl seduced by the soldier, the woman who receives a letter, the painter in the process of painting . . .) nonetheless refer to the vast distances [*parcours*] displayed on a map. I studied maps, said Fromentin "not in geography but in painting."[14] And just as trajectories are no more real than becomings are imaginary, there is something unique in their joining together that belongs only to art. Art is defined, then, as an impersonal process in which the work is composed somewhat like a *cairn,* with stones carried in by different voyagers and beings in becoming (rather than ghosts) [*devenants plutôt que revenants*] that may or may not depend on a single author.

Only a conception such as this can tear art away from the personal process of memory and the collective ideal of commemoration. To an archaeology-art, which penetrates the millennia in order to reach the immemorial, is opposed a cartography-art built on "things of forgetting and places of passage." The same thing happens when sculpture ceases to be monumental in order to become hodological: it is not enough to say that it is a landscape and that it lays out a place or territory. What it lays out are paths—it is itself a voyage. A sculpture follows the paths that give it an outside; it works only with nonclosed curves that divide up and traverse the organic body and has no other memory than that of the material (hence its procedure of direct cutting and its frequent utilization of wood). Carmen Perrin clears out erratic blocks from the greenery that integrates them into the undergrowth and delivers them to the memory of the glacier that carried them there, not in order to assign an origin to them but to make their *displacement* something visible.[15] One might object that a walking tour, as an art of paths, is no more satisfactory than the museum as a monumental or commemorative art. But there is something that distinguishes cartography-art from a walking tour in an essential way: it is characteristic of this new sculpture to assume a position on external trajectories, but this position depends primarily on paths internal to the work itself; the external path is a creation that does not exist before the work, and depends on its internal relations. One circles around a sculpture, and the viewing axes that belong to it make us grasp the body, sometimes along its entire length, sometimes in an astonishing foreshortening, sometimes in two or more diverging directions: its position in the surrounding space is strictly dependent on these internal trajectories. It is as if the real path were intertwined with virtual paths that give it new courses or trajectories. A map of virtualities, drawn up by art, is superimposed onto the real map, whose distances [*parcours*] it transforms. Such internal paths or courses are implied not only in sculpture, but in any work of art, including music: in each case, the choice of a particular path can determine a variable position of the work in space. Every work is made up of a plurality of trajectories that coexist and are readable only on a map, and that change direction depending on the trajectories that are retained.[16] These internalized trajectories are inseparable from becomings. *Trajectories and becomings:* art makes each of them present in the other, it renders their mutual presence perceptible. Thus defined, it invokes Dionysus as the god of places of passage and things of forgetting.

10
Bartleby; or, The Formula

"Bartleby" is neither a metaphor for the writer nor the symbol of anything whatsoever. It is a violently comical text, and the comical is always literal. It is like the novellas of Kleist, Dostoyevsky, Kafka, or Beckett, with which it forms a subterranean and prestigious lineage. It means only what it says, literally. And what it says and repeats is *I would prefer not to*. This is the formula of its glory, which every loving reader repeats in turn. A gaunt and pallid man has uttered the formula that drives everyone crazy. But in what does the literality of the formula consist?

We immediately notice a certain mannerism, a certain solemnity: *prefer* is rarely employed in this sense, and neither Bartleby's boss, the attorney, nor his clerks normally use it ("queer word, I never use it myself"). The usual formula would instead be *I had rather not*. But the strangeness of the formula goes beyond the word itself. Certainly it is grammatically correct, syntactically correct, but its abrupt termination, NOT TO, which leaves what it rejects undetermined, confers upon it the character of a radical, a kind of limit-function. Its repetition and its insistence render it all the more unusual, entirely so. Murmured in a soft, flat, and patient voice, it attains to the irremissible, by forming an inarticulate block, a single breath. In all these respects, it has the same force, the same role as an *agrammatical* formula.

Linguists have rigorously analyzed what is called "agrammaticality." A number of very intense examples can be found in the work of the American poet e. e. cummings—for instance, "he danced his did," as if one said in French *il dansa son mit* ("he danced his began") instead

68

of *il se mit à danser* ("he began to dance"). Nicolas Ruwet explains that this presupposes a series of ordinary grammatical variables, which would have an agrammatical formula as their limit: *he danced his did* would be a limit of the normal expressions *he did his dance, he danced his dance, he danced what he did* . . .[1] This would no longer be a portmanteau word, like those found in Lewis Carroll, but a "portmanteau-construction," a breath-construction, a limit or tensor. Perhaps it would be better to take an example from the French, in a practical situation: someone who wants to hang something on a wall and holds a certain number of nails in his hand exclaims, J'EN AI UN DE PAS ASSEZ ("I have one not enough"). This is an agrammatical formula that stands as the limit of a series of correct expressions: *J'en ai de trop, Je n'en ai pas assez, Il m'en manque un* . . . ("I have too many," "I don't have enough," "I am one short" . . .). Would not Bartleby's formula be of this type, at once a stereotypy of Bartleby's and a highly poetic expression of Melville's, the limit of a series such as "I would prefer this. I would prefer not to do that. That is not what I would prefer . . ."? Despite its quite normal construction, it has an anomalous ring to it.

I WOULD PREFER NOT TO. The formula has several variants. Sometimes it abandons the conditional and becomes more curt: I PREFER NOT TO. Sometimes, as in its final occurrences, it seems to lose its mystery by being completed by an infinitive, and coupled with *to:* "I prefer to give no answer," "I would prefer not to be a little reasonable," "I would prefer not to take a clerkship," "I would prefer to be doing something else" . . . But even in these cases we sense the muted presence of the strange form that continues to haunt Bartleby's language. He himself adds, "but I am not a particular case," "there is nothing particular about me," *I am not particular,* in order to indicate that whatever else might be suggested to him would be yet another particularity falling under the ban of the great indeterminate formula, I PREFER NOT TO, which subsists once and for all and in all cases.

The formula occurs in ten principal circumstances, and in each case it may appear several times, whether it is repeated verbatim or with minor variations. Bartleby is a copyist in the attorney's office; he copies ceaselessly, "silently, palely, mechanically." The first instance takes place when the attorney tells him to proofread and collate the two clerks' copies: I WOULD PREFER NOT TO. The second, when the attorney tells Bartleby to come and reread his own copies. The third, when the attorney invites Bartleby to reread with him personally, tête à tête. The fourth, when the attorney wants to send him on an errand. The fifth, when he asks him to go into the next room. The sixth, when the attorney enters his study one Sunday afternoon and discovers that Bartleby has been sleeping there. The seventh, when the attorney satisfies himself by asking questions. The eighth, when Bartleby has stopped copying, has renounced all copying, and the attorney asks him to leave. The ninth, when the attorney makes a second attempt to get rid of him. The tenth, when Bartleby is forced out of the office, sits on the banister of the landing while the panic-stricken attorney proposes other, unexpected occupations to him (a clerkship in a dry goods store, bartender, bill collector, traveling companion to a young gentleman . . .). The formula bourgeons and proliferates. At each occurrence, there is a stupor surrounding Bartleby, as if one had heard the Unspeakable or the Unstoppable. And there is Bartleby's silence, as if he had said everything and exhausted language at the same time. With each instance, one has the impression that the madness is growing: not Bartleby's madness in "particular," but the madness around him, notably that of the attorney, who launches into strange propositions and even stranger behaviors.

Without a doubt, the formula is ravaging, devastating, and leaves nothing standing in its wake. Its contagious character is immediately evident: Bartleby "ties the tongues" of others. The queer words, *I would prefer,* steal their way into the language of the clerks and of the attorney himself ("So you have got the word, too"). But this contamination is not the essential point; the essential point is its effect on Bartleby: from the moment he says I WOULD PREFER NOT TO (collate), he is no longer *able* to copy either. And yet he will never say that he prefers not to (copy): he has simply passed beyond this stage. And doubtless he does not realize this immediately, since he continues copying until after the sixth instance. But when he does notice it, it seems obvious, like the delayed reaction that was already implied in the first statement of the formula: "Do you not see the reason for yourself?" he says to the attorney. The effect of the formula-block is not only to impugn what Bartleby prefers not to do, but also to render what he was doing impossible, what he was supposed to prefer to continue doing.

It has been noted that the formula, I prefer not to, is neither an affirmation nor a negation. Bartleby "does not refuse, but neither does he accept, he advances and then withdraws into this advance, barely exposing himself in a nimble retreat from speech."[2] The attorney would be relieved if Bartleby did not want to, but Bartleby does not refuse, he simply rejects a nonpreferred (the proofreading, the errands . . .). And he does not accept either, he does not affirm a preference that would consist in continuing to copy, he simply posits its impossibility. In short, the formula that successively refuses every other act has already engulfed the act of copying, which it no longer even needs to refuse. The formula is devastating because it eliminates the preferable just as mercilessly as any nonpreferred. It not only abolishes the term it refers to, and that it rejects, but also abolishes the other term it seemed to preserve, and that becomes impossible. In fact, it renders them indistinct: it hollows out an ever expanding zone of indiscernibility or indetermination between some nonpreferred activities and a preferable activity. All particularity, all reference is abolished. The formula annihilates "copying," the only reference in relation to which something might or might not be preferred. I would prefer nothing rather than something: not a will to nothingness, but the growth of a nothingness of the will. Bartleby has won the right to survive, that is, to remain immobile and upright before a blind wall. Pure patient passivity, as Blanchot would say. Being as being, and nothing more. He is urged to say yes or no. But if he said no (to collating, running errands . . .), or if he said yes (to copying), he would quickly be defeated and judged useless, and would not survive. He can survive only by whirling in a suspense that keeps everyone at a distance. His means of survival is to prefer *not* to collate, but thereby also *not* to prefer copying. He had to refuse the former in order to render the latter impossible. The formula has two phases and continually recharges itself by passing again and again through the same states. This is why the attorney has the vertiginous impression, each time, that everything is starting over again from zero.

The formula at first seems like the bad translation of a foreign language. But once we understand it better, once we hear it more clearly, its splendor refutes this hypothesis. Perhaps it is the formula that carves out a kind of foreign language within language. It has been suggested that e. e. cummings's agrammaticalities can be considered as having issued from a dialect differing from Standard English, and whose rules of creation can be abstracted. The same goes for Bartleby: the rule would lie in this logic of negative preference, a negativism beyond all negation. But if it is true that the masterpieces of literature always form a kind of foreign language within the language in which they are written, what wind of madness, what psychotic breath thereby passes into language as a whole? Psychosis characteristically brings into play a *procedure* that treats an ordinary language, a standard language, in a manner that makes it "render" an original and unknown language, which would perhaps be a projection of God's language, and would carry off language as a whole. Procedures of this type appear in France in Roussel and Brisset, and in America in Wolfson. Is this not the schizophrenic vocation of American literature: to make the English language, by means of driftings, deviations, de-taxes or sur-taxes (as opposed to the standard syntax), slip in this manner? To introduce a bit of psychosis into English neurosis? To invent a new universality? If need be, other languages will be summoned into English in order to make it echo this divine language of storm and thunder. Melville invents a foreign language that runs beneath English and carries it off: it is the OUTLANDISH or Deterritorialized, the language of the Whale. Whence the interest of studies of *Moby-Dick* that are based on Numbers and Letters, and their cryptic meaning, to set free at least a skeleton of the inhuman or superhuman originary language.[3] It is as if three operations were linked together: a certain treatment of language; the result of this treatment, which tends to constitute an original language within language; and the effect, which is to sweep up language in its entirety, sending it into flight, pushing it to its very limit in order to discover its Outside, silence or music. A great book is always the inverse of another book that could only be written in the soul, with silence and blood. This is the case not only with *Moby-Dick* but also with *Pierre,* in which Isabelle affects language with an incomprehensible murmur, a kind of *basso continuo* that carries the whole of language on the chords and tones of its guitar. And it is also the angelic or adamic Billy Budd, who suffers from a stuttering that denatures language but also gives rise to the musical and celestial Beyond of language as a whole. It is like the "persistent horrible twittering squeak" that muddles the resonance of words, while the sister is getting the violin ready to respond to Gregor.

Bartleby also has an angelic and Adamic nature, but his case seems different because he has no general Procedure, such as stuttering, with which to treat language. He makes do with a seemingly normal, brief Formula, at best a localized tick that crops up in certain circumstances. And yet the result and the effect are the same: to carve out a kind of foreign language within language, to make the whole confront silence, make it topple into silence. *Bartleby* announces the long silence, broken only by the music of poems, into which Melville will enter and from which, except for *Billy Budd,* he will never emerge.[4] Bartleby himself had no other escape than to remain silent and withdraw behind his partition every time he uttered the formula, all the way up until his final silence in prison. After the formula there is nothing left to say: it functions as a procedure, overcoming its appearance of particularity.

The attorney himself concocts a theory explaining how Bartleby's formula ravages language as a whole. All language, he suggests, has references or assumptions. These are not exactly what language designates, but what permit it to designate. A word always presupposes other words that can replace it, complete it, or form alternatives with it: it is on this condition that language is distributed in such a way as to designate things, states of things and actions, according to a set of objective, explicit conventions. But perhaps there are also other implicit and subjective conventions, other types of reference or presupposition. In speaking, I do not simply indicate things and actions; I also commit acts that assure a relation with the interlocutor, in keeping with our respective situations: I command, I interrogate, I promise, I ask, I emit "speech acts." Speech acts are self-referential (I command by saying "I order you . . ."), while constative propositions refer to other things and other words. It is this double system of references that Bartleby ravages.

The formula I PREFER NOT TO excludes all alternatives, and devours what it claims to conserve no less than it distances itself from everything else. It implies that Bartleby stop copying, that is, that he stop reproducing words; it hollows out a zone of indetermination that renders words indistinguishable, that creates a vacuum within language [*langage*]. But it also stymies the speech acts that a boss uses to command, that a kind friend uses to ask questions or a man of faith to make promises. If Bartleby had refused, he could still be seen as a rebel or insurrectionary, and as such would still have a social role. But the formula stymies all speech acts, and at the same time, it makes Bartleby a pure outsider [*exclu*] to whom no social position can be attributed. This is what the attorney glimpses with dread: all his hopes of bringing Bartleby back to reason are dashed because they rest on a *logic of presuppositions* according to which an employer "expects" to be obeyed, or a kind friend listened to, whereas Bartleby has invented a new logic, *a logic of preference,* which is enough to undermine the presuppositions of language as a whole. As Mathieu Lindon shows, the formula "disconnects" words and things, words and actions, but also speech acts and words—it severs language from all reference, in accordance with Bartleby's absolute vocation, *to be a man without references,* someone who appears suddenly and then disappears, without reference to himself or anything else.[5] This is why, despite its conventional appearance, the formula functions as a veritable agrammaticality.

Bartleby is the Bachelor, about whom Kafka said, "He has only as much ground as his two feet take up, only as much of a hold as his two hands encompass"—someone who falls asleep in the winter snow to freeze to death like a child, someone who does nothing but take walks, yet who could take them anywhere, without moving.[6] Bartleby is the man without references, without possessions, without properties, without qualities, without particularities: he is too smooth for anyone to be able to hang any particularity on him. Without past or future, he is instantaneous. I PREFER NOT TO is Bartleby's chemical or alchemical formula, but one can read inversely I AM NOT PARTICULAR as its indispensable complement. The entire nineteenth century will go through this search for the man without a name, regicide and parricide, the modern-day Ulysses ("I am No One"): the crushed and mechanized man of the great metropolises, but from which one expects, perhaps, the emergence of the Man of the Future or New World Man. And, in an identical messianism, we glimpse him, sometimes as a Proletarian, sometimes as an American. Musil's novel will also follow this quest, and will invent the new logic of which *The Man without Qualities* is both the thinker and the product.[7] And though the derivation of Musil from Melville seems certain to us, it should be sought not in "Bartleby," but rather in *Pierre; or, the Ambiguities.* The incestuous couple Ulrich-Agathe is like the return of the Pierre-Isabelle couple; in both cases, the silent sister, unknown or forgotten, is not a substitute for the mother, but on the contrary the abolition of sexual difference as particularity, in favor of an androgynous relationship in which both Pierre and Ulrich are or become woman. In Bartleby's case, might not his relation with the attorney be equally mysterious, and in turn mark the possibility of a becoming, of a new man? Will Bartleby be able to conquer the place where he takes his walks?

Perhaps Bartleby is a madman, a lunatic or a psychotic ("an innate and incurable disorder" of the soul). But how can we know, if we do not take into account the anomalies of the attorney, who continues to behave in the most bizarre ways? The attorney had just received an important professional promotion. One will recall that President

Schreber unleashed his own delirium only after receiving a promotion, as if this gave him the audacity to take the risk. But what is the attorney going to risk? He already has two scriveners who, much like Kafka's assistants, are inverted doubles of each other, the one normal in the morning and drunk in the afternoon, the other in a perpetual state of indigestion in the morning but almost normal in the afternoon. Since he needs an extra scrivener, he hires Bartleby after a brief conversation *without any references* because his pallid aspect seemed to indicate a constancy that could compensate for the irregularities of the two others. But on the first day he places Bartleby in a strange arrangement: Bartleby is to sit in the attorney's own office, next to some folding doors separating it from the clerk's office, between a window that faces the side of a neighboring building and a high screen, green as a prairie, as if it were important that Bartleby be able to hear, but without being seen. Whether this was a sudden inspiration on the attorney's part or an agreement reached during the short conversation, we will never know. But the fact is that, caught in this arrangement, the invisible Bartleby does an extraordinary amount of "mechanical" work. But when the attorney tries to make him leave his retreat, Bartleby emits his formula, and at this first occurrence, as with those that follow, the attorney finds himself disarmed, bewildered, stunned, thunderstruck, without response or reply. Bartleby stops copying altogether and remains on the premises, a fixture. We know to what extremes the attorney is forced to go in order to rid himself of Bartleby: he returns home, decides to relocate his office, then takes off for several days and hides out, avoiding the new tenant's complaints. What a strange flight, with the wandering attorney living in his rockaway . . . From the initial arrangement to this irrepressible, Cain-like flight, everything is bizarre, and the attorney behaves like a madman. Murder fantasies and declarations of love for Bartleby alternate in his soul. What happened? Is it a case of shared madness, here again, another relationship between doubles, a nearly acknowledged homosexual relation ("yes, Bartleby . . . I never feel so private as when I know you are here . . . I penetrate to the predestinated purpose of my life . . .")?[8]

One might imagine that hiring Bartleby was a kind of pact, as if the attorney, following his promotion, had decided to make this person, without objective references, a man of confidence [*un homme de confiance*] who would owe everything to him. He wants to make him *his* man. The pact consists of the following: Bartleby will sit near his master and copy, listening to him but without being seen, like a night bird who cannot stand to be looked at. So there is no doubt that once the attorney wants to draw (without even doing it on purpose) Bartleby from behind his screen to correct the copies with the others, he breaks the pact. This is why Bartleby, once he "prefers not to" correct, is already unable to copy. Bartleby will expose himself to view even more than he is asked to, planted in the middle of the office, but he will no longer do any copying. The attorney has an obscure feeling about it, since he assumes that if Bartleby refuses to copy, it is because his vision is impaired. And in effect, exposed to view, Bartleby for his part no longer sees, no longer looks. He has acquired what was, in a certain fashion, already innate in him: the legendary infirmity, one-eyed and one-armed, which makes him an autochthon, someone who is born to and stays in a particular place, while the attorney necessarily fills the function of the traitor condemned to flight. Whenever the attorney invokes philanthropy, charity, or friendship, his protestations are shot through with an obscure guilt. In fact, it is the attorney who broke the arrangement he himself had organized, and from the debris Bartleby pulls a trait of expression, I PREFER NOT TO, which will proliferate around him and contaminate the others, sending the attorney fleeing. But it will also send language itself into flight, it will open up a zone of indetermination or indiscernibility in which neither words nor characters can be distinguished—the fleeing attorney and the immobile, petrified Bartleby. The attorney starts to vagabond while Bartleby remains tranquil, but it is precisely because he remains tranquil and immobile that Bartleby is treated like a vagabond.

Is there a relation of identification between the attorney and Bartleby? But what is this relation? In what direction does it move? Most often, an identification seems to bring into play three elements, which are able to interchange or permutate: a form, image, or representation, a portrait, a model; a subject (or at least a virtual subject); and the subject's efforts to assume a form, to appropriate the image, to adapt itself to this image and the image to itself. It is a complex operation that passes through all of the adventures of resemblance, and that always risks falling into neurosis or turning into narcissism. A "mimetic rivalry," as it is sometimes called. It mobilizes a paternal function in general: an image of the father par excellence, and the subject is a son, even if the determinations are interchangeable. The bildungsroman

[*roman de formation*], or one could just as easily say the reference novel [*roman de reference*], provides numerous examples.

Certainly, many of Melville's novels begin with images or portraits, and seem to tell the story of an upbringing under a paternal function: *Redburn*, for instance. *Pierre; or, The Ambiguities* begins with an image of the father, with a statue and a painting. Even *Moby-Dick* begins by amassing information at the beginning in order to give the whale a form and sketch out its image, right down to the dark painting hanging in the inn. "Bartleby" is no exception to the rule. The two clerks are like paper images, symmetrical opposites, and the attorney fills the paternal function so well that one can hardly believe the story is taking place in New York. Everything starts off as in an English novel, in Dickens's London. But in each case, something strange happens, something that blurs the image, marks it with an essential uncertainty, keeps the form from "taking," but also undoes the subject, sets it adrift and abolishes any paternal function. It is only here that things begin to get interesting. The statue of the father gives way to his much more ambiguous portrait, and then to yet another portrait that could be of anybody or nobody. All referents are lost, and the formation [*formation*] of man gives way to a new, unknown element, to the mystery of a formless, nonhuman life, a *Squid*. Everything began *à l'anglaise* but continues *à l'américaine*, following an irresistible line of flight. Ahab can say with good reason that he is fleeing from everywhere. The paternal function is dropped in favor of even more obscure and ambiguous forces. The subject loses its texture in favor of an infinitely proliferating patchwork: the American patchwork becomes the law of Melville's oeuvre, devoid of a center, of an upside down or right side up. It is as if the traits of expression escaped form, like the abstract lines of an unknown writing, or the furrows that twist from Ahab's brow to that of the Whale, or the "horrible contortions" of the flapping lanyards that pass through the fixed rigging and can easily drag a sailor into the sea, a subject into death.[9] In *Pierre; or, The Ambiguities*, the disquieting smile of the unknown young man in the painting, which so resembles the father's, functions as a trait of expression that emancipates itself, and is just as capable of undoing resemblance as it is of making the subject vacillate. I PREFER NOT TO is also a trait of expression that contaminates everything, escaping linguistic form and stripping the father of his exemplary speech, just as it strips the son of his ability to reproduce or copy.

It is still a process of identification, but rather than following the adventures of the neurotic, it has now become psychotic. A little bit of schizophrenia escapes the neurosis of the Old World. We can bring together three distinctive characteristics. In the first place, the formless trait of expression is opposed to the image or to the expressed form. In the second place, there is no longer a subject that tries to conform to the image, and either succeeds or fails. Rather, a zone of indistinction, of indiscernibility, or of ambiguity seems to be established between two terms, as if they had reached the point immediately preceeding their respective differentiation: not a similitude, but a slippage, an extreme proximity, an absolute contiguity; not a natural filiation, but an unnatural alliance. It is a "hyperborean," "arctic" zone. It is no longer a question of Mimesis, but of becoming. Ahab does not imitate the whale, he becomes Moby-Dick, he enters into the zone of proximity [zone de voisinage] where he can no longer be distinguished from Moby-Dick, and strikes himself in striking the whale. Moby-Dick is the "wall, shoved near" with which he merges. Redburn renounces the image of the father in favor of the ambiguous traits of the mysterious brother. Pierre does not imitate his father, but reaches the zone of proximity where he can no longer be distinguished from his half sister, Isabelle, and becomes woman. While neurosis flounders in the nets of maternal incest in order to identify more closely with the father, psychosis liberates incest with the sister as a becoming, a free identification of man and woman: in the same way Kleist emits atypical, almost animal traits of expression—stutterings, grindings, grimaces—that feed his passionate conversation with his sister. This is because, in the third place, psychosis pursues its dream of establishing a function of universal fraternity that no longer passes through the father, but is built on the ruins of the paternal function, a function that presupposes the dissolution of all images of the father, following an autonomous line of alliance or proximity that makes the woman a sister, and the other man, a brother, like the terrible "monkey-rope" uniting Ishmael and Queequeg as a married couple. These are the three characteristics of the American Dream, which together make up the new identification, the New World: the Trait, the Zone, and the Function.

We are in the process of melding together characters as different as Ahab and Bartleby. Yet does not everything instead set them in opposition to each other? Melvillian psychiatry constantly invokes two poles: *monomaniacs* and *hypochondriacs*, demons and angels, torturers and victims, the Swift and the Slow, the Thundering and the Petrified, the Unpunishable (beyond all punishment) and the Irresponsible (beyond all responsibility). What is Ahab doing when he lets loose his harpoons of fire and madness? He is breaking a pact. He is betraying the Whalers' Law, which says that any healthy whale encountered must be hunted, without choosing one over another. But Ahab, thrown into his indiscernible becoming, makes a choice—he pursues his identification with Moby-Dick, putting his crew in mortal danger. This is the monstrous preference that Lieutenant Starbuck bitterly objects to, to the point where he even dreams of killing the treacherous captain. Choosing is the Promethean sin *par excellence*.[10] This was the case with Kleist's Penthesilea, an Ahab-woman who, like her indiscernible double Achilles, had chosen her enemy, in defiance of the law of the Amazons forbidding the preference of one enemy over another. The priestess and the Amazons consider this a betrayal that madness sanctions in a cannibal identification. In his last novel, *Billy Budd,* Melville himself brings another monomaniacal demon into the picture with Claggart: the master-at-arms. We should have no illusions about Claggart's subordinate function: his is no more a case of psychological wickedness than Captain Ahab's. It is a case of metaphysical perversion that consists in choosing one's prey, preferring a chosen victim with a kind of love rather than observing the maritime law that requires him to apply the same discipline to everyone. This is what the narrator suggests when he recalls an ancient and mysterious theory, an exposé of which is found in Sade: secondary, sensible Nature is governed by the Law (or laws), while *innately depraved beings* participate in a terrible supersensible Primary Nature, original and oceanic, which, knowing no Law, pursues its own irrational aim through them. Nothingness, Nothingness.[11] Ahab will break through the wall, even if there is nothing behind it, and will make nothingness the object of his will: "To me, the white whale is that wall, shoved near to me. Sometimes I think there's naught beyond. But 'tis enough."[12] Melville says that only the eye of a *prophet,* and not a psychologist, is capable of discerning or diagnosing such obscure beings as these creatures of the abyss, without being able to prevent their mad enterprise, the "mystery of iniquity" . . .

We are now in a position to classify Melville's great characters. At one pole, there are those monomaniacs or demons who, driven by the will to nothingness, make a monstrous choice: Ahab, Claggart, Babo . . . But at the other pole are those angels or saintly hypochondriacs, almost stupid, creatures of innocence and purity, stricken with a constitutive weakness but also with a strange beauty. Petrified by nature, they prefer . . . no will at all, a nothingness of the will rather than a will to nothingness (hypochondriacal "negativism"). They can only survive by becoming stone, by denying the will and sanctifying themselves in this suspension.[13] Such are Cereno, Billy Budd, and above all Bartleby. And although the two types are opposed in every way—the former innate traitors and the latter betrayed in their very essence; the former monstrous fathers who devour their children, the latter abandoned sons without fathers—they haunt one and the same world, forming alternations within it, just as Melville's writing, like Kleist's, alternates between stationary, fixed processes and mad-paced procedures: *style*, with its succession of catatonias and accelerations . . . This is because both poles, both types of characters, Ahab and Bartleby, *belong to this Primary Nature*, they inhabit it, they constitute it. Everything sets them in opposition, and yet they are perhaps the same creature—primary, original, stubborn, seized from both sides, marked merely with a "plus" or a "minus" sign: Ahab and Bartleby. Or in Kleist, the terrible Penthesilea and the sweet little Catherine, the first beyond conscience, the second before conscience: she who chooses and she who does not choose, she who howls like a she-wolf and she who would prefer-not-to speak.[14]

There exists, finally, a third type of character in Melville, the one on the side of the Law, the guardian of the divine and human laws of secondary nature: the prophet. Captain Delano lacks the prophet's eye, but Ishmael in *Moby-Dick*, Captain Vere in *Billy Budd*, and the attorney in *Bartleby* all have this power to "See": they are capable of grasping and understanding, as much as is possible, the beings of Primary Nature, the great monomaniacal demons or the saintly innocents, and sometimes both. Yet they themselves are not lacking in ambiguity, each in his own way. Though they are able to see into the Primary Nature that so fascinates them, they are nonetheless representatives of secondary nature and its laws. They bear the paternal image—they seem like good fathers, benevolent fathers (or at least protective big brothers, as Ishmael is toward Queequeg). But they cannot ward off the demons, because the latter are too quick for the law, too surprising. Nor can they save the innocent, the irresponsible: they immolate them in the name of the Law, they make the sacrifice of Abraham. Behind their paternal mask, they have a kind of double identification: with the innocent, toward whom they feel a genuine love, but also with the demon, since they break their pact with the innocent they love, each in his own manner. They betray, then, but in a different way than does Ahab or Claggart: the latter broke the law, whereas Vere or the attorney, in the name of the law, break an implicit and almost unavowable agreement (even Ishmael seems to turn away from his savage brother Queequeg). They continue to cherish the innocent they have condemned: Captain Vere will die muttering the name of Billy Budd, and the final words of the attorney's narrative will be, "Ah, Bartleby! Ah, humanity!" which does not indicate a connection, but rather an alternative in which he has had to choose the all-too-human law over Bartleby. Torn between the two Natures, with all their contradictions, these characters are extremely important, but do not have the stature of the two others. Rather, they are Witnesses, narrators, interpreters. There is a problem that escapes this third type of character, a very important problem that is settled between the other two.

The Confidence-Man (much as one says the Medicine-Man) is sprinkled with Melville's reflections on the novel. The first of these reflections consists in claiming the rights of a superior irrationalism (chapter 14). Why should the novelist believe he is obligated to explain the behavior of his characters, and to supply them with reasons, whereas life for its part never explains anything and leaves in its creatures so many indeterminate, obscure, indiscernible zones that defy any attempt at clarification? It is life that justifies; it has no need of being justified. The English novel, and even more so the French novel, feels the need to rationalize, even if only in the final pages, and psychology is no doubt the last form of rationalism: the Western reader awaits the final word. In this regard, psychoanalysis has revived the claims of reason. But even if it has hardly spared the great novelistic works, no great novelist contemporaneous with psychoanalysis has taken much interest in it. The founding act of the American novel, like that of the Russian novel, was to take the novel far from the order of reasons, and to give birth to characters who exist in nothingness, survive only in the void, defy logic and psychology and keep their mystery until the end. Even their soul, says Melville, is "an immense and terrifying void," and Ahab's body is an "empty shell." If they have a formula, it is certainly not explanatory. I PREFER NOT TO remains just as much a cabalistic formula as that of the Underground Man, who can not keep two and two from making four, but who will not RESIGN himself to it either (*he prefers that two and two not make four*). What counts for a great novelist—Melville, Dostoyevsky, Kafka, or Musil— is that things remain enigmatic yet nonarbitrary: in short, a new logic, definitely a logic, but one that grasps the innermost depths of life and death without leading us back to reason. The novelist has the eye of a prophet, not the gaze of a psychologist. For Melville, the three great categories of characters belong to this new logic, just as much as this logic belongs to them. Once it has reached that sought-after Zone, the hyperborean zone, far from the temperate regions, the novel, like life, needs no justification.[15] And in truth, there is no such thing as reason; it exists only in bits and pieces. In *Billy Budd*, Melville defines mono-maniacs as the Masters of reason, which is why they are so difficult to surprise; but this is because theirs is a delirium of action, because they make use of reason, make it serve their own sovereign ends, which in truth are highly unreasonable. Hypochondriacs are the Outcasts of reason, without our being able to know if they have excluded them-selves from it in order to obtain something reason can not give them— the indiscernible, the unnameable with which they will be able to merge. In the end, even prophets are only the Castaways of reason: if Vere, Ishmael, or the attorney clings so tightly to the debris of reason, whose integrity they try so hard to restore, it is because they have *seen* so much, and because what they have seen has marked them forever.

But a second remark by Melville (chapter 44) introduces an essen-tial distinction between the characters in a novel. Melville says that we must above all avoid confusing true Originals with characters that are simply remarkable or singular, particular. This is because the particu-lars, who tend to be quite populous in a novel, have characteristics that determine their form, properties that make up their image; they are influenced by their milieu and by each other, so that their actions and reactions are governed by general laws, though in each case they retain a particular value. Similarly, the sentences they utter are their own, but they are nonetheless governed by the general laws of language. By contrast, we do not even know if an original exists in an absolute sense, apart from the primordial God, and it is already something extraordinary when we encounter one. Melville admits that it is diffi-cult to imagine how a novel might include several of them. Each origi-nal is a powerful, solitary Figure that exceeds any explicable form: it projects flamboyant traits of expression that mark the stubbornness of a thought without image, a question without response, an extreme and nonrational logic. Figures of life and knowledge, they know something inexpressible, live something unfathomable. They have nothing general about them, and are not particular—they escape knowledge, defy psychology. Even the words they utter surpass the general laws of language (presuppositions) as well as the simple particularities of speech, since they are like the vestiges or projections of a unique, original language [langue], and bring all of language [langage] to the limit of silence and music. There is nothing particular or general about Bartleby: he is an Original.

Originals are beings of Primary Nature, but they are inseparable from the world or from secondary nature, where they exert their effect: they reveal its emptiness, the imperfection of its laws, the mediocrity of particular creatures . . . the world as masquerade (this is what Musil, for his part, will call "parallel action"). The role of prophets, who are not originals, is to be the only ones who can recognize the wake that originals leave in the world, and the unspeakable confusion and trouble they cause in it. The original, says Melville, is not subject to the influence of his milieu; on the contrary, he throws a livid white light on his surroundings, much like the light that "accompanies the beginning of things in Genesis." Originals are sometimes the immobile source of this light—like the foretopman high up on the mast, Billy Budd the bound, hanged man who "ascends" with the glimmering of the dawn, or Bartleby standing in the attorney's office—and sometimes its dazzling passage, a movement too rapid for the ordinary eye to follow, the lightning of Ahab or Claggart. These are the two great original Figures that one finds throughout Melville, the panoramic shot and the tracking shot, stationary process and infinite speed. And even though these are the two elements of music, though stops give rhythm to movement and lightning springs from immobility, is it not this contradiction that separates the originals, their two types? What does Jean-Luc Godard mean when, in the name of cinema, he asserts that between a tracking shot and a panoramic shot there lies a "moral problem"? Perhaps it is this difference that explains why a great novel cannot, it seems, include more than a single original. Mediocre novels have never been able to create the slightest original character. But how could even the greatest novel create more than one at a time? Ahab or Bartleby . . . It is like the great Figures of the painter Francis Bacon, who admits that he has not yet found a way of bringing together two figures in a single painting.[16] And yet Melville will find a way. If he finally broke his silence in the

end to write *Billy Budd,* it is because this last novel, under the pene-
trating eye of Captain Vere, brings together two originals, the demonic
and the petrified. The problem was not to link them together through
a plot—an easy and inconsequential thing to do, since it would be
enough for one to be the victim of the other—but to make them *work
together* in the picture (if *Benito Cereno* was already an attempt in this
direction, it was a flawed one, under the myopic and blurred gaze of
Delano).

What then is the biggest problem haunting Melville's oeuvre? To
recover the already-sensed identity? No doubt, it lies in reconciling the
two originals *but thereby also in reconciling the original with secondary humanity,* the inhuman with the human. Now what Captain
Vere and the attorney demonstrate is that there are no good fathers.
There are only monstrous, devouring fathers, and petrified, fatherless
sons. If humanity can be saved, and the originals reconciled, it will
only be through the dissolution or decomposition of the paternal function. So it is a great moment when Ahab, invoking Saint Elmo's fire,
discovers that the father is himself a lost son, an orphan, whereas the
son is the son of nothing, or of everyone, a brother.[17] As Joyce will say,
paternity does not exist, it is an emptiness, a nothingness—or rather, a
zone of uncertainty haunted by brothers, by the brother and sister. The
mask of the charitable father must fall in order for Primary Nature to
be appeased, and for Ahab and Claggart to recognize Bartleby and
Billy Budd, releasing through the violence of the former and the stupor
of the latter the fruit with which they were laden: the fraternal relation
pure and simple. Melville will never cease to elaborate on the radical
opposition between fraternity and Christian "charity" or paternal
"philanthropy." To liberate man from the father function, to give birth
to the new man or the man without particularities, to reunite the original and humanity by constituting a society of brothers as a new universality. In the society of brothers, alliance replaces filiation and the
blood pact replaces consanguinity. Man is indeed the blood brother of
his fellow man, and woman, his blood sister: acccording to Melville,
this is the *community of celibates,* drawing its members into an unlimited becoming. A brother, *a* sister, all the more true for no longer being
"his" or "hers," since all "property," all "proprietorship," has disappeared. A burning passion deeper than love, since it no longer has
either substance or qualities, but traces a zone of indiscernibility in
which it passes through all intensities in every direction, extending all

the way to the homosexual relation between brothers, and passing through the incestuous relation between brother and sister. This is the most mysterious relation, the one in which Pierre and Isabelle are swept up, the one that draws Heathcliff and Catherine along in *Wuthering Heights,* each one becoming Ahab and Moby-Dick by turns: "Whatever our souls are made of, his and mine are the same. . . . My love for Heathcliff resembles the eternal rocks beneath—a source of little visible delight, but necessary. . . . I *am* Heathcliff—he's always always in my mind—not as a pleasure, any more than I am always a pleasure to myself—but as my own being . . ."[18]

How can this community be realized? How can the biggest problem be resolved? But is it not already resolved, by itself, precisely because it is not a personal problem, but a historical, geographic, or political one? It is not an individual or particular affair, but a collective one, the affair of a people, or rather, of all peoples. It is not an Oedipal phantasm but a political program. Melville's bachelor, Bartleby, like Kafka's, must "find the place where he can take his walks". . . America.[19] The American is one who is freed from the English paternal function, the son of a crumbled father, the son of all nations. Even before their independence, Americans were thinking about the combination of States, the State-form most compatible with their vocation. But their vocation was not to reconstitute an "old State secret," a nation, a family, a heritage, or a father. It was above all to constitute a universe, a society of brothers, a federation of men and goods, a community of anarchist individuals, inspired by Jefferson, by Thoreau, by Melville. Such is the declaration in *Moby-Dick* (chapter 26): if man is the brother of his fellow man, if he is worthy of trust or "confidence," it is not because he belongs to a nation or because he is a proprietor or shareholder, but only insofar as he is Man, when he has lost those characteristics that constitute his "violence," his "idiocy," his "villainy," when he has no consciousness of himself apart from the proprieties of a "democratic dignity" that considers all particularities as so many ignominious stains that arouse anguish or pity. America is the potential of the man without particularities, the Original Man. Already in *Redburn*:

> You can not spill a drop of American blood without spilling the blood of the whole world. Be he Englishman, Frenchman, German, Dane, or Scot; the European who scoffs at an American, calls his own brother *Raca,* and stands in danger of the judgment. We are not a

narrow tribe of men, with a bigoted Hebrew nationality—whose blood has been debased in the attempt to enoble it, by maintaining an exclusive succession among ourselves. . . . We are not a nation, so much as a world; for unless we may claim all the world for our sire, like Melchisedec, we are without father or mother. . . . We are the heirs of all time, and with all nations we divide our inheritance . . .[20]

The picture of the nineteenth-century proletarian looks like this: the advent of the communist man or the society of comrades, the future Soviet, being without property, family, or nation, has no other determination than that of being man, *Homo tantum*. But this is also the picture of the American, executed by other means, and the traits of the former often intermingle with or are superimposed over those of the latter. America sought to create a revolution whose strength would lie in a universal immigration, émigrés of the world, just as Bolshevik Russia would seek to make a revolution whose strength would lie in a universal proletarization, "Proletarians of the world" . . . the two forms of the class struggle. So that the messianism of the nineteenth century has two heads and is expressed no less in American *pragmatism* than in the ultimately Russian form of socialism.

Pragmatism is misunderstood when it is seen as a summary philosophical theory fabricated by Americans. On the other hand, we understand the novelty of American thought when we see pragmatism as an attempt to transform the world, to think a new world or new man insofar as they *create themselves*. Western philosophy was the skull, or the paternal Spirit that realized itself in the world as totality, and in a knowing subject as proprietor. Is it against Western philosophy that Melville directs his insult, "metaphysical villain"? A contemporary of American transcendentalism (Emerson, Thoreau), Melville is already sketching out the traits of the pragmatism that will be its continuation. It is first of all the affirmation of a world in *process,* an *archipelago.* Not even a puzzle, whose pieces when fitted together would constitute a whole, but rather a wall of loose, uncemented stones, where every element has a value in itself but also in relation to others: isolated and floating relations, islands and straits, immobile points and sinuous lines—for Truth always has "jagged edges." Not a skull but the vertebral column, a spinal cord; not a uniform piece of clothing but a Harlequin's coat, even white on white, an infinite patchwork with multiple joinings, like the jacket of Redburn, White Jacket or the Great Cosmopolitan: the American invention *par excellence,* for the Americans invented patchwork, just as the Swiss are said to have invented the cuckoo clock. But to reach this point, it was also necessary for the knowing subject, the sole proprietor, to give way to a community of explorers, the brothers of the archipelago, who replace knowledge with belief, or rather with "confidence"—not belief in another world, but confidence in this one, and in man as much as in God ("I am going to attempt the ascent of Ofo *with hope, not with faith*. . . . I will follow my own path . . .").

Pragmatism is this double principle of archipelago and hope.[21] And what must the community of men consist of in order for truth to be possible? *Truth* and *trust*. [22] Like Melville before it, pragmatism will fight ceaselessly on two fronts: against the particularities that pit man against man and nourish an irremediable mistrust; but also against the Universal or the Whole, the fusion of souls in the name of great love or charity. Yet, what remains of souls once they are no longer attached to particularities, what keeps them from melting into a whole? What remains is precisely their "originality," that is, a sound that each one *produces,* like a ritornello at the limit of language, but that it produces only when it takes to the open road (or to the open sea) with its body, when it leads its life without seeking salvation, when it embarks upon its incarnate voyage, without any particular aim, and then encounters other voyagers, whom it recognizes by their sound. This is how Lawrence described the new messianism, or the *democratic* contribution of American literature: against the European morality of salvation and charity, a morality of life in which the soul is fulfilled only by taking to the road, with no other aim, open to all contacts, never trying to save other souls, turning away from those that produce an overly authoritarian or groaning sound, forming even fleeting and unresolved chords and accords with its equals, with freedom as its sole accomplishment, always ready to free itself so as to complete itself.[23] According to Melville or Lawrence, brotherhood is a matter for original souls: perhaps it begins only with the death of the father or God, but it does not derive from this death, it is a whole other matter—"all the subtle sympathizings of the incalculable soul, from the bitterest hate to passionate love."

This requires a new perspective, an archipelago-perspectivism that conjugates the panoramic shot and the tracking shot, as in *The Encantadas.* It requires an acute perception, both visual and auditory, as *Benito Cereno* shows, and must replace the concept with the "percept," that is, with a perception in becoming. It requires a new community, whose members are capable of trust or "confidence," that is, of a belief in themselves, in the world, and in becoming. Bartleby the bachelor must embark upon his voyage and find his sister, with whom he will consume the ginger nut, the new host. Bartleby lives cloistered in the office and never goes out, but when the attorney suggests new occupations to him, he is not joking when he responds, "There is too much confinement . . ." And if he is prevented from making his voyage, then the only place left for him is prison, where he dies of "civil disobedience," as Thoreau says, "the only place where a free man can stay with honor."[24] William and Henry James are indeed brothers, and *Daisy Miller*, the new American maiden, asks for nothing more than a little confidence, and allows herself to die because even this meager request remains unfulfilled. And what was Bartleby asking for if not a little confidence from the attorney, who instead responds to him with charity and philanthropy—all the masks of the paternal function? The attorney's only excuse is that he draws back from the becoming into which Bartleby, through his lonely existence, threatens to drag him: *rumors* are already spreading . . . The hero of pragmatism is not the successful businessman, it is Bartleby, and it is Daisy Miller, it is Pierre and Isabelle, the brother and sister.

The dangers of a "society without fathers" have often been pointed out, but the only real danger is the return of the father.[25] In this respect, it is difficult to separate the failure of the two revolutions, the American and the Soviet, the pragmatic and the dialectical. Universal emigration was no more successful than universal proletarization. The Civil War already sounded the knell, as would the liquidation of the Soviets later on. The birth of a nation, the restoration of the nation-state—and the monstrous fathers come galloping back in, while the sons without fathers start dying off again. Paper images—this is the fate of the American as well as the Proletarian. But just as many Bolsheviks could hear the diabolical powers knocking at the door in 1917, the pragmatists, like Melville before them, could see the masquerade that the society of brothers would lead to. Long before Lawrence, Melville and Thoreau were diagnosing the American evil, the new cement that would rebuild the wall: paternal authority and filthy charity. Bartleby therefore lets himself die in prison. In the beginning, it was Benjamin Franklin, the hypocritical *lightning-rod Merchant*, who instituted the magnetic

American prison. The city-ship reconstitutes the most oppressive law, and brotherhood exists among the topmen only when they remain immobile, high up on the masts (*White Jacket*). The great community of celibates is nothing more than a company of bons vivants, which certainly does not keep the rich bachelor from exploiting the poor and pallid workers, by reconstituting the two unreconciled figures of the monstrous father and the orphaned daughters (*The Paradise of Bachelors and the Tartarus of Maids*). The American confidence-man appears everywhere in Melville's work. What malignant power has turned the trust into a company as cruel as the abominable "universal nation" founded by the Dog-Man in *The Encantadas*? *The Confidence-Man*, in which Melville's critique of charity and philanthropy culminates, brings into play a series of devious characters who seem to emanate from a "great Cosmopolitan" in patchwork clothing, and who ask for no more than . . . a little human confidence, in order to pull off a multiple and rebounding confidence game.

Are these false brothers sent by a diabolical father to restore his power over *overly credulous* Americans? But the novel is so complex that one could just as easily say the opposite: this long procession [*théorie*] of con men would be a comic version of authentic brothers, such as *overly suspicious* Americans see them, or rather have already become incapable of seeing them. This cohort of characters, including the mysterious child at the end, is perhaps the society of Philanthropists who dissimulate their demonic project, but perhaps it is also the community of brothers that the Misanthropes are no longer able to recognize in passing. For even in the midst of its failure, the American Revolution continues to send out its fragments, always making something take flight on the horizon, even sending itself to the moon, always trying to break through the wall, to take up the experiment once again, to find a brotherhood in this enterprise, a sister in this becoming, a music in its stuttering language, a pure sound and unknown chords in language itself. What Kafka would say about "small nations" is what Melville had already said about the great American nation: it must become a patchwork of all small nations. What Kafka would say about minor literatures is what Melville had already said about the American literature of his time: because there are so few authors in America, and because its people are so indifferent, the writer is not in a position to succeed as a recognized master. Even in his failure, the writer remains all the more the bearer of a collective enunciation, which no longer forms part of literary history and preserves the rights of a people to come, or of a human becoming. [26] A schizophrenic vocation: even in his catatonic or anorexic state, Bartleby is not the patient, but the doctor of a sick America, the *Medicine-Man,* the new Christ or the brother to us all.

11
An Unrecognized Precursor to Heidegger: Alfred Jarry

Pataphysics (*epi meta ta phusika*) has as its exact and explicit object the great Turning, the overcoming of metaphysics, the rising up beyond or before, "the science of that which is superinduced upon metaphysics, whether in itself or outside of itself, extending as far beyond metaphysics as the latter extends beyond physics."[1] We can thus consider Heidegger's work as a development of pataphysics in conformity with the principles of Sophrotates the Armenian, and of his first disciple, Alfred Jarry. The great resemblances, memorial or historical, concern the *Being of phenomena, planetary technology,* and the *treatment of language.*

I. In the first place, pataphysics as the overcoming of metaphysics is inseparable from a phenomenology, that is, from a new sense and a new comprehension of phenomena. There is a striking resemblance between the two authors. The phenomenon can no longer be defined as an appearance, nor can it be defined as an apparition, as in Husserl's phenomenology. The apparition refers to a consciousness to which it appears, and can still exist in a form different from the one it makes appear. The phenomenon, on the contrary, is that which shows itself in itself.[2] A watch *appears* round whenever one reads the time (utensility); or again, independently of its utility, and by virtue of the demands of consciousness alone (everyday banality), the facade of a house appears square, in accordance with the constants of reduction. But the *phenomenon* is the watch as an infinite series of ellipses, or the facade as an infinite series of trapezoids: a world made up of remarkable singularities, or a world that shows itself (whereas apparitions are only singularities reduced to the ordinary, appearing ordinarily to consciousness).[3] The phenomenon, on this account, does not refer to a consciousness, but to a Being, the Being of the phenomenon that consists precisely in its self-showing [*se-montrer*]. The Being of the phenomenon is the "*epiphenomenon*," nonuseful and unconscious, the object of pataphysics. The epiphenomenon is the Being of the phenomenon, whereas the phenomenon is only a being, or life. It is not Being, but the phenomenon that is perception—it perceives or is perceived—whereas Being is thinking.[4] No doubt Being, or the epiphenomenon, is nothing other than the phenomenon, but it differs from it absolutely: it is the self-showing of the phenomenon.

Metaphysics is an error that consists in treating the epiphenomenon as another phenomenon, another being, another life. In truth, rather than considering Being as a superior being that would ground the constancy of other perceived beings, we must think of it as an Emptiness or a Non-Being, through the transparency of which singular variations come into play, "an iridescent mental kaleidoscope (that) thinks itself."[5] Beings could even seem to be a degeneration of Being, and life, a degeneration of thought; or, even more, one could say that beings cross out Being, they put it to death and destroy it, or that life kills thought—so that we are not yet thinking. "To remain at peace with my consciousness while glorifying thought, I want Being to disappear, to resolve itself into its opposite." This disappearance or dissipation, however, does not come from the outside. If Being is the self-showing of beings, it does not show itself, but ceaselessly withdraws; it is itself in withdrawal or retreating. Better yet: withdrawing or turning away is the only manner by which it shows itself *as* Being, since it is only the self-showing of the phenomenon or beings.

II. Because it confuses Being with beings, metaphysics in its entirety stands in the withdrawal of Being, or forgetfulness. Technology as the effective mastery of Being is the heir to metaphysics: it completes metaphysics, it realizes it. Action and life "have killed thought, therefore let us Live, and in so doing we will become Masters." In this sense, it is Ubu who represents the fat being, the outcome of metaphysics as planetary technology and a completely mechanized science, the science

of machines in all its sinister frenzy. Anarchy is the bomb, or the comprehension of technology. Jarry puts forward a curious conception of
anarchism: "Anarchy Is," but it makes Being lower itself to the being
of science and technology (Ubu himself will become an anarchist in
order to better ensure that he is obeyed).[6] More generally, Jarry's entire
oeuvre ceaselessly invokes science and technology; it is populated with
machines and places itself under the sign of the *Bicycle*. The bicycle is
not a simple machine, but the simple model of a Machine appropriate
to the times.[7] And it is the Bicycle that transforms the Passion, as the
Christian metaphysics of the death of God, into an eminently technical
relay race.[8] The Bicycle, with its chain and its gears, is the essence of
technology: it envelops and develops, it brings about the great Turning
of the earth. The bicycle is the frame, like Heidegger's "fourfold."

If the problem is a complex one, however, it is because technology
and technologized science, for both Jarry and Heidegger, do not simply
entail the withdrawal or forgetting of Being. Being also shows itself in
technology by the very fact that it withdraws from it, insofar as it withdraws. But *this* can only be comprehended pataphysically (ontologically), and not metaphysically. This is why Ubu invents pataphysics at
the same time as he promotes planetary technology: he comprehends
the essence of technology—the comprehension Heidegger imprudently
credited to national socialism. What Heidegger finds in Nazism (a
populist tendency), Jarry finds in anarchism (a right-wing tendency). In
both authors, technology seems to be the site of a combat in which
Being is sometimes lost in forgetting or in withdrawal, while at other
times, on the contrary, it shows itself or unveils itself in it. It is not
enough to oppose Being to its forgetting or withdrawal, since what
defines the loss of Being is rather the forgetting of forgetting, the
withdrawal of the withdrawal, whereas withdrawal and forgetting are
the manner by which Being shows itself, or is *able* to show itself. The
essence of technology is not technology, and "must harbour in itself
the growth of the saving power."[9] Thus, it is the culmination of metaphysics in technology that makes possible the overcoming of metaphysics, that is, pataphysics. Hence the importance of the theory of
science and the experimentations with machines as integral parts of
pataphysics: planetary technology is not simply the loss of Being, but
the possibility of its salvation.

Being shows itself twice: once in relation to metaphysics, in an *immemorial past*, one that retreats before every historical past—the al-

ways Already-thought of the Greeks; and a second time in relation to technology, in an *unassignable future,* a pure imminence or the possibility of a thought always still-to-come.[10] This is what appears in Heidegger with the notion of *Ereignis,* which is like the eventuality of an Event, a Possibility of Being, a *Possest,* a Still-to-come that goes beyond the presence of the present no less than the immemorial of memory. And in his last writings, Heidegger no longer even speaks of metaphysics or the overcoming of metaphysics, since Being in turn must be overcome in favor of a Being-Power that is no longer linked to technology.[11] Jarry will likewise stop speaking of pataphysics once he discovers the Possible beyond Being, in *The Supermale,* as the novel of the future; and in his final work, *The Sword Knot [La Dragonne],* he will show how the Possible surpasses both the present and the past to produce a new dawn.[12] Now for Jarry, this opening of the possible also needs a technologized science: this can already be seen from the limited viewpoint of pataphysics itself. And if Heidegger defined technology by the rising of a "standing-reserve" [*fonds*] that effaces the object in favor of a possibility of Being—the airplane *in every one of its constituent parts* as the possibility of flying—Jarry for his part considers science and technology as the rising of an "ether," or the unveiling of courses that correspond to the molecular potentialities or virtualities of *all the parts of an object:* the bicycle, or more precisely the bicycle's frame, is an excellent atomic model, inasmuch as it is made up of "rigid, articulated rods and wheels driven by a rapid rotative movement."[13] The "physick stick" [*bâton à physique*] is the technical being par excellence, which describes the set of its virtual lines: circular, rectilinear, crossed. It is in this sense that pataphysics already entails a great theory of machines, and already goes beyond the virtualities of beings toward the possibility of Being (Ubu sends his technical inventions to an office whose boss is Mr. Possible), following a tendency that will culminate in *The Supermale.*

Planetary technology is thus the site of possible reversals, conversions, or turnings. In effect, science treats time as an independent variable; this is why machines are essentially machines for exploring time, the "tempomotive" rather than the "locomotive." From a technological standpoint, it is science that first makes a pataphysical reversal of time possible: the succession of three stases—past, present, and future—gives way to the *co-presence or simultaneity* of the three exstases, the Being of the past, the Being of the present, the Being of the future. Presence is the Being of the present, but also the Being of the past and the future. *Ethernity* does not designate the eternal, but the donation or excretion of time, the temporalization of time that occurs simultaneously in these three dimensions (Zeit-Raum). Moreover, the machine starts by transforming succession into simultaneity, before leading to the final transformation "in reverse," when the Being of time in its entirety is converted into Being-Power, into the possibility of Being as Future. Jarry is perhaps recalling his Professor Bergson when he takes up the theme of Duration [*Durée*], which he first defines as an immobility in temporal succession (conservation of the past), and then as an exploration of the future, or an opening toward what is to come. "Duration is the transformation of a succession into a reversion—in other words: the becoming of a memory." This is a profound reconciliation of the Machine with Duration.[14] And this reversion also implies a reversal in the relationship between man and machine. Not only are the indices of virtual speed reversed to infinity, but the bicycle becomes more rapid than the train, as in the great race in *The Supermale;* but the relationship between man and machine gives way to a relationship between the machine and *the Being of man* (*Dasein* or Supermale), inasmuch as the Being of man is more powerful than the machine, and succeeds in "stoking" it. The Supermale is the Being of man that is no longer aware of the distinction between man and woman: woman as a whole enters into the machine, is absorbed by the machine, and man alone becomes the celibate capacity, or the Being-Power, the emblem of scissiparity, "far removed from earthly sexes" and "the firstborn of the future."[15]

III. *Being shows itself*, but only inasmuch as it never ceases to withdraw (the past); *the More and Less than Being occurs,* but only by ceaselessly receding, by possibilizing itself (the future).[16] In other words, Being does not merely show itself in beings, but in something that shows its inevitable withdrawal; and the more and less than Being, in something that shows its inexhaustible possibility. This something, or the Thing, is the *Sign.* For if it is true that science or technology already contain a possibility for salvation, they remain incapable of deploying it, and must give way to the Beautiful and Art, which sometimes extend technology by crowning it, as with the Greeks, and sometimes transmute or convert it. According to Heidegger, the technical being (the machine) was already more than an object, since it made the ground appear; but the poetic being (the Thing, the Sign) went even further, because it brought into being a world that was groundless.[17] In this transition from science to art, in this reversion of science into art, Heidegger perhaps rediscovers a problem familiar to the late nineteenth century, one that would be encountered in a different manner by Renan (another Breton precursor to Heidegger), by neoimpressionism, and by Jarry himself. Jarry would follow a similar path when he developed his strange thesis on anarchy: by making-disappear, anarchy could only operate technically, with machines, whereas Jarry prefers the aesthetic stage of crime, and ranks Quincy above Vaillant.[18] More generally, according to Jarry, the technical machine makes virtual lines emerge, which bring together the atomic components of beings, whereas the poetic sign deploys all the possibilities or capabilities of Being that, when brought together in their original unity, constitute "the thing." We know that Heidegger will identify this grandiose nature of the sign with the *Quadriparti*, the mirror-play of the world, the ringing of the ring, the "Fourfold" [*das Geviert*].[19] But Jarry had already deployed the great heraldic Act of the four heralds, with the coat of arms as the mirror, and the organization of the world, *Perhinderion*, as the Cross of Christ, or the Frame of the original Bicycle, which ensures the transition from technology to the Poetic[20]—which is what Heidegger failed to recognize in the play of the world and its four paths. This was also the case with the "physick-stick": from the machine or engine, it becomes the thing that bears the artistic sign, when it forms a cross with itself "in each quarter of every one of its revolutions."

Jarry's thought is above all a theory of the Sign: the sign neither designates nor signifies, but shows . . . It is the same as the thing, but is not identical to it; it shows the thing. The question is knowing how and why the sign thus understood is necessarily linguistic, or rather under what conditions it becomes language.[21] The first condition is that we must form a poetic conception of language, and not a technical or scientific one. Science presupposes the idea of diversity, a *tower of Babel of languages*, in which order would have to be introduced by grasping their virtual relations. But we, on the contrary, will consider only two languages in principle, as if they were the only languages in the world, a living language and a dead language, the latter being put to work in the former—agglutinations in the second inspiring new emergences or reemergences in the first. The dead language seems to create anagrams in the living language. Heidegger kept rather strictly to German and Greek (or to High German): he put an ancient Greek or an old German to work within contemporary German, but precisely in order to obtain a new German . . . The old language *affects* the present language, which under this condition produces a language still to come: the three exstases. Ancient Greek is caught up in agglutinations of the type "*legô*-I speak" and "*legô*-I harvest, I gather," in such a way that the German "*sagen*-to speak" recreates "*sagen*-to show by gathering." Or again, in the most famous example, the agglutination "*lethé*-forgetfulness" and "*aletheia*-the true" will activate in German the obsessive couplet "veiling-unveiling." Or again "*chraô-cheir*," which is almost Breton. Or again the old Saxon "*wuon*" (to live somewhere), in its agglutination with "*freien*" (to save, to preserve), will disengage "*bauen*" (to live in peace) from the current meaning of "*bauen*." Jarry seems to have proceeded in the same manner. But Jarry, though he often invoked Greek, as shown by Pataphysics, instead introduced Latin, or old French, or an ancestral dialect, or perhaps Breton into the French language, in order to bring to light a French of the future that found in a symbolism close to that of Mallarmé and Villiers something analogous to what Heidegger found in Hölderlin.[22] And injected into the French, "*si vis pacem*" will give "civil," and "industria," "1, 2, 3": only two languages *against the Tower of Babel,* one of which works or plays within the other to produce the language of the future, Poetry par excellence, which shines forth particularly in the description of Dr. Faustroll's islands, with its music-words and sonorous harmonies.[23]

We have heard the news that not one of Heidegger's etymologies is correct, not even Lethé or Aletheia.[24] But is this a well-posed problem? Has not every scientific criterion of etymology been repudiated in advance, in favor of a pure and simple Poetry? It is sometimes said that these are nothing more than word plays. But is it not contradictory to expect some sort of linguistic correctness from a project that explicitly sets out to go beyond scientific and technical being toward poetic being? Strictly speaking, it is not a question of etymology, but of bringing about agglutinations in the other-language [*l'autre-langue*] so as to emerge in the-language [*la-langue*]. Undertakings like those of Heidegger or Jarry should not be compared with linguistics, but rather with the analogous undertakings of Roussel, Brisset, or Wolfson. The difference consists in this: Wolfson maintains the Tower of Babel, and makes use of every language minus *one* to constitute the language of the future in which this *one* must disappear; Roussel on the contrary makes use of only one language, but he carves out from it, as the equivalent of another language, homophonous series, which say something else entirely with similar sounds; and Brisset makes use of one language in order to pull out syllabic or phonic elements that may be present in other languages, but that say the same thing, and that in turn form the secret language of the Origin or the Future. Jarry and Heidegger have yet another procedure: they work in principle with two languages, activating a dead language within a living language, in such a way that the living language is transformed and transmuted. If we use the term *element* to designate an abstraction capable of taking on variable values, we could say that a linguistic element A affects element B in such a way as to turn it into element C. The affect (A) produces in the current language (B) a kind of foot stomping, a stammering, an obsessional tom-tom, like a repetition that never ceases to create something new (C). Under the impulse of the affect, our language is set whirling, and in whirling it forms a language of the future, as if it were a foreign language, an eternal reiteration, but one that leaps and jumps. We stomp within the turning question, but this turning is the bud of the new language. *"Is it from the Greek or from the Negro, Father Ubu?"*[25] From one element to the other, between the old language and the present language being affected, between the current language and the new one being formed, there are intervals and empty spaces, but they are filled with immense visions, insane scenes and landscapes: the unveiling of Heidegger's world, the procession of Dr. Faustroll's islands, or the sequence of "Ymagier's" engravings.

Such is the response: language does not have signs at its disposal, but acquires them by creating them, when a $language_1$ acts within a $language_2$ so as to produce in it a $language_3$ an unheard of and almost foreign language. The first injects, the second stammers, the third suddenly starts with a fit. Then language has become Sign or poetry, and one can no longer distinguish between language, speech, or word. And a language is never made to produce a new language within itself without language as whole in turn being taken to a limit. The limit of language is the Thing in its muteness—vision. The thing is the limit of language, as the sign is the language of the thing. When a language is hollowed out by its turning within language, it finally completes its mission: the Sign shows the Thing, and effectuates the nth power of language, for

"where word breaks off no thing may be."[26]

12

The Mystery of Ariadne according to Nietzsche

Dionysus sings:

> "Be wise, Ariadne! . . .
> You have little ears, you have ears like mine:
> Put a clever word into them!
> Must we not first hate each other if we are to love each other? . . .
>
> I am your labyrinth."[1]

Just as other women are between two men, Ariadne is between Theseus and Dionysus.[2] She passes from Theseus to Dionysus. She began by hating Dionysus the Bull. But abandoned by Theseus, whom she had nonetheless guided through the labyrinth, she is carried off by Dionysus, and discovers another labyrinth. "Who besides me knows what Ariadne is?"[3] Is this to say: Wagner-Theseus, Cosima-Ariadne, Nietzsche-Dionysus? The question "*who?*" does not refer to persons, but to forces and wills.[4]

Theseus appears to be the model for a text in the second part of *Zarathustra,* "On Those Who Are Sublime." It concerns the hero, cunning and skillful at solving riddles, passing through the labyrinth and subduing the bull. This sublime man prefigures the theory of the higher man in the fourth part: he is called "the ascetic of the spirit," a name that will later be applied to one of the fragments on the higher man ("The Magician"). The characteristics of the sublime man match up with the attributes of the higher man in general: his serious spirit, his heaviness, his taste for bearing burdens, his contempt for the earth, his inability to laugh and play, his enterprise of revenge.

We know that Nietzsche's theory of the higher man is a critique that sets out to expose the deepest and most dangerous mystification of humanism. The higher man claims to carry humanity to perfection, to completion. He claims to recuperate all the properties of man, to overcome alienation, to realize the total man, to put man in the place of God, to turn man into a power of affirmation that affirms itself. But in truth, man, even the higher man, does not know what it means to affirm. He merely presents a caricature of affirmation, a ridiculous travesty. He believes that to affirm means to bear, to assume, to endure an ordeal, to take on a burden. He measures positivity in terms of the weight he bears and confuses affirmation with the exertion of his tense muscles.[5] Everything heavy is real, everything that bears is affirmative and active! Moreoever, instead of the bull, the higher man's animals are the ass and the camel, beasts of the desert who inhabit the desolate face of the earth and who know how to bear burdens. Theseus, the sublime or higher man, subdues the bull, but he is far inferior to it, having merely the same neck: "He should act like a bull, and his happiness should smell of the earth, and not of contempt for the earth. I would like to see him as a white bull, walking before the plowshare, snorting and bellowing; and his bellowing should be in praise of everything earthly. . . . To stand with relaxed muscles and unharnessed will: that is most difficult for all of you who are sublime."[6] The sublime or higher man subdues monsters, poses riddles, but knows nothing of the riddle and the monster that he himself is. He does not know that to affirm is not to bear, carry, or harness oneself to that which exists, but on the contrary to unburden, unharness, and set free that which lives. It is not to burden life with the weight of higher or even heroic values, but to create new values that would be those of life, values that make life light or affirmative. "He must still discard his heroic will; he shall be elevated, not merely sublime."[7] Theseus does not understand that the bull (or the rhinoceros) possesses the only true superiority: a light, prodigious beast deep in the heart of the labyrinth, but who also feels at ease in high places, a beast who unharnesses and affirms life.

According to Nietzsche, the will to power has two tonalities: affirmation and negation; and forces have two qualities: action and reaction. What the higher man presents as affirmation is no doubt the most profound being of man, but it is only the extreme combination of negation with reaction, of negative will with reactive force, of nihilism with bad conscience and *ressentiment*. The products of nihilism are made to be borne, and it is reactive forces that bear them. Whence the illusion of a false affirmation. The higher man claims knowledge as his authority: he claims to explore the labyrinth or the forest of knowledge. But knowledge is only a disguise for morality; the thread in the labyrinth is the moral thread. Morality, in turn, is a labyrinth, a disguise for the ascetic and religious ideal. From the ascetic ideal to the moral ideal, from the moral ideal to the ideal of knowledge, it is the same enterprise that is being pursued, that of killing the bull, that is, of denying life, crushing it beneath a weight, reducing it to its reactive forces. The sublime man no longer even needs a God to harness man. In the end, man replaces God with humanism; the ascetic ideal with the moral ideal and the ideal of knowledge. Man burdens himself, he puts on his own harness—all in the name of heroic values, in the name of man's values.

There are a number of higher men: the soothsayer, the two kings, the man with leeches, the magician, the last pope, the ugliest man, the voluntary beggar, and the shadow. They form a procession [*théorie*], a series, a farandole. This is because they are distinguished by the place they occupy along the thread, by the form of their ideal, by the specific weight of their reaction and the tonality of their negativity. But they all amount to the same thing: they are powers of the false, a parade of forgers, as if the false necessarily referred to the false. Even the truthful man is a forger because he conceals his motives for willing the truth, his somber passion for condemning life. Perhaps only Melville is comparable to Nietzsche for having created a prodigious chain of forgers, higher men emanating from the "great Cosmopolitan," each of whom guarantees or even exposes the swindle of the other, but always in a way that reinforces the power of the false.[8] Is not the false already in the model, in the truthful man, as much as in the simulations?

As long as Ariadne loves Theseus, she participates in this life-denying enterprise. Under his false appearances of affirmation, Theseus—the model—is the power to deny, the Spirit of negation, the confidence-man. Ariadne is the Anima, the Soul, but the reactive soul or the force of *ressentiment*. Her splendid song remains a complaint, and in *Zarathustra*, where it first appears, it is put into the mouth of the Magician, the forger par excellence, an abject old man who dons the mask of a little girl. Ariadne is the sister, but the sister who feels *ressentiment* against her brother the bull. A pathetic appeal runs through all of Nietzsche's work: Beware of sisters. It is Ariadne who holds the thread to the labyrinth, the thread of morality. Ariadne is the Spider, the tarantula. Here again Nietzsche cries out: "Hang yourself with this thread!"[9] Ariadne will have to fulfill this prophecy (in certain traditions, Ariadne, abandoned by Theseus, does indeed hang herself).[10]

But what does this mean: Ariadne abandoned by Theseus? It means that the combination of the negative will with the force of reaction, of the spirit of reaction with the reactive soul, is not nihilism's last word. The moment arrives when the will to negation breaks its alliance with the forces of reaction, abandons them and even turns against them. Ariadne hangs herself, Ariadne wants to perish. Now this fundamental moment ("midnight") heralds a double transmutation, as if completed nihilism gave way to its opposite: reactive forces, themselves denied, become active; negation is converted and becomes the thunderclap of a pure affirmation, the polemical and ludic mode of a will that affirms and enters into the service of an excess of life. Nihilism "defeated by itself." Our aim is not to analyze this transmutation of nihilism, this double conversion, but simply to see how the myth of Ariadne expresses it. Abandoned by Theseus, Ariadne senses the approach of Dionysus. Dionysus the Bull is pure and multiple affirmation, the true affirmation, the affirmative will; he bears nothing, unburdens himself completely, makes everything that lives lighter. He is able to do what the higher man cannot: to laugh, play, and dance, in other words, to affirm. He is the Light One who does not recognize himself in man, especially not in the higher man or sublime hero, but only in the overman, in the overhero, in something other than man. It was necessary that Ariadne be abandoned by Theseus: "For this is the soul's secret: only when the hero has abandoned her is she approached in a dream by the overhero."[11] Under the caress of Dionysus, the soul becomes active. She was so heavy with Theseus but becomes lighter with Dionysus, unburdened, delicate, elevated to the sky. She learns that what she formerly thought to be an activity was only an enterprise of revenge, mistrust, and surveillance (the thread), the reaction of the bad conscience and *ressentiment;* and more profoundly, what she believed to be an affirmation was only a travesty, a manifestation of heaviness, a way of believing oneself strong because one bears and assumes. Ariadne realizes how she had been deceived: she thought it was a Greek she had encountered, but Theseus was not a true Greek. He was, rather, a kind of German *avant la lettre*.[12] Ariadne understands her deception at a moment when it no longer concerns her: Dionysus, who is a true Greek, is approaching; the Soul becomes active, and at the same time, the Spirit reveals the true nature of affirmation. Ariadne's song then takes on its full meaning: the transmutation of Ariadne at the approach of Dionysus, Ariadne being the Anima that now corresponds to the Spirit that says yes. Dionysus adds a final couplet to Ariadne's song, which becomes a dithyramb. In keeping with Nietzsche's general method, the meaning and nature of the song change depending on who sings it—the magician behind Ariadne's mask, Ariadne herself in Dionysus's ear.

Why does Dionysus need Ariadne, or to be loved? He sings a song of solitude, he seeks a fiancée.[13] For if Dionysus is the god of affirmation, there must be a second affirmation in order for affirmation itself to be affirmed. Affirmation must divide in two so that it can redouble [*Il faut qu'elle se dédouble pour pouvoir redoubler*]. Nietzsche clearly distinguishes the two affirmations when he says "Eternal affirmation of being, eternally I am your affirmation."[14] Dionysus is the affirmation of Being, but Ariadne is the affirmation of affirmation, the second affirmation or the becoming-active. From this point of view, all the symbols of Ariadne change meaning when they are related to Dionysus rather than being deformed by Theseus. Not only does Ariadne's song cease to be the expression of *ressentiment* in order to become an active search, an already affirmative question ("Who are you? . . . Me—you want me? me—all of me? . . .")[15] but the labyrinth is no longer the labyrinth of knowledge and morality, the labyrinth is no longer the path pursued by the one who, holding a thread, is going to kill the bull. The labyrinth has become the white bull himself, Dionysus the Bull: "I am your labyrinth." More precisely, the labyrinth is now the ear of Dionysus, the labyrinthine ear. Ariadne must have ears like those of Dionysus in order to hear the Dionysian affirmation, but she must also respond to the affirmation in the ear of Dionysus himself. Dionysus says to Ariadne: "You have little ears, you have ears like mine, put a clever word into them!"—yes. Dionysus also has occasion to say to Ariadne, in jest: "I find a kind of humor in your ears . . . why are they not longer?" In this way, Dionysus reminds her of her errors when she loved Theseus: she believed that to affirm meant to bear a weight, to do as the ass does. But in truth, with Dionysus, Ariadne has acquired small ears: the round ear, propitious to the eternal return.

The labyrinth is no longer architectural; it has become sonorous and musical. It was Schopenhauer who defined architecture in terms of two forces, that of bearing and that of being borne, support and load, even if the two tend to merge together. But music appears to be the opposite of this, when Nietzsche separates himself more and more from the old forger, Wagner the magician: music is Lightness [*la Légère*], pure weightlessness.[16] Does not the entire triangular story of Ariadne bear witness to an anti-Wagnerian lightness, closer to Offenbach and Strauss than to Wagner? To make the roofs dance, to balance the beams—this is what is essential to Dionysus the musician.[17] Doubtless there is also an Apollonian, even Theseusian side to music, but it is a music that is distributed according to territories, milieus, activities, ethoses: a work song, a marching song, a dance song, a song for repose, a drinking song, a lullaby . . . almost little "hurdy-gurdy songs," each with its own particular weight.[18] In order for music to free itself, it will have to pass over to the other side—there where the territories tremble, where the structures collapse, where the ethoses get mixed up, where a powerful song of the earth is unleashed, the great ritornello that transmutes all the airs it carries away and makes return.[19] *Dionysus knows no other architecture than that of routes and trajectories.* Was this not already the distinctive feature of the lied: to set out from the territory at the call or wind of the earth? Each of the higher men leaves his domain and makes his way toward Zarathustra's cave. But only the dithyramb spreads itself out over the earth and embraces it in its entirety. Dionysus has no territory because he is everywhere on the earth.[20] The sonorous labyrinth is the song of the earth, the Ritornello, the eternal return in person.

But why oppose the two sides as the true and the false? Is it not the same power of the false on both sides, and is not Dionysus a great forger, the greatest "in truth," the Cosmopolitan? Is not art the highest power of the false? Between the high and the low, from one side to the other, there is a considerable difference, a distance that must be affirmed. The spider is always respinning its web and the scorpion never stops stinging; each higher man is fixated on his own feat, which he rehearses like a circus act (and this is precisely how the fourth part of *Zarathustra* is organized, much like Raymond Roussel's gala of Incomparables, or a puppet show, or an operetta). This is because each of these mimes has an invariable model, a fixed form, that can always be called true, though it is just as "false" as its reproductions. It is like the forger of paintings: what he copies from the original painting is an attributable form that is just as false as the copies; what escapes him is the metamorphosis or transformation of the original, the impossibility of attributing any particular form to it, in short, creation. This is why the higher men are merely the lowest degrees of the will to power: "May men higher than you stride over you! You signify steps."[21] With them the will to power represents only a will to deceive, a will to take, a will to dominate, a sickly, exhausted life that brandishes prostheses. Their very roles are prostheses they use to prop themselves up. Only Dionysus, the creative artist, attains the power of metamorphosis that makes him become, attesting to a surging forth of life. *He carries the power of the false to a degree that is no longer effected in a form, but in a transformation*—"the gift-giving virtue," or the creation of possibilities of life: transmutation. The will to power is like energy: an energy capable of transforming itself is called noble. Those that merely know how to disguise or travesty themselves, that is, to take on and maintain a form that is always the same, are vile or base.

To pass from Theseus to Dionysus is, for Ariadne, a clinical matter, a question of health and healing. And for Dionysus as well. Dionysus needs Ariadne. Dionysus is pure affirmation; Ariadne is the Anima, affirmation divided in two, the "yes" that responds to "yes." But, divided in two [*dédoublée*], affirmation returns to Dionysus as the affirmation that redoubles [*redouble*]. It is in this sense that the eternal return is the product of the union of Dionysus and Ariadne. As long as Dionysus is alone, he still fears the thought of the Eternal Return, because he is afraid that it brings back reactive forces, the enterprise of denying life, the little man (whether higher or sublime). But when Dionysian affirmation finds its full development in Ariadne, Dionysus in turn learns something new: that the thought of the Eternal Return is consoling, and at the same time, that the Eternal Return itself is selective. The Eternal Return does not occur without a transmutation. The Eternal Return, as the being of becoming, is the product of a double affirmation that only makes what affirms itself return, and only makes what is active become. Neither reactive forces nor the will to deny will return: they are eliminated by the transmutation, by the Eternal Return as selection. Ariadne has forgotten Theseus; he is no longer even a bad memory. Theseus will never come back. The Eternal Return is active and affirmative: it is the union of Dionysus and Ariadne. For this reason, Nietzsche compares it not only to the circular ear, but also to the wedding ring: the labyrinth is the ring, the ear, the Eternal Return itself that expresses what is active or affirmative. The labyrinth is no longer the path on which one gets lost, but the path that returns. The labyrinth is no longer that of knowledge or morality, but the labyrinth of life and of Being as *living* being. As for the product of Dionysus and Ariadne's union, it is the overman or the overhero, the opposite of the higher man. The overman is the living being of caves and summits, the only child conceived through the ear, the son of Ariadne and the Bull.

13
He Stuttered

It is sometimes said that bad novelists feel the need to vary their dialogic markers [*indicatifs*] by substituting for "he said" expressions like "he murmured," "he stammered," "he sobbed," "he giggled," "he cried," "he stuttered," all of which indicate different voice intonations. And in fact, with regard to these intonations, the writer seems to have only two possibilities: either *to do it* (as did Balzac, when he made Father Grandet stutter in his dealings with business matters, or when he made Nucingen speak in a contorted patois; in each case we can clearly sense Balzac's pleasure). Or else *to say it without doing it,* to be content with a simple indication that the reader is allowed to fill in: thus, Masoch's heroes are constantly murmuring, and their voice *must* be a barely audible murmur; Melville's Isabelle has a voice that must not rise above a murmur, and the angelic Billy Budd cannot stir without our having to reconstitute his "stutter or even worse";[1] Kafka's Gregor squeaks more than he speaks, but this is according to the testimony of others.

However, there seems to be a third possibility: when *saying is doing.*[2] This is what happens when the stuttering no longer affects preexisting words, but itself introduces the words it affects; these words no longer exist independently of the stutter, which selects and links them together through itself. It is no longer the character who stutters in speech; it is the writer who becomes *a stutterer in language.* He makes the language as such stutter: an affective and intensive language, and no longer an affectation of the one who speaks. A poetic operation such as this seems to be very distant from the previous cases; but it is perhaps less distant from the second case than we might think. For when an author is content with an external marker that leaves the *form of expression* intact ("he stuttered . . ."), its efficacy will be poorly understood unless there is a corresponding *form of content*—an atmospheric quality, a milieu that acts as the conductor of words—that brings together within itself the quiver, the murmur, the stutter, the tremolo, or the vibrato, and makes the indicated affect reverberate through the words. This, at least, is what happens in great writers like Melville, in whom the hum of the forests and caves, the silence of the house, and the presence of the guitar are evidence of Isabelle's murmurings, and her soft, "foreign intonations"; or Kafka, who confirms Gregor's squeaking through the trembling of his feet and the oscillations of his body; or even Masoch, who doubles the stammering of his characters with the heavy suspense of the boudoir, the hum of the village, or the vibrations of the steppe. The affects of language here become the object of an indirect effectuation, and yet they remain close to those that are made directly, when there are no characters other than the words themselves. "What was it my family wished to say? I do not know. It had been stuttering since birth, and yet it had something to say. This congenital stuttering weighs heavily on me and many of my contemporaries. We were not taught to speak but to stammer—and only by listening to the swelling noise of the century and being bleached by the foam on the crest of its wave did we acquire a language."[3]

Is it possible to make language stutter without confusing it with speech? Everything depends on the way we consider language. If we extract it like a homogeneous system in equilibrium, or close to equilibrium, defined by constant terms and relations, it is obvious that the disequilibriums and variations can only affect speech (nonpertinent variations of the intonation type). But if the system appears in perpetual disequilibrium or bifurcation, if each of its terms in turn passes through a zone of continuous variation, then the language itself will begin to vibrate and stutter, but without being confused with speech, which never assumes more than one variable position among others, or moves in more than one direction. If language merges with speech, it is only with a very particular kind of speech, a poetic speech that actualizes these powers of bifurcation and variation, of heterogenesis and modulation, that are proper to language. The linguist Guillaume, for example, considers each term of a language not as a constant in relation to other constants, but as a series of differential positions or points of view on a specifiable dynamism: the indefinite article *a* covers the entire zone of variation included in a movement of particulariza-tion, and the definite article *the* covers the entire zone generated by the movement of generalization.[4] It is a stuttering, with every position of *a* or *the* constituting a zone of vibration. Language trembles from head to toe. This is the principle of a poetic comprehension of language itself: it is as if the language were stretched along an abstract and infi-nitely varied line. Even with respect to pure science, the question must be posed thus: Can we make progress if we do not enter into *regions far from equilibrium?* Physics attests to this. Keynes made advances in political economy because he related it to the situation of a "boom," and no longer one of equilibrium. This is the only way to introduce desire into the corresponding field. Must language then be put into a state of *boom,* close to a *crash?* Dante is admired for having "listened to stammerers" and studied "speech impediments," not only to derive speech effects from them, but in order to undertake a vast phonetic, lexical, and even syntactic creation.[5]

This is not a situation of bilingualism or multilingualism. We can easily conceive of two languages mixing with each other, with inces-sant transitions from one to the other; yet each of them nonetheless remains a homogenous system in equilibrium, and their mixing takes place in speech. But this is not how great authors proceed, even though Kafka is a Czech writing in German, and Beckett an Irishman (often) writing in French, and so on. They do not mix two languages together, not even a minor language and a major language, though many of them are linked to minorities as a sign of their vocation. What they do, rather, is invent a *minor use* of the major language within which they express themselves entirely; they *minorize* this language, much as in music, where the minor mode refers to dynamic combinations in per-petual disequilibrium. They are great writers by virtue of this minori-zation: they make the language take flight, they send it racing along a witch's line, ceaselessly placing it in a state of disequilibrium, making it bifurcate and vary in each of its terms, following an incessant modula-tion. This exceeds the possibilities of speech and attains the power of the language, or even of language in its entirety. This means that a great writer is always like a foreigner in the language in which he ex-presses himself, even if this is his native tongue. At the limit, he draws his strength from a mute and unknown minority that belongs only to him. He is a foreigner in his own language: he does not mix another language with his own language, he carves out a nonpreexistent foreign language *within* his own language. He makes the language itself scream, stutter, stammer, or murmur. What better compliment could one receive than that of the critic who said of *Seven Pillars of Wisdom*: this is not English. Lawrence made English stumble in order to extract from it the music and visions of Arabia. And what language did Kleist awaken deep within German by means of grimaces, slips of the tongue, screechings, inarticulate sounds, extended liaisons, and brutal accelerations and decelerations, at the risk of horrifying Goethe, the greatest representative of the major language, and in order to attain these truly strange ends: petrified visions and a vertiginous music.[6]

Language is subject to a double process, that of choices to be made and that of sequences to be established: disjunction or the selection of similars, connection or the consecution of combinables. As long as language is considered as a system in equilibrium, the disjunctions are necessarily exclusive (we do not say "passion," "ration," "nation" at the same time, but must choose between them), and the connections, progressive (we do not combine a word with its own elements, in a kind of stop-start or forward-backward jerk). But far from equilibrium, *the disjunctions become included or inclusive, and the connections, reflexive,* following a rolling gait that concerns the process of language and no longer the flow of speech. Every word is divided, but into itself (*pas-rats, passions-rations*); and every word is combined, but with itself (*pas-passe-passion*). It is as if the entire language started to roll from right to left, and to pitch backward and forward: *the two stutterings.* If Gherasim Luca's speech is eminently poetic, it is because he makes stuttering an affect of language and not an affectation of speech. The entire language spins and varies in order to disengage a final block of sound, a single breath at the limit of the cry, JE T'AIME PASSIONNÉMENT ("I love you passionately").

> Passionné nez passionnem je
> je t'ai je t'aime je
> je je jet je t'ai jetez
> je t'aime passionnem t'aime.[7]

Luca the Romanian, Beckett the Irishman. Beckett took this art of inclusive disjunctions to its highest point, an art that no longer selects but affirms the disjointed terms through their distance, without limiting one by the other or excluding one from the other, laying out and passing through the entire set of possibilities. Hence, in *Watt*, the ways in which Knott puts on his shoes, moves about his room, or changes his furniture. It is true that, in Beckett, these affirmative disjunctions usually concern the bearing or gait of the characters: an ineffable manner of walking, while rolling and pitching. But this is how the transfer from the form of expression to a form of content is brought about. But we could equally well bring about the reverse transition by supposing that the characters speak like they walk or stumble, for speaking is no less a movement than walking: the former goes beyond speech toward language, just as the latter goes beyond the organism toward a body without organs. A confirmation of this can be found in one of Beckett's poems that deals specifically with the connections of language and makes stuttering the poetic or linguistic power par excellence.[8] Beckett's procedure, which is different from Luca's, is as follows: he places himself in the middle of the sentence and makes the sentence grow out from the middle, adding particle upon particle (*que de ce, ce ceci-ci, loin là là-bas à peine quoi . . .*) so as to pilot the block of a single expiring breath (*voulais croire entrevoir quoi . . .*). Creative stuttering is what makes language grow from the middle, like grass; it is what makes language a rhizome instead of a tree, what puts language in perpetual disequilibrium: *Ill Seen, Ill Said* (content and expression). Being well spoken has never been either the distinctive feature or the concern of great writers.

There are many ways to grow from the middle, or to stutter. Péguy does not work with asignifying particles, but rather with highly significative terms: substantives, each of which defines a zone of variation until it reaches the neighborhood of another substantive, which determines another zone (Mater *purissima, catissima, inviolata,* Virgo *potens, clemens, fidelis*). Péguy's repetitions give words a vertical thickness and make them perpetually recommence the "unrecommenceable." In Péguy, stuttering embraces the language so well that it leaves the words intact, complete, and normal, but it uses them as if they were themselves the disjointed and decomposed members of a superhuman stuttering. Péguy is like a thwarted stutterer. In Roussel, there is yet another procedure, for the stuttering no longer affects particles or complete terms, but propositions, perpetually inserted into the middle of the sentence, each within the preceding sentence, following a proliferating system of parentheses—to the point where there are five parentheses inside each other, so that "with each additional increase this internal development could not fail to overwhelm the language it enriched. The invention of each verse was the destruction of the whole and stipulated its reconstitution."[9]

This is therefore a ramified variation of language. Each variable state is like a point on a ridge line, which then bifurcates and is continued along other lines. It is a syntactic line, syntax being constituted by the curves, rings, bends, and deviations of this dynamic line as it passes through the points, from the double viewpoint of disjunctions and connections. It is no longer the formal or superficial syntax that governs the equilibriums of language, but a syntax in the process of becoming, a creation of syntax that gives birth to a foreign language within language, a grammar of disequilibrium. But in this sense it is inseparable from an end, it tends toward a limit that is itself no longer either syntactic or grammatical, even when it still seems to be so formally: hence Luca's formula, "je t'aime passionnément," which explodes like a scream at the end of long stuttering series (or the "I prefer not to" in *Bartleby,* which has even absorbed all the prior variations; or e. e. cummings's "he danced his did," which is extracted from variations that are assumed to be merely virtual). Such expressions are taken as inarticulate words, blocks of a single breath. This final limit eventually abandons any grammatical appearance in order to appear in its raw state in Artaud's breath-words: Artaud's deviant syntax, to the extent that it sets out to strain the French language, reaches the destination of its own tension in these breaths or pure intensities that mark a limit of language. Or again, sometimes this takes place in different books. In Céline, *Journey to the End of the Night* places the native language in disequilibrium, *Death on the Installment Plan* develops the new syntax in affective variations, while *Guignol's Band* achieves the ultimate aim: exclamatory sentences and suspensions that do away with all syntax in favor of a pure dance of words. The two aspects are nonetheless correlative: the tensor and the limit, the tension in language and the limit of language.

The two aspects are effected in an infinity of tonalities, but always together: a limit of language that subtends the entire language, and a line of variation or subtended modulation that brings language to this limit. And just as the new language is not external to the initial language, the asyntactic limit is not external to language as a whole: it is *the outside* of language, but is not outside it. It is a painting or a piece of music, but a music of words, a painting with words, a silence in words, as if the words could now discharge their content: a grandiose vision or a sublime sound. What is specific to the drawings and paintings of great writers (Hugo, Michaux . . .) is not that these works are literary, for they are not literary at all; they attain pure visions, but visions that are still related to language in that they constitute an ultimate aim, an outside, an inverse, an underside, an inkstain or unreadable handwriting. Words paint and sing, but only at the limit of the path they trace through their divisions and combinations. Words create silence. The sister's violin takes up Gregor's squeaking, and the guitar reflects Isabelle's murmur; the melody of a singing bird about to die drowns out the stuttering of Billy Budd, the sweet "barbarian." *When a language is so strained* that it starts to stutter, or to murmur or stammer . . . *then language in its entirety reaches the limit* that marks its outside and makes it confront silence. When a language is strained in this way, language in its entirety is submitted to a pressure that makes it fall silent. Style—the foreign language within language—is made up of these two operations; or should we instead speak with Proust of a nonstyle, that is, of "the elements of a style to come which do not yet exist"? Style is the economy of language.[10] To make one's language stutter, face to face, or face to back, and at the same time to push language as a whole to its limit, to its outside, to its silence—this would be like the *boom* and the *crash*.

Everyone can talk about his memories, invent stories, state opinions in his language; sometimes he even acquires a beautiful style, which gives him adequate means and makes him an appreciated writer. But when it is a matter of digging under the stories, cracking open the opinions, and reaching regions without memories, when the self must be destroyed, it is certainly not enough to be a "great" writer, and the means must remain forever inadequate. Style becomes nonstyle, and one's language lets an unknown foreign language escape from it, so that one can reach the limits of language itself and become something other than a writer, conquering fragmented visions that pass through the words of a poet, the colors of a painter, or the sounds of a musician. "The only thing the reader will see marching past him are *inadequate means*: fragments, allusions, strivings, investigations. Do not try to find a well-polished sentence or a perfectly coherent image in it, what is printed on the pages is an embarrassed word, a stuttering . . ."[11] Biely's stuttering work, *Kotik Letaiev,* is flung into a becoming-child that is not a "self" but the cosmos, the explosion of the world: a childhood that is not my own, that is not a memory but a block, an anonymous and infinite fragment, a becoming that is always contemporary.[12] Biely, Mandelstam, Khlebnikov: a Russian trinity thrice the stutterer and thrice crucified.

14

The Shame and the Glory: T. E. Lawrence

The desert and its perception, or the perception of the Arabs in the desert, seem to pass through Goethean moments. In the beginning, there is light, but it is not yet perceived. It is instead a pure transparency, invisible, colorless, unformed, untouchable. It is the Idea, the God of the Arabs. But the Idea, or the abstract, has no transcendence. The Idea is extended throughout space, it is like the Open: "beyond there lay nothing but clear air."[1] Light is the opening that creates space. Ideas are forces that are exerted on space following certain directions of movement: entities or hypostases, not transcendences. The revolt, the rebellion, is light because it is space (it is a question of extending it in space, of opening up as much space as possible) and it is an Idea (what is essential is predication). The men of the rebellion are the prophet and the knight-errant, Feisal and Auda, he who preaches the Idea and he who crosses space.[2] The "Movement": this is what the revolt is called.

What comes to occupy this space is haze, solar haze. The rebellion itself is a gas, a vapor. Haze is the first state of nascent perception; it creates mirages in which things rise and fall, as if under the action of a piston, and men levitate, as if hung from a rope. To see through a haze is to have blurred vision—the rough outlines of a hallucinatory perception, a cosmic gray.[3] Does the gray then divide in two, producing black when the shadow spreads or the light disappears, but also white when the luminosity itself becomes opaque? Goethe defined white as the "fortuitously opaque flash of pure transparency"; white is the ever-renewed accident of the desert, and the Arab world is painted in black and white.[4] But these are still only the conditions of perception, which will be fully actualized when colors appear, that is, when white darkens into yellow and black lightens into blue: sand and sky, whose intensification produces a blinding crimson in which the world burns, and eyesight is replaced by suffering. Sight and suffering, two entities . . .: "in the night, waking up, there had been no sight, only pain in his eyes."[5] From gray to red, there is the appearing and disappearing of the world in the desert, all the adventures of the visible and its perception. The Idea in space is vision, which passes from a pure and invisible transparency to the crimson fire in which all sight burns.

"The union of dark cliffs, pink floors, and pale green shrubbery was beautiful to eyes sated with months of sunlight and sooty shadow. When evening came, the declining sun crimsoned one side of the valley with its glow, leaving the other in purple gloom."[6] Lawrence is one of the greatest portrayers of landscapes in literature. Rumm the sublime, the absolute vision, the landscape of the mind.[7] And color is movement, no less than the line; it is deviation, displacement, sliding, obliquity. Color and line are born together and meld into each other. Sandstone or basalt landscapes are made up of colors and lines, but they are always in movement, the broad strokes being colored in coats, and the colors being drawn in broad strokes. Forms of thorns and blisters follow upon each other, while at the same time colors are given names, from pure transparency to hopeless gray. Faces correspond to the landscapes, they appear and disappear in these brief pictures, which makes Lawrence one of the great portraitists: "Though usually merry, he had a quick vein of suffering in him . . ."; "his streaming hair and the ruined face of a tired tragedian . . ."; "his mind, like a pastoral landscape, had four corners to its view: cared-for, friendly, limited, displayed . . ."; "upon his coarse eyelashes the eyelids sagged down in tired folds, through which, from the overhead sun, a red light glittered into his eye-sockets and made them look like fiery pits in which the man was slowly burning."[8]

The finest writers have singular conditions of perception that allow them to draw on or shape aesthetic percepts like veritable visions, even if they return from them with red eyes. Melville's perceptions are impregnated from within by the ocean, so much so that the ship seems unreal compared with the empty sea and is imposed on sight like "a shadowy tableau just emerged from the deep."[9] But is it enough to invoke the objectivity of a milieu that distorts things, and that makes perception flicker or scintillate? Are there not rather *subjective conditions* that certainly require a favorable and objective milieu, are deployed in it, can coincide with it, but nonetheless retain an irresistible and irreducible difference from it? It is by virtue of a subjective disposition that Proust finds his percepts in a current of air passing under a door, and is left cold by the beauties others bring to his attention.[10] In Melville, there is a private ocean of which the sailors are unaware, even if they have a foreboding of it: it is there that Moby-Dick swims, and it is he who is cast into the ocean from the outside, but in order to transmute its perception and to "abstract" a Vision from it. In Lawrence, there is a private desert that drives him to the Arabian deserts, among the Arabs, and that coincides on many points with their own perceptions and conceptions, but that retains an unmasterable difference that inserts them into a completely different and secret Figure. Lawrence speaks Arabic, he dresses and lives like an Arab, even under torture he cries out in Arabic, but he does not imitate the Arabs, he never renounces his difference, which he already experiences as a betrayal.[11] Beneath his young groom's suit, "suspect immaculate silk," he ceaselessly betrays his Bride. And Lawrence's difference does not simply stem from the fact that he is English, in the service of England; for he betrays England as much as Arabia, in a nightmare-dream where everything is betrayed at once. But neither is it his personal difference, since Lawrence's undertaking is a cold and concerted destruction of the ego, carried to its limit. Every mine he plants also explodes within himself, he is himself the bomb he detonates. It is an infinitely secret *subjective disposition,* which must not be confused with a national or personal character, and which leads him far from his own country, under the ruins of his devastated ego.

No problem is more important than the nature of this disposition that carries Lawrence along, freeing him from the "chains of being." Even a psychoanalyst would hesitate to say that this subjective disposition is homosexuality, or more precisely, the hidden love that Lawrence, in his splendid dedicatory poem, makes the motivating force of his action—though homosexuality is no doubt included in the disposition. Nor should we assume that it is a disposition to betray—though betrayal perhaps follows from it. It would rather be a question of a profound desire, a tendency to project—into things, into reality, into the future, and even into the sky—an image of himself and others so intense that *it has a life of its own*: an image that is always stitched together, patched up, continually growing along the way, to the point where it becomes fabulous.[12] It is a machine for manufacturing giants, what Bergson called a fabulatory function.

Lawrence says that he sees through a haze, that he cannot immediately perceive either forms or colors, that he can only recognize things through direct contact; that he is hardly a man of action, that he is interested in Ideas rather than ends and their means; that he has hardly any imagination and does not like dreams . . . And in these negative characterizations, there are already numerous motifs that link him with the Arabs. But what inspires him, what carries him along, is to be a "diurnal dreamer," to be a truly dangerous man, one who defines himself neither in relation to the real or action, nor in relation to the imaginary or dreams, but solely in relation to the force through which he projects images into the real, images he was able to draw from himself and his Arab friends.[13] Did these images correspond to what they really were? Those who criticize Lawrence for ascribing himself an importance he never had are simply revealing their personal pettiness, their aptitude for denigration as much as their inaptitude in comprehending a text. For Lawrence does not hide the fact that he gives himself a very local role, caught up in a fragile network; he underscores the insignificance of many of his undertakings, as when he plants mines that do not go off and cannot remember where he planted them. As for his final success, in which he takes a certain pride without sustaining any illusions about it, it lies in his having led the Arab partisans to Damascus before the arrival of the Allied troops—under conditions somewhat analogous to those that would be reproduced at the end of the Second World War, when resistance fighters seized the official buildings of a liberated city, and even had time to neutralize the representatives of a compromise at the last minute.[14] In short, it is not some sort of contemptible individual mythomania that compels Lawrence to project grandiose images on his path, beyond his often modest undertakings. The projection machine is inseparable from the movement of the Revolt itself: it is subjective, but it refers to the subjectivity of the revolutionary group. And Lawrence's writing, his style, makes use of this machine in its own way, or rather acts as its relay: the subjective disposition, that is to say, the force through which the images are projected, is inseparably political, erotic, and artistic. Lawrence himself shows how his writing project is linked to the Arab movement: lacking a literary technique, he needs the mechanism of revolt and preaching to become a writer.[15]

The images Lawrence projects into the real are not inflated images that would sin by a false extension, but are valid solely through the pure intensity, whether dramatic or comic, that the writer is able to give the event. And the image he offers of himself is not a deceptive image, because it has no need to correspond to a preexisting reality. As Genet says of this type of projection, behind the image there is nothing, an "absence of being," an emptiness that bears witness to a dissolved ego. There is nothing behind the images, even the bloody and harrowing ones, *except the mind that regards them with a strange coldness.*[16] There are thus two books in *Seven Pillars of Wisdom*, two books that are intertwined with each other: the first concerns the images projected into the real, leading a life of their own; the second concerns the mind that contemplates them, given over to its own abstractions.

But the mind that contemplates is not itself empty, and the abstractions are the eyes of the mind. The mind's serenity is beset by thoughts that claw away at it. The mind is a Beast with multiple eyes, always ready to leap on the animal bodies it perceives. Lawrence insists on his passion for abstraction, which he shares with the Arabs: both Lawrence and the Arabs will gladly interrupt an action in order to follow an Idea they come across. I am the manservant of the abstract.[17] Abstract ideas are not dead things, they are entities that inspire powerful spatial dynamisms; in the desert they are intimately linked up with the projected images—things, bodies, or beings. This is why *Seven Pillars* is the object of a double reading, a double theatricality. Such is Lawrence's special disposition—a gift for making entities live passionately in the desert, alongside people and things, in the jerking rhythm of a camel's gait. Perhaps this gift confers something unique on Lawrence's language, something that sounds like a foreign language, less Arabic than a phantom German that is inscribed in his style, endowing the English language with new powers (an English that does not flow, said Forster, but is granular, uneven, constantly changing regime, full of abstractions, stationary processes, and frozen visions).[18] In any case, the Arabs were enchanted by Lawrence's capacity for abstraction. One feverish evening, his febrile mind inspired in him a half-delirious discourse denouncing *Omnipotence* and *Infinity,* imploring these entities to hit us even harder in order to fortify us with the weapons of their own ruin, and exalting the importance of being beaten: Nondoing is our only victory, and Failure our sovereign freedom. "To the clear-sighted, failure was the only goal . . ."[19] What is most curious is that his listeners were so filled with enthusiasm that they decided to join the Revolt on the spot.

One moves from images to *entities*. In the final analysis, then, this is Lawrence's subjective disposition: a world of entities that passes through the desert, that *doubles the images,* intermingling with them and giving them a visionary dimension. Lawrence says that he knows these entities intimately, but their *character* escapes him. Character must not be confused with an ego. At the most profound level of subjectivity, there is not an ego but rather a singular composition, an idiosyncrasy, a secret cipher marking the unique chance that *these* entities had been retained and willed, that *this* combination had been thrown and not another. It is this combination that is named Lawrence. A dice throw, a Will that throws the dice. *Character* is the Beast: mind, will, desire, a desert-desire that brings together heterogenous entities.[20] The problem then becomes: What are these subjective entities, and how are they combined? Lawrence devotes the grandiose chapter 103 to this problem. Of all the entities, none appears with greater insistence than Shame and Glory, Shame and Pride. Perhaps it is their relationship that permits him to decipher the secret of *character*. Never before has shame been sung like this, in so proud and haughty a manner.

Every entity is multiple, and at the same time is linked with various other entities. Shame is first of all the shame of betraying the Arabs, since Lawrence never stops guaranteeing English promises that he knows perfectly well will not be kept. Though he is honest, Lawrence still feels the shame of preaching national freedom to men of another nation: an unlivable situation. Lawrence constantly lives like a confidence man: "I must take up again my mantle of fraud."[21] But he already experiences a kind of compensatory fidelity by betraying his own race and his government a little, since he is training partisans capable, he hopes, of forcing the English to keep their word (hence the importance of entering Damascus). Mingled with shame, his pride lies in seeing the Arabs so noble, so beautiful, so charming (even when they in turn betray a little), so opposed in every respect to the English soldiers.[22] For in keeping with the demands of guerrilla warfare, he is training warriors and not soldiers. As the Arabs join the Revolt, they are molded more and more on the projected images that individualize them, and make giants of them. "Our confidence game glorified them. The more we condemned and distrusted ourselves, the more we were able to be proud of them, our creatures. Our will blew them before us like straw, and they were not straw, but the bravest, simplest, most gay of men." For Lawrence, the first great theoretician of guerrilla warfare, the dominating opposition is between the raid and the battle, between partisans and armies. The problem of guerrilla warfare merges with that of the desert: it is the problem of individuality or subjectivity, even if it is a group subjectivity, in which the fate of freedom is at stake, whereas the problem of wars and armies is the organization of an anonymous mass subjected to objective rules, which set out to turn the men into "types."[23] The shame of battles, which soil the desert—the only battle Lawrence fights against the Turks, out of weariness, turns into an ignoble and useless slaughter. The shame of armies, whose members are worse than convicts, and merely attract whores.[24] It is true that groups of partisans sometimes have to form an army, or at least be integrated into an army, if they want to achieve a decisive victory; but at that point they cease to exist as free men and rebels. For almost half of *Seven Pillars,* we are made to witness the long obliteration of the partisan period—the camels are replaced by automatic machine guns and Rolls-Royces, and the guerrilla chiefs by experts and politicians. Even comfort and success create shame. Shame has many contradictory motifs. At the end, as he steps aside, filled with his own solitude, with two mad laughs, Lawrence can say with Kafka: "It was as if the shame of it must outlive him."[25] Shame enlarges the man.

There are many shames in one, but there are also other shames. How is it possible to command without shame? To command is to steal souls in order to deliver them over to suffering. A leader cannot be legitimized by the crowd that believes in him—"fervent hopes united in myopic multitudes"—if he does not take on the suffering and sacrifice himself. But shame survives even in this redemptive sacrifice, for one has now taken the place of others. The redeemer takes delight in his own sacrifice, but "he wounds his brothers' virility": he has not sufficiently immolated his own ego, which prevents others from themselves taking on the role of the redeemer. This is why "the virile disciples are ashamed": it is as if Christ had deprived the thieves of the glory that could have been theirs. The shame of the redeemer because he "cast down the bought."[26] These are the sort of clawed thoughts that tear away at Lawrence's brain and make *Seven Pillars* an almost mad book.

Must we then choose servitude? But what could be more shameful than to be subject to one's inferiors? The shame is doubled when man has to depend on animals, not only in his biological functions, but for his most human projects. Lawrence mounts his horse only when absolutely necessary, and he prefers to walk in bare feet on sharp coral, not only to harden himself but also because he is ashamed to depend on a form of existence whose very resemblance to us is enough to remind us of what we are in the eyes of God.[27] Despite the admiring or comic portrait he gives of several camels, his hatred erupts when the fever abandons him to their stench and abjection.[28] And in armies, there are servitudes that make us depend on men who are no less inferior to us than the beasts. A forced and shameful servitude—such is the problem of armies. And if it is true that *Seven Pillars* poses the question, How can one live and survive in the desert as a free subjectivity? Lawrence's other book, *The Mint*, asks, "Can I again become a man like others by binding myself to my equals?" How can one live and survive in an army as an anonymous "type," objectively determined down to the smallest detail?[29] Lawrence's two books can perhaps be read as an exploration of two ways, like Parmenides' poem. When Lawrence plunges into anonymity and is engaged as a simple soldier, he passes from one way to the other. *The Mint* is in this sense the song of shame, just as *Seven Pillars* is the song of glory. But just as glory is already filled with shame, perhaps shame has a glorious outcome. Glory is so compromised by shame that servitude becomes glorious—but only on the condition that it is taken on voluntarily. There is always glory to extract from shame, a "glorification of humanity's cross." It is a voluntary servitude that Lawrence demands of himself, a kind of arrogant masochistic contract that he calls on with all his goodwill: a subjection, and not an enslavement.[30] It is voluntary servitude that defines a subject-group in the desert—for example, Lawrence's own bodyguard.[31] But it is also what transmutes the abject dependence on the army into a splendid and free servitude: hence the lesson of *The Mint*, in which Lawrence goes from the shame of the Prison to the glory of the officers' school. Lawrence's two ways, his two very different questions, meet up in voluntary servitude.

The third aspect of shame, without a doubt the most essential one, is the shame of the body. Lawrence admires the Arabs because they *distrust* the body; "in successive waves they had been dashing themselves against the coasts of the flesh" throughout their entire history.[32] But

shame is something more than distrust: Lawrence insists on his difference from the Arabs. He has shame because he thinks the mind,
though distinct, is inseparable from the body; the two are irremediably
linked.[33] In this sense, the body is not even a means or a vehicle for the
mind, but rather a "molecular sludge" that adheres to all the mind's
actions. When we act, the body lets itself be forgotten. But when it is
reduced to a state of sludge, on the contrary, one has the strange feeling that it finally makes itself visible and attains its ultimate aim.[34] *The
Mint* opens with this shame of the body and its marks of infamy. In
two famous episodes, Lawrence reaches the limit of horror: in his own
body, tortured and raped by the soldiers of the bey; and in the bodies
of the agonized Turks, who limply raise their hands to show they are
still alive.[35] The idea that horror nonetheless has an aim stems from the
fact that molecular sludge is the body's final state, which the mind contemplates with a certain attraction, finding in it the security of a final
level that it cannot pass beyond.[36] The mind depends on the body;
shame would be nothing without this dependency, this attraction for
the abject, this voyeurism of the body. Which means that the mind is
ashamed *of* the body in a very special manner; in fact, it is ashamed *for*
the body. It is as if it were saying to the body: You make me ashamed,
You ought to be ashamed . . . "A bodily weakness which made my animal self crawl away and hide until the shame was passed."[37]

Being ashamed for the body implies a very particular conception
of the body. According to this conception, the body has autonomous
external reactions. The body is an animal. What the body does it does
alone. Lawrence makes Spinoza's formula his own: we do not know
what a body can do! In the midst of his tortures, an erection; even in
the state of sludge, there are convulsions that jolt the body, like the
reflexes that still animate a dead frog. And there are the gestures of the
dying, that attempt at raising their hands that makes all the agonizing
Turks ripple together, as if they had practiced the same theatrical gesture, provoking Lawrence's mad laughter. For all the more reason, in
its normal state, the body never ceases to act and react *before the mind
moves it*. One might perhaps recall William James's theory of the emotions, which has often been subject to absurd refutations.[38] James suggests a paradoxical order: (1) I perceive a lion, (2) my body trembles,
(3) I am afraid; (1) the perception of a situation, (2) the modification
of the body, a reenforcement or a weakening, (3) the emotion of consciousness or the mind. James is perhaps wrong to confuse this order

with a causality, and to believe that the emotion of the mind is merely the result or effect of corporeal modifications. But the order is correct: I am in an exhausting situation; my body "crouches down and crawls"; my mind is ashamed. The mind begins by coldly and curiously regarding what the body does, it is first of all a witness; then it is affected, it becomes an impassioned witness, that is, it experiences for itself affects that are not simply effects of the body, but veritable *critical entities* that hover over the body and judge it.[39]

Spiritual entities or abstract ideas are not what we think they are: they are emotions or affects. They are innumerable, and do not simply consist of shame, though shame is one of the principal entities. There are cases where the mind is ashamed *of* the body, but also cases where the body makes *it* laugh, or indeed charms *it*, as with the young and handsome Arabs ("the love-locks plaited tightly over each temple in long horns, made them look like Russian dancers").[40] It is always the mind that is ashamed, cracks, or extracts pleasure or glory, while the body "continues to toil away obstinately." Affective critical entities do not cancel each other out, but can coexist and intermingle, composing the *character* of the mind, constituting not an ego but a center of gravity that is displaced from one entity to the next, following the secret threads of this marionette theater. Perhaps this is what glory is: a hidden will that makes entities communicate, and extracts them at the favorable moment.

Entities rise up and act on the mind when it contemplates the body. These are acts of subjectivity. They are not only the eyes of the mind, but its Powers and its Words. What we hear in Lawrence's style is the shock of entities. But because their only object is the body, they provoke, at the limit of language, the apparition of great visual and sonorous images—images that hollow out these bodies, whether animate or inanimate, in order to humiliate and magnify them at the same time, as in the opening of *Seven Pillars:* "At night we were stained by dew, and shamed into pettiness by the innumerable silences of stars."[41] It is as if the entities populate a private desert that is applied to the external desert, and projects fabulous images onto it through the bodies of men, beasts, and rocks. Entities and Images, Abstractions and Visions combine to make of Lawrence another William Blake. Lawrence does not lie, and even in pleasure he experiences all kinds of shame in relation to the Arabs: the shame of disguising himself, of sharing their misery, of commanding them, of deceiving them . . . He is ashamed of the Arabs, for the Arabs, before the Arabs. Yet Lawrence bears the shame within himself, for all time, from birth, as a profound component of his Character. And it is through this profound shame that the Arabs set about playing the glorious role of an expiation, a voluntary purification; Lawrence himself helps them transform their paltry undertakings into a war of resistance and liberation, even if the latter must fail through betrayal (the failure in turn doubles the splendor or purity). The English, the Turks, the whole world distrusts them; but it is as if the Arabs, insolent and cheerful, *leap beyond shame* and capture the reflection of Vision and Beauty. They bring a strange freedom into the world, where glory and shame enter into an almost spiritual combat. This is where Jean Genet has many points in common with Lawrence: the impossibility of identifying with the Arab (Palestinian) cause; the shame of not being able to do so; the deeper shame that comes from elsewhere, cosubstantial with being; and the revelation of an insolent beauty that shows, as Genet says, at what point "the coming out of shame was easy," as least for a moment . . .[42]

15

To Have Done with Judgment

From Greek tragedy to modern philosophy, an entire doctrine of judgment has been elaborated and developed. What is tragic is less the action than the judgment, and what Greek tragedy instituted at the outset was a tribunal. Kant did not invent a true critique of judgment; on the contrary, what the book of this title established was a fantastic subjective tribunal. Breaking with the Judeo-Christian tradition, it was Spinoza who carried out the critique, and he had four great disciples to take it up again and push it further: Nietzsche, D. H. Lawrence, Kafka, Artaud. These four had personally, singularly suffered from judgment. They experienced that infinite point at which accusation, deliberation, and verdict converge. Nietzsche moved like a condemned man from room to room, against which he set a grandiose defiance; Lawrence lived under the accusations of immoralism and pornography that were brought against the least of his watercolors; Kafka showed himself to be "diabolical in all innocence" in order to escape from the "tribunal in the hotel" where his infinite engagements were being judged.[1] And who suffered more from judgment in its harshest form, the terror of psychiatric expertise, than Artaud-Van Gogh?

It was Nietzsche who was able lay bare the condition of judgment: "the consciousness of being in debt to the deity," the adventure of debt as it becomes *infinite* and thus unpayable.[2] Man does not appeal to judgment, he judges and is judgable only to the extent that his existence is subject to an infinite debt: the infinity of the debt and the immortality of existence each depend on the other, and together constitute "the doctrine of judgment."[3] The debtor must survive if his debt is to be infinite. Or as Lawrence says, Christianity did not renounce power, but rather invented a new form of power as the Power to judge: the destiny of man is "postponed" at the same time that judgment becomes a final authority.[4] The doctrine of judgment appears in the Apocalypse or the Last Judgment, just as it appears in the theater of *America*. Kafka, for his part, locates the infinite debt in an "apparent aquittal," and the deferred destiny in an "unlimited postponement," both of which keep the judges beyond our experience and our comprehension.[5] Artaud will never cease to pit the operation of having done with the judgment of God against the infinite. For all four, the logic of judgment merges with the psychology of the priest, as the inventor of the most somber organization: I want to judge, I have to judge . . . It is not as if the judgment itself were postponed, put off until tomorrow, pushed back to infinity; on the contrary, it is the act of postponing, of carrying to infinity, that makes judgment possible. The condition of judgment lies in a supposed relation between existence and the infinite in the *order* of time. The power to judge and to be judged is given to whomever stands in this relation. Even the judgment of knowledge envelops an infinity of space, time, and experience that determines the existence of phenomena in space and time ("every time that . . ."). But the judgment of knowledge in this sense implies a prior moral and theological form, according to which a relation was established between existence and the infinite following an order of time: the existing being as having a debt to God.

But what then can be distinguished from judgment? Would it be enough to invoke a "prejudicative" that would be both its ground and its horizon? And would this be the same thing as an antijudicative, understood as Antichrist—less a ground than a collapse, a landslide, a loss of horizons? Existing beings confront each other, and obtain redress by means of *finite* relations that merely constitute the *course* of time. Nietzsche's greatness lies in having shown, without any hesitation, that *the creditor-debtor relation was primary in relation to all exchange*.[6] One begins by promising, and becomes indebted not to a god but to a partner, depending on the forces that pass between the parties, which provoke a change of state and create something new in them: an affect. Everything takes place between parties, and the ordeal is not a judgment of God, since there is neither god nor judgment.[7] Where Mauss and then Lévi-Strauss still hesitated, Nietzsche did not hesitate: there exists a justice that is opposed to all judgment, according to which bodies are marked by each other, and the debt is inscribed directly on the body following the *finite blocks* that circulate in a territory. The law [*le droit*] does not have the immobility of eternal things, but is ceaselessly displaced among families that either have to draw blood or pay with it. Such are the terrible signs that lacerate bodies and stain them, the incisions and pigments that reveal in the flesh of each person what they owe and are owed: an entire *system of cruelty,* whose echo can be heard in the philosophy of Anaximander and the tragedy of Aeschylus.[8] In the doctrine of judgment, by contrast, our debts are inscribed in an autonomous book without our even realizing it, so that we are no longer able to pay off an account that has become infinite. We are dispossessed, expelled from our territory, inasmuch as the book has already collected the dead signs of a Proprietorship that claims to be eternal. The bookish doctrine of judgment is moderate only in appearence, because it in fact condemns us to an endless servitude and annuls any liberatory process. Artaud will give sublime developments to the system of cruelty, a writing of blood and life that is opposed to the writing of the book, just as justice is opposed to judgment, provoking a veritable inversion of the sign.[9] Is this not also the case with Kafka, when to the great book of *The Trial* he opposes the machine of "The Penal Colony"—a writing in bodies that testifies both to an ancient order and to a justice in which obligation, accusation, defense, and verdict all merge together? The system of cruelty expresses the finite relations of the existing body with the forces that affect it, whereas the doctrine of infinite debt determines the relationships of the immortal soul with judgments. The system of cruelty is everywhere opposed to the doctrine of judgment.

Judgment did not appear on a soil that, even had it been quite different, would have favored its blossoming. Ruptures and bifurcations were necessary. The debt had to be owed to the gods; it had to be related, no longer to the forces of which we were the guardians, but to the gods who were supposed to have given us these forces. Many circuitous paths had to be taken, for at the outset the gods were passive witnesses or plaintive litigants who could not judge (as in Aeschylus's *Eumenides*). It was only gradually that the gods and men together raised themselves to the activity of judging—for better or for worse, as can be seen in Sophocles' plays. At bottom, a doctrine of judgment presumes that the gods give *lots* to men, and that men, depending on their lots, are fit for some particular *form,* for some particular organic *end.*

What form does my lot condemn me to? But also, Does my lot correspond to the form I aspire to? This is the essential effect of judgment: existence is cut into lots, the affects are distributed into lots, and then related to higher forms (this is a constant theme in both Nietzsche and Lawrence: the denunciation of this claim to "judge" life in the name of higher values). Men judge insofar as they value their own lots, and are judged insofar as a form either confirms or dismisses their claim. They judge and are judged at the same time, and take equal delight in judging and being judged. Judgment burst in on the world in the form of the *false judgment* leading to delirium and madness, when man is mistaken about his lot, and in the form the *judgment of God,* when the form imposes another lot. *Ajax* would be a good example. The doctrine of judgment, in its infancy, has as much need of the false judgment of man as it does of the formal judgment of God. A final bifurcation takes place with Christianity: there are no longer any lots, for it is our judgments that make up our only lot; and there is no longer any form, for it is the judgment of God that constitutes the infinite form. At the limit, dividing oneself into lots and punishing oneself become the characteristics of the new judgment or modern tragedy. Nothing is left but judgment, and every judgment bears on another judgment. Perhaps *Oedipus* prefigures this new state in the Greek world. And what is modern about a theme like *Don Juan* is less the comic action than this new form of judgment. This second movement of the doctrine of judgment, in very general terms, can be expressed in the following manner: we are no longer debtors of the gods through forms or ends, but have become in our entire being the infinite debtors of a single God. The doctrine of judgment has reversed and replaced the system of affects. These characteristics are found even in the judgment of knowledge or experience.

The world of judgment establishes itself as in a dream. It is the dream that makes the lots turn (Ezekiel's wheel) and makes the forms pass in procession. In the dream, judgments are hurled into the void, without encountering the resistance of a milieu that would subject them to the exigencies of knowledge or experience; this is why the question of judgment is first of all knowing whether one is dreaming or not. Moreover, Apollo is both the god of judgment and the god of dreams: it is Apollo who judges, who imposes limits and emprisons us in an organic form, it is the dream that emprisons life within these forms in whose name life is judged. The dream erects walls, it feeds on death and creates shadows, shadows of all things and of the world, shadows of ourselves. But once we leave the shores of judgment, we also repudiate the dream in favor of an "intoxication," like a high tide sweeping over us.[10] What we seek in states of intoxication—drinks, drugs, ecstasies—is an antidote to both the dream and judgment. Whenever we turn away from judgment toward justice, we enter into a dreamless sleep. What the four authors denounce in the dream is a state that is still too immobile, and too directed, too governed. Groups that are deeply interested in dreams, like psychoanalysts or surrealists, are also quick to form tribunals that judge and punish in reality: a disgusting mania, frequent in dreamers. In his reservations concerning surrealism, Artaud insists that it is not thought that collides with the kernel of a dream, but rather dreams that bounce off a kernel of thought that escapes them.[11] The peyote rites, according to Artaud, and the songs of the Mexican forest, according to Lawrence, are not dreams, but states of intoxication or sleep. This dreamless sleep is not a state in which we fall asleep, but one that traverses the night and inhabits it with a frightening clarity. It is not daylight, but Lightning: "In the dream of the night I see gray dogs, creeping forward to devour the dream."[12] This dreamless sleep, in which one does not fall asleep, is Insomnia, for only insomnia is appropriate to the night, and can fill and populate it.[13] The dream is rediscovered, no longer as a dream of sleep or a daydream, but as an insomniac dream. *The new dream has become the guardian of insomnia.* As in Kafka, it is no longer a dream one has while sleeping, but a dream one has *alongside* insomnia: "I'll send [to the country] my clothed body. . . . For I myself am meanwhile lying in my bed, smoothly covered over with the yellow-brown blanket . . ."[14] The insomniac can remain motionless, whereas the dream has taken the real movement upon itself. This dreamless sleep in which one nonetheless does not fall asleep, this insomnia that nonetheless sweeps the dream along as far as the insomnia extends—such is the state of Dionysian intoxication, its way of escaping judgment.

The physical system of cruelty is also opposed to the theological doctrine of judgment from a third aspect, at the level of the body. This is because judgment implies a veritable organization of the bodies through which it acts: organs are both judges and judged, and the judgment of God is nothing other than the power to organize to infinity. Whence the relationship between judgment and the sense organs. The body of the physical system is completely different; it escapes judgment all the more inasmuch as it is not an "organism," and is deprived of this organization of the organs through which one judges and is judged. Where we once had a vital and living body, God has made us into an organism, woman has turned us into an organism. Artaud presents this "body without organs" that God has stolen from us in order to palm off an organized body without which his judgment could not be exercised.[15] The body without organs is an affective, intensive, anarchist body that consists solely of poles, zones, thresholds, and gradients. It is traversed by a powerful, nonorganic vitality. Lawrence paints the picture of such a body, with the sun and moon as its poles, with its planes, its sections, and its plexuses.[16] Moreover, when Lawrence assigns his characters a double determination, it would seem that the first is a personal, organic feeling, but the second is a powerful, inorganic affect that comes to pass on this vital body: "The more exquisite the music, the more perfectly he produced it, in sheer bliss; and at the same time, the more intense was the maddened exasperation within him."[17] Lawrence ceaselessly describes bodies that are organically defective or unattractive—like the fat retired toreador or the skinny, oily Mexican general—but that are nonetheless traversed by this intense vitality that defies organs and undoes their organization. This nonorganic vitality is the relation of the body to the imperceptible forces and powers that seize hold of it, or that it seizes hold of, just as the moon takes hold of a woman's body. In Artaud, the anarchist Heliogabalus will constantly bear witness to this confrontation between forces and powers as so many becomings: becoming-mineral, becoming-vegetable, becoming-animal. The way to escape judgment is to make yourself a body without organs, to find your body without organs. This had already been Nietzsche's project: to define the body in its becoming, in its intensity, as the power to affect or to be affected, that is, as *Will to Power*. And if Kafka, at first sight, does not seem to take part in this current, his work nonetheless makes two worlds or two bodies coexist, each of which reacts upon and enters into the other: a body of judgment, with its organization, its segments (contiguity of offices), its differentiations (bailiffs, lawyers, judges . . .), its hierarchies (classes of judges, of bureaucrats); but also a body of justice in which the segments are dissolved, the differentiations lost, and the hierarchies thrown into confusion, a body that retains nothing but intensities that make up uncertain zones, that traverse these zones at full speed and confront the powers in them . . . on this anarchic body restored to itself (*"Justice* wants nothing from you, it receives you when you come and dismisses you when you go . . .").[18]

A fourth characteristic of the system of cruelty follows from this: combat, combat everywhere; it is combat that replaces judgment. And no doubt the combat appears as a combat *against* judgment, against its authorities and its personae. But more profoundly, it is the combatant himself who is the combat: the combat is *between* his own parts, between the forces that either subjugate or are subjugated, and between the powers that express these relations of force. Thus, all of Kafka's works could be entitled "Description of a Combat": the combat against the castle, against judgment, against his father, against his fiancées. All gestures are defenses or even attacks, evasions, ripostes, anticipations of a blow one does not always see coming, or of an enemy one is not always able to identify: hence the importance of the body's postures. But these external combats, these *combats-against,* find their justification in the *combats-between* that determine the composition of forces in the combatant. The combat against the Other must be distinguished from the combat between Oneself. The combat-against tries to destroy or repel a force (to struggle against "the diabolical powers of the future"), but the combat-between, by contrast, tries to take hold of a force in order to make it one's own. The combat-between is the process through which a force enriches itself by seizing hold of other forces and joining itself to them in a new ensemble: a becoming. Kafka's love letters can be seen as a combat against the fiancée, whose disquieting carnivorous forces they seek to repel. But they are also a combat *between* the fiancé's forces and the animal forces he joins with so as to better flee the force he fears falling prey to, or the vampiric forces he will use to suck the woman's blood before she devours him. All these associations of forces constitute so many becomings—a becoming-animal, a becoming-vampire, perhaps even a becoming-woman—that can only be obtained through combat.[19]

In Artaud, the combat is against God, the thief or the forger, but this undertaking is possible only because the combatant at the same time wages the combat of the principles or powers that are actualized in the stone, the animal, or the woman, so that it is only by becoming (by becoming-stone, becoming-animal, or becoming-woman) that the combatant can lash out "against" his enemy, in league with all the allies this other combat has given to him.[20] A similar theme appears constantly in Lawrence. Men and women often treat each other as enemies, but this is the most mediocre aspect of their combat, fit for a domestic scene. More profoundly, man and woman are two flows that must struggle, that can either seize hold of each other alternately, or separate while devoting themselves to chastity, which is itself a force, a flow.[21] Lawrence meets up with Nietzsche intensely—everything good is the result of a combat—and their common master is the thinker of combat, Heraclitus.[22] Neither Artaud nor Lawrence nor Nietzsche has anything to do with the Orient and its ideal of noncombat; their highest places are Greece, Etruria, and Mexico, places where things come and become in the course of the combat that composes their forces. But whenever someone wants to make us renounce combat, what he is offering us is a "nothingness of the will," a deification of the dream, a cult of death, even in its mildest form—that of the Buddha or Christ as a person (independently of what Saint Paul makes of him).

But neither is combat a "will to nothingness." Combat is not war. War is only a combat-against, a will to destruction, a judgment of God that turns destruction into something "just." The judgment of God is on the side of war, and not combat. Even when it takes hold of other forces, the force of war begins by mutilating these forces, reducing them to their lowest state. In war, the will to power merely means that the will wants strength [*puissance*] as a maximum of power [*pouvoir*] or domination. For Nietzsche and Lawrence, war is the lowest degree of the will to power, its sickness. Artaud begins by evoking the relation of war between America and the USSR; Lawrence describes the imperialism of death, from the ancient Romans to the modern fascists.[23] They do so in order to show more clearly that this is *not* the way combat works. Combat, by contrast, is a powerful, nonorganic vitality that supplements force with force, and enriches whatever it takes hold of. A baby vividly displays this vitality, this obstinate, stubborn, and indomitable will to live that differs from all organic life. With a young child, one already has an organic, personal relationship, but not with a baby, who concentrates in its smallness the same energy that shatters paving stones (Lawrence's baby tortoise).[24] With a baby, one has nothing but an affective, athletic, impersonal, vital relationship. The will to power certainly appears in an infinitely more exact manner in a baby than in a man of war. For the baby is combat, and the *small* is an irreducible locus of forces, the most revealing test of forces. All four authors are caught up in processes of "miniaturization" or "minorization": Nietzsche, who thinks the game or the child-player; Lawrence or "the little Pan"; Artaud *le mômo,* "a child's ego, a little child consciousness"; Kafka, "the great shameful man who makes himself very small."[25]

A power is an idiosyncrasy of forces, such that the dominant force is transformed by passing into the dominated forces, and the dominated by passing into the dominant—a center of metamorphosis. This is what Lawrence calls a *symbol:* an intensive compound that vibrates and expands, that has no meaning, but makes us whirl about until we harness the maximum of possible forces in every direction, each of which receives a new meaning by entering into relation with the others. A decision is not a judgment, nor is it the organic consequence of a judgment: it springs vitally from a whirlwind of forces that leads us into combat. It resolves the combat without suppressing or ending it. It is the lightning flash appropriate to the night of the symbol. The four authors of whom we are speaking could be called symbolists. *Zarathustra,* the book of symbols, the combative book par excellence. In Nietzsche's aphorisms and Kafka's parables, there appears an analogous tendency to multiply and enrich forces, to attract a maximum of forces, each of which reacts upon the others. Between the theater and the plague, Artaud creates a symbol in which each of these two forces intensifies and energizes the other. Let us take the horse, the apocalyptic beast, as an example: the horse that laughs, in Lawrence; the horse that sticks his head through the window and looks at you, in Kafka; the horse "that is the sun," in Artaud; or even the ass that says *Yea-Yuh,* in Nietzsche—these are all figures that constitute so many symbols through the building-up of forces, through the constitution of compounds of power.

Combat is not a judgment of God, but the way to have done with God and with judgment. No one develops through judgment, but through a combat that implies no judgment. Existence and judgment seem to be opposed on five points: *cruelty versus infinite torture, sleep or intoxication versus the dream, vitality versus organization, the will to power versus a will to dominate, combat versus war.* What disturbed us was that in renouncing judgment we had the impression of depriving ourselves of any means of distinguishing between existing beings, between modes of existence, as if everything were now of equal value. But is it not rather judgment that presupposes preexisting criteria (higher values), criteria that preexist for all time (to the infinity of time), so that it can neither apprehend what is new in an existing being, nor even sense the creation of a mode of existence? Such a mode is created vitally, through combat, in the insomnia of sleep, and not without a certain cruelty toward itself: nothing of all this is the result of judgment. Judgment prevents the emergence of any new mode of existence. For the latter creates itself through its own forces, that is, through the forces it is able to harness, and is valid in and of itself inasmuch as it brings the new combination into existence. Herein, perhaps, lies the secret: to bring into existence and not to judge. If it is so disgusting to judge, it is not because everything is of equal value, but on the contrary because what has value can be made or distinguished only by defying judgment. What expert judgment, in art, could ever bear on the work to come? It is not a question of judging other existing beings, but of sensing whether they agree or disagree with us, that is, whether they bring forces to us, or whether they return us to the miseries of war, to the poverty of the dream, to the rigors of organization. As Spinoza had said, it is a problem of love and hate and not judgment; "my soul and body are one. . . . What my soul loves, I love. What my soul hates, I hate. . . . All the subtle sympathizings of the incalculable soul, from the bitterest hate to passionate love."[26] This is not subjectivism, since to pose the problem in terms of force, and not in other terms, already surpasses all subjectivity.

16

Plato, the Greeks

Platonism appears as a selective doctrine, as a selection among claimants or rivals.[1] Every thing or every being lays claim to certain qualities. It is a question of judging the well-foundedness or legitimacy of these claims. The Idea is posited by Plato as that which possesses a quality firsthand (necessarily and universally); it then allows us to determine, after certain tests, which things possess that quality secondhand, thirdhand, and so forth, depending on the nature of their participation. Such is the doctrine of judgment. The legitimate claimant is the participant, the one who possesses the quality secondhand and whose claim is thereby validated by the Idea. Platonism is the philosophical Odyssey, which will be continued in Neoplatonism. It confronts sophism as its enemy, but also as its limit and its double: because he lays claim to anything and everything, there is the great risk that the sophist will scramble the selection and pervert the judgment.

This problem finds its source in the City. Because they refuse any imperial or barbarian transcendence, the Greek societies or cities form fields of immanence (even in the case of the tyrannies). These fields are filled and populated by societies of friends, that is, by free rivals whose claims in each case enter into a competitive *agôn*, and are exercised in diverse domains: love, athletics, politics, the magistratures. In such a regime, opinion obviously assumes a decisive importance. This is particularly clear in the case of Athens and its democracy: *autochtonie, philia, doxa* are its three fundamental traits, and constitute the conditions under which philosophy was born and developed. In spirit, philosophy can criticize these traits, surpass and correct them, but it nonetheless remains indexed to them. As Vernant has shown, the Greek philosopher invokes an order that is immanent to the cosmos. He presents himself as a friend of wisdom (and not as a wise man, as in the East). He sets out to "rectify" or secure the opinion of men. These characteristics survive in Western societies, even if they have taken on a new meaning, which explains the permanence of philosophy in the economy of our democratic world: the field of immanence of "capital"; the society of brothers or comrades, to which every revolution appeals (and the free competition among brothers); and the reign of opinion.

But what Plato criticizes in the Athenian democracy is the fact that anyone can lay claim to anything; whence his enterprise of restoring criteria of selection among rivals. It will be necessary for him to erect a new type of transcendence, one that differs from imperial or mythical transcendence (although Plato makes use of myth by giving it a special function). He will have to invent a transcendence that can be exercised and situated *within* the field of immanence itself. This is the meaning of the theory of Ideas. And modern philosophy will continue to follow Plato in this regard, encountering a transcendence at the heart of immanence as such. The poisoned gift of Platonism is to have introduced transcendence into philosophy, to have given transcendence a plausible philosophical meaning (the triumph of the judgment of God). This enterprise runs up against numerous paradoxes and aporias, which concern, precisely, the status of the *doxa* (*Theataetus*), the nature of friendship and love (*Symposium*), and the irreducibility of an immanence of the earth (*Timaeus*).

Every reaction against Platonism is a restoration of immanence in its full extension and in its purity, which forbids the return of any transcendence. The question is whether such a reaction abandons the project of a selection among rivals, or on the contrary, as Spinoza and Nietzsche believed, draws up completely different methods of selection. Such methods would no longer concern claims as acts of transcendence, but the manner in which an existing being is filled with immanence (the Eternal Return as the capacity of something or someone to return eternally). Selection no longer concerns the claim, but power: unlike the claim, power is modest. In truth, only the philosophies of pure immanence escape Platonism—from the Stoics to Spinoza or Nietzsche.

17

Spinoza and the Three "Ethics"

*"I'm not some sort of Spinoza to jump around doing
entrechats."*   —Chekhov, "The Wedding"[1]

On a first reading, the *Ethics* can appear to be a long, continuous
movement that goes in an almost straight line, with an incomparable
power and serenity, passing again and again through definitions, axioms, postulates, propositions, demonstrations, corollaries, and scholia,
carrying everything along in its grandiose course. It is like a river that
sometimes broadens and sometimes branches into a thousand streams;
sometimes speeding up and sometimes slowing down, but always maintaining its radical unity. And Spinoza's Latin, which appears so scholarly, seems to constitute the ageless ship that follows the eternal river.
But as emotions invade the reader, or after a second reading, these two
impressions prove to be erroneous. This book, one of the greatest in
the world, is not what it seems at first glance: it is not homogenous,
rectilinear, continuous, serene, navigable, a pure language without style.

The *Ethics* sets forth three elements, which are not only contents
but forms of expression: Signs or affects; Notions or concepts; Essences
or percepts. They correspond to the three kinds of knowledge, which
are also modes of existence and expression.

A sign, according to Spinoza, can have several meanings, but it is
always an *effect*. An effect is first of all the trace of one body upon
another, the state of a body insofar as it suffers the action of another
body. It is an *affectio*—for example, the effect of the sun on our body,
which "indicates" the nature of the affected body and merely "en-

velops" the nature of the affecting body. We have knowledge of our affections through the ideas we have, sensations or perceptions, sensations of heat and color, the perception of form and distance (the sun is
above us, it is a golden disk, it is two hundred feet away . . .). We will
call them, for convenience, *scalar* signs, since they express our state at
a moment in time and are thus distinguished from another type of sign.
This is because our present state is always a slice of our duration, and
as such determines an increase or decrease, an expansion or restriction
of our existence in duration in relation to the preceding state, however
close it may be. It is not that we compare the two states in a reflective
operation; rather, each state of affection determines a passage to a
"more" or a "less": the heat of the sun fills me or, on the contrary, its
burning repulses me. Affection is therefore not only the instantaneous effect of a body upon my own, but also has an effect on my own
duration—a pleasure or pain, a joy or sadness. These are passages, becomings, rises and falls, continuous variations of power [*puissance*]
that pass from one state to another. We will call them *affects,* strictly
speaking, and no longer affections. They are signs of increase and decrease, signs that are *vectorial* (of the joy-sadness type) and no longer
scalar like the affections, sensations or perceptions.

In fact, there are an even greater number of types of signs. There
are four principal types of scalar signs. The first, which are sensory
or perceptive physical effects that merely envelop the nature of their
cause, are essentially *indicative,* and indicate our own nature rather
than some other thing. In a second case, our nature, being finite, simply retains some selected characteristic from what affects it (man as a
vertical animal, or a reasonable animal, or an animal that laughs).
These are *abstractive* signs. In the third case, the sign always being an
effect, we take the effect for an end, or the idea of the effect for the
cause (since the sun heats, we believe that it was made "in order to"
warm us; since the fruit tastes bitter, Adam believes that it "should
not" be eaten). These are moral effects or *imperative* signs: Do not eat
this fruit! Get out in the sun! The last of the scalar signs, finally, are
imaginary effects: our sensations and perceptions make us conceive of
suprasensible beings who would be their final cause, and conversely
we imagine these beings in the inordinately enlarged image of what
affects us (God as an infinite sun, or as a Prince or Legislator). These
are *hermeneutic or interpretive* signs. The prophets, who were the great
specialists in signs, combined abstractive, imperative, and interpretive

signs in marvelous ways. In this regard, a famous chapter of the *Tractatus Theologico-Politicus* joins together the power of the comic with the depth of its analysis. There are thus four scalar signs of affection, which could be called sensible indices, logical icons, moral symbols, and metaphysical idols.

In addition, there are two kinds of vectorial signs of affect, depending on whether the vector is one of increase or decrease, growth or decline, joy or sadness. These two sorts of signs could be called augmentative powers and diminutive servitudes. We could also add to these a third sort: ambiguous or fluctuating signs, when an affection increases or diminishes our power at the same time, or affects us with joy and sadness at the same time. There are thus six signs, or seven, which ceaselessly enter into various combinations with each other. In particular, the scalars are necessarily combined with the vectorials. Affects always presuppose the affections from which they are derived, although they cannot be reduced to them.

The common characteristics of all these signs are associability, variability, and equivocity or analogy. The affections vary according to the chains of association between bodies (the sun hardens clay and softens wax, the horse is not the same for the warrior and for the peasant). The moral effects themselves vary according to peoples; and the prophets each had personal signs that appealed to their imaginations. As for interpretations, they are fundamentally equivocal depending on the variable association that is made between something given and something that is not given. It is an equivocal or analogical language that ascribes to God an infinite intellect and will, in an enlarged image of our own intellect and our own will—an equivocity similar to the one found between the dog as a barking animal and the Dog as a celestial constellation. If signs like words are conventional, it is precisely because they act on natural signs and simply classify their variability and equivocity: conventional signs are Abstractions that fix a relative constant for variable chains of association. The conventional-natural distinction is therefore not determinative for signs, any more than is the distinction between the social State and the state of nature; even vectorial signs can depend on conventions, as rewards (augmentation) and punishments (diminution). Vectorial signs in general, that is, affects, enter into variable associations as much as do affections: what is growth for one part of the body can be a diminution for another part, what is servitude for one part is power for another, and a rise can be followed by a fall and conversely.

Signs *do not have objects as their direct referents.* They are states of bodies (affections) and variations of power (affects), each of which refers to the other. Signs refer to signs. They have as their referents confused mixtures of bodies and obscure variations of power, and follow an order that is established by Chance or by the fortuitous encounter between bodies. Signs are effects: the effect of one body upon another in space, or affection; the effect of an affection on a duration, or affect. Like the Stoics, Spinoza breaks causality into two distinct chains: effects between themselves, on the condition that one in turn grasp causes between themselves. Effects refer to effects just as signs refer to signs: consequences separated from their premises. We must also understand "effect" optically and not merely causally. Effects or signs are *shadows* that play on the surface of bodies, always between two bodies. The shadow is always on the edge. It is always a body that casts a shadow on another body. We have knowledge of bodies only through the shadows they cast upon us, and it is through our own shadow that we know ourselves, ourselves and our bodies. Signs are *effects of light* in a space filled with things colliding with each other at random. If Spinoza differs essentially from Leibniz, it is because the latter, under a baroque inspiration, saw the Dark ("fuscum subnigrum") as a matrix or premise, from which chiaroscuro, colors, and even light emerge. In Spinoza, on the contrary, everything is light, and the Dark is only a shadow, a simple effect of light, a limit of light on the bodies that reflect it (affection) or absorb it (affect). Spinoza is closer to Byzantium than to the baroque. In place of a light that emerges by degrees from the shadow through the accumulation of red, we instead have a light that creates degrees of blue shadow. Chiaroscuro is itself an effect of the brightening or darkening of the shadow: it is the variations of power or vectorial signs that constitute degrees of chiaroscuro, the augmentation of power being a brightening, and the diminution of power, a darkening.

If we consider the second aspect of the *Ethics,* we see a determining opposition to signs emerge: *common notions are concepts of objects,* and objects are causes. Light is no longer reflected or absorbed by bodies that produce shadows, it makes bodies transparent by revealing their intimate "structure" *(fabrica)*. This is the second aspect of light; and the intellect is the true apprehension of the structures of the body, whereas the imagination merely grasped the shadow of one body upon another. Here again it is a question of optics, but it is now an optical geometry. In effect, the structure is geometrical and consists of solid lines, but they are constantly being formed and deformed, acting as cause. What constitutes the structure is a composite relation of movement and rest, of speed and slowness, which is established between the infinitely small parts of a transparent body. Since the parts always come in larger or smaller infinities, there is in each body an infinity of relations that are composed and decomposed, in such a way that the body in turn enters into a more vast body under a new composite relation or, on the contrary, makes smaller bodies come out from under their composite relations. Modes are geometric but fluid structures that are transformed and deformed in the light at variable speeds. Structure is rhythm, that is, the linking of figures that compose and decompose their relations. It causes disagreements between bodies when the relations decompose, and agreements when the relations compose a new body. But the structure moves in both directions simultaneously. Chyle and lymph are two bodies determined by two relations that constitute blood under a composite relation, although a poison may decompose the blood. If I learn to swim or dance, my movements and pauses, my speeds and slownesses, must take on a rhythm common to that of the sea or my partner, maintaining a more or less durable adjustment. The structure always has several bodies in common, and refers to a concept of the object, that is, to a common notion. *The structure or object is formed by at least two bodies,* each of which in turn is formed by two or more bodies, to infinity, while in the other direction they are united into ever larger and more composite bodies, until one reaches the unique object of Nature in its entirety, an infinitely transformable and deformable structure, universal rhythm, *Facies totius Naturae,* infinite mode. Common notions are universals, but they are "more or less" so depending on whether they form the concept of at least two bodies, or that of all possible bodies (to be in space, to be in movement and at rest . . .).

Understood in this way, modes are projections. Or rather, the variations of an object are projections that *envelop* a relation of movement and rest as their invariant (involution). And since each relation involves all the others to infinity, following an order that varies with each case, this order is the profile or projection that in each case envelops the face of Nature in its entirety, or the relation of all relations.[2]

Modes, as projections of light, are also colors, *coloring causes.* Colors enter into relations of complementarity and contrast, which means that each of them, at the limit, reconstitutes the whole, and that they all merge together in whiteness (infinite mode) following an order of composition, or stand out from it in the order of decomposition. What Goethe said about whiteness must be said of every color: it is the opacity characteristic of pure transparency.[3] The solid and rectilinear structure is necessarily colored in, because it is the opacity that is revealed when light renders the body transparent. In this way, a difference in kind is established *between color and shadow, between the coloring cause and the effect of shadow:* the first adequately "completes" the light, while the second abolishes it in the inadequate. Vermeer is said to have replaced chiaroscuro by the complementarity and contrast of colors. It is not that the shadow disappears, but it subsists as an effect that can be isolated from its cause, a separated consequence, an extrinsic sign distinct from colors and their relations.[4] In Vermeer, one sees the shadow detach itself and move forward so as to frame or border the luminous background from which it originates ("The Maidservant Pouring Milk," "The Young Lady with a Pearl Necklace," "The Love Letter"). This is the way Vermeer set himself in opposition to the tradition of chiaroscuro; and in all these respects Spinoza remains infinitely closer to Vermeer than to Rembrandt.

The distinction between signs and concepts thus seems irreducible and insurmountable, much as in Aeschylus: "He is going to express himself, no longer in a mute language, nor through the smoke of a fire burning on a peak, but in clear terms . . ."[5] Signs or affects are inadequate ideas and passions; common notions or concepts are adequate ideas from which true actions ensue. If one refers to the cleavage in causality, signs refer to signs as effects refer to effects, following an *associative chain* that depends on the order of the simple chance encounter between physical bodies. But insofar as concepts refer to concepts, or causes to causes, they follow what must be called an *automatic chain,* determined by the necessary order of relations or proportions, and by the determinate succession of their transformations and deformations. Contrary to our initial thesis, it therefore seems that signs or affects are not and cannot be a positive element in the *Ethics,* and even less a form of expression. The kind of knowledge they constitute is hardly a knowledge, but rather an experience in which one randomly encounters confused ideas of bodily mixtures, brute imperatives to avoid this mixture and seek another, and more or less delirious interpretations of these situations. Rather than a form of expression, this is a material and affective language, one that resembles cries rather than the discourse of the concept. It seems, then, that if signs-affects intervene in the *Ethics,* it is only to be severely criticized, denounced, and sent back to their night, out of which light reappears or in which it perishes.

This cannot, however, be the case. Book II of the *Ethics* explains the common notions by beginning with "the most universal" notions (those that agree with all bodies). It presumes that concepts are already given; hence the impression that they owe nothing to signs. But when one asks *how* we manage to form a concept, or how we rise from effects to causes, it is clear that at least certain signs must serve as a springboard for us, and that certain affects must give us the necessary vitality (Book V). From a random encounter of bodies, we can select the idea of those bodies that agree with our own and give us joy, that is, that increase our power. And it is only when our power has sufficiently increased, to a point that undoubtedly varies with each case, that we come into possession of this power and become capable of forming a concept, beginning with the least universal concept (the agreement of our body with *one* other), even if we subsequently attain ever larger concepts following the order of the composition of relations. There is thus a *selection* of the passional affects, and of the ideas on which they depend, which must liberate joys, vectorial signs of the augmentation of power, and ward off sadnesses, signs of diminution. This selection of the affects is the very condition for leaving the first kind of knowledge, and for attaining the concept through the acquisition of a sufficient power. The signs of augmentation remain passions and the ideas that they presuppose remain inadequate; yet they are the precursors of the notions, the dark precursors.[6] Furthermore, even when we have attained common notions, as well as the actions that follow from them as active affects of a new type, the inadequate ideas and passional affects (i.e., signs) will not disappear entirely, nor even the inevitable sadnesses. They will subsist, they will double the notions, but will lose their exclusive or tyrannical character to the profit of notions and actions. There is thus something in signs that at the same time prepares for and doubles the concepts. The rays of light are both prepared for and accompanied by these processes that continue to operate in the shadows. *Values of chiaroscuro are reintroduced* in Spinoza, because joy as a passion is a sign of brightening that leads us to the light of the notions. And the *Ethics* cannot dispense with this passional form of expression that operates through signs, for it alone is capable of bringing about the indispensable selection without which we would remain condemned to the first kind.

This selection is extremely hard, extremely difficult. The joys and sadnesses, increases and decreases, brightenings and darkenings are often ambiguous, partial, changing, intermixed with each other. And above all, there exist people who can only establish their Power [*Pouvoir*] on sadness and affliction, on the diminution of the power of others, on the darkening of the world. They act as if sadness were a promise of joy, and already a joy in itself. They institute a cult of sadness, of servitude or impotence, of death. They never cease to emit and impose signs of sadness, which they present as ideals and joys to the souls they have made ill. Hence the infernal couple, the Despot and the Priest, terrible "judges" of life. The selection of signs or affects as the primary condition for the birth of the concept does not merely imply the personal effort each person must make on his or her own behalf (Reason), but a passional struggle, an inexpiable affective combat in which one risks death, in which signs confront signs and affects clash with affects in order that a little joy might be saved that could make us leave the shadow and change kind. The cries of the language of signs are the mark of this battle of the passions, of joys and sadnesses, of increases and decreases of power.

The *Ethics*, or at least most of the *Ethics*, is written in common notions, beginning with the most general notions and ceaselessly developing their consequences. It presupposes that the common notions are already acquired or given. The *Ethics* is the discourse of the concept. It is a discursive and deductive system, which is why it can appear to be a long, tranquil, and powerful river. The definitions, axioms, postulates, propositions, demonstrations, and corollaries form a grandiose course. And when one of these elements deals with inadequate ideas or passions, it does so in order to denounce their insufficiency, to repress them as far as possible like so many sediments on the riverbanks. But there is another element that only ostensibly has the same nature as the preceding elements. These are the "scholia," which are nonetheless inserted into the demonstrative chain, even though the reader quickly realizes that they have a completely different tone. They have another style, almost another language. They operate in the shadows, trying to distinguish between what prevents us from reaching common notions and what, on the contrary, allows us to do so, what diminishes and what augments our power, the sad signs of our servitude and the joyous signs of our liberations. They denounce the personae that lie behind our diminutions of power, those that have an interest in maintaining and propagating sadness, the despot and the priest. They herald the sign or condition of the new man, one who has sufficiently augmented his power in order to form concepts and convert his affects into actions.

The scholia are ostensive and polemical. If it is true that the scholia most often refer to other scholia, we can see that in themselves they constitute a specific chain, distinct from that of the demonstrative and discursive elements. Conversely, the demonstrations do not refer to the scholia, but to other demonstrations, definitions, axioms, and postulates. If the scholia are inserted into the demonstrative chain, it is therefore less because they form a part of it than because they intersect and reintersect with it, by virtue of their own nature. It is like a broken chain, discontinuous, subterranean, volcanic, which at irregular intervals comes to interrupt the chain of demonstrative elements, the great and continuous fluvial chain. Each scholium is like a lighthouse that exchanges its signals with the others, at a distance and across the flow of the demonstrations. It is like a language of fire that is distinguishable from the language of the waters. It no doubt appears to be the same Latin, but one could almost believe that the Latin of the scholia is translated from the Hebrew. On their own, the scholia form a book of Anger and Laughter, as if it were Spinoza's anti-Bible. It is the book of Signs, which never ceases to accompany the more visible Ethics, the book of the Concept, and which only emerges for its own sake at explosive points. Nonetheless, it is a perfectly positive element and an autonomous form of expression in the composition of the double Ethics. The two books, the two *Ethics* coexist, the one developing the free notions conquered in the light of transparencies, while the other, at the deepest level of the obscure mixture of bodies, carries on the combat between servitudes and liberations. At least two *Ethics*, which have one and the same meaning but not the same language, like two versions of the language of God.

Robert Sasso accepts the principle of a difference in kind between the chain of scholia and the demonstrative linkages. But he notes that there is no reason to consider the demonstrative linkage itself as a homogenous flow, continuous and rectilinear, whose progress would be sheltered from turbulences and accidents. This is not only because the scholia, by interrupting the course of the demonstrations, happen to break its flow at various points. It is the concept in itself, says Sasso, that passes through extremely variable moments: definitions, axioms, postulates, demonstrations that are sometimes slower, sometimes more rapid.[7] And certainly Sasso is correct. One can discern *stations, arms, elbows, loops,* speedings up and slowings down, and so on. The prefaces and appendices, which mark the beginning and end of the great Parts, are like the stations along the river where the ship takes on new passengers and drops off old ones; they often mark the juncture between the demonstrations and the scholia. Arms appear when a single proposition can be demonstrated in several ways. And elbows appear when the flow changes direction: a single substance is posited for all the attributes by means of an elbow, whereas upstream each attribute could have one and only one substance. In the same way, an elbow introduces the physics of bodies. The corollaries, for their part, constitute derivations that loop back onto the demonstrated proposition. Finally, the series of demonstrations attests to relative speeds and slownesses, depending on whether the river widens or narrows its course— for example, Spinoza will always maintain that one cannot begin with God, with the idea of God, but that one must reach it *as quickly as possible.* One could identify many other demonstrative figures. Yet whatever their variety, there is a single river that persists throughout all its states, and forms the *Ethics* of the concept or the second kind of knowledge. This is why we believe that the difference between the scholia and the other elements is more important, because in the final analysis it is what accounts for the differences between the demonstrative elements. The river would not have so many adventures without the subterranean action of the scholia. It is they that give shape to the demonstrations, and ensure the turnings. The entire *Ethics* of the concept, in all its variety, has need of an *Ethics* of signs in all their specificity. The variety in the course of the demonstrations does not correspond term by term to the jolts and pressures of the scholia, and yet it presupposes and envelops them.

But perhaps there is yet a third *Ethics,* represented by Book V, incarnated in Book V, or a least in the greater part of Book V. Unlike the other two, which coexist throughout the entire course, it occupies a precise place, the final one. Nonetheless it was there from the start as the focus, the focal point that was already at work before it appeared. Book V must be seen as being coextensive with all the others; we have the impression of reaching it at the end, but it was there all the time, for all time. This is the third element of Spinoza's logic: no longer signs or affects, nor concepts, but Essences or Singularities, Percepts. It is the third state of light: no longer signs of shadow, nor of light as color, but light in itself and for itself. The common notions (concepts) are revealed by the light that traverses bodies and makes them transparent; they therefore refer to geometrical structures or figures (*fabrica*), which are all the more full of life in that they are transformable and deformable in a projective space, subordinated to the exigencies of a projective geometry like that of Desargues. But essences have a completely different nature: *pure figures of light* produced by a substantial Luminosity (and no longer geometrical figures revealed by light).[8] It has often been noted that Platonic and even Cartesian ideas remained "tactilo-optical": it fell to Plotinus in relation to Plato, and Spinoza in relation to Descartes, to attain a purely optical world. The common notions, insofar as they concern relations of projection, are already optical figures (although they still retain a minimum of tactile references). But essences are pure figures of light: they are in themselves "contemplations," that is to say, they contemplate as much as they are contemplated, in a unity of God, the subject or the object (*percepts*). The common notions refer to relations of movement and rest that constitute relative speeds; essences on the contrary are absolute speeds that do not compose space by projection, but occupy it all at once, in a single stroke.[9] One of the most considerable of Jules Lagneau's contributions is to have shown the importance of speeds in thought, as Spinoza conceives of it, although Lagneau reduces absolute speed to a relative speed.[10] These are nonetheless the two characteristics of essences: *absolute and no longer relative speed, figures of light and no longer geometric figures revealed by light.* Relative speed is the speed of the affections and the affects: the speed of an action of one body upon another in space, the speed of the passage from one state to another in duration. What the notions grasp are the relations between relative speeds.

But absolute speed is the manner in which an essence surveys [*survole*] its affects and affections in eternity (speed of power).

For Book V alone to constitute a third *Ethics,* it is not enough for it to have a specific object; it would also have to adopt a method distinct from the two others. But this does not seem to be the case, since it contains only demonstrative elements and scholia. Yet the reader has the impression that the geometric method here assumes a strange and wild demeanor, which could almost make one believe that Book V was only a provisional version, a rough sketch: the propositions and demonstrations are traversed by such violent hiatuses, and include so many ellipses and contractions, that the syllogisms seem to be replaced by simple "enthymemes."[11] And the more one reads Book V, the more one realizes that these features are neither imperfections in the elaboration of the method nor shortcuts, but are perfectly adapted to essences insofar as they surpass any order of discursivity or deduction. They are not simple operations of fact, but an entire procedure in principle. This is because, at the level of concepts, the geometric method is a method of exposition that requires completeness and saturation: this is why the common notions are expounded for themselves, starting with the most universal, as in an axiomatic, without one having to wonder how in fact we attain even a *single* common notion. But the geometric method of Book V is a method of invention that will proceed by intervals and leaps, hiatuses and contractions, somewhat like a dog searching rather than a reasonable man explaining. Perhaps it surpasses all demonstration inasmuch as it operates in the "undecidable."

When mathematicians are not given over to the constitution of an axiomatic, their style of invention assumes strange powers, and the deductive links are broken by large discontinuities, or on the contrary are violently contracted. No one denies the genius of Desargues, but mathematicians like Huygens or Descartes had difficulty understanding him. His demonstration that every plane is the "polar" of a point, and every point the "pole" of a plane, is so rapid that one has to fill in everything it skips over. No one has described this jolting, jumping, and colliding thought—which grasps singular essences in mathematics—better than Evariste Galois, who himself met with a great deal of incomprehension from his peers: analysts "do not deduce, they combine, they compose; when they arrive at the truth, it is by crashing in from all sides that they happen to stumble on it."[12] Once again, these features do not appear as simple imperfections in the exposition, so that it can be done "more quickly," but as powers of a new order of thought that conquers an absolute speed. It seems to us that Book V bears witness to this type of thought, which is irreducible to the one developed by the common notions in the course of the first four books. If, as Blanchot says, books have as their correlate "the absence of the book" (or a more secret book made of flesh and blood), Book V would be this absence or this secret in which signs and concepts vanish, and things begin to write by themselves and for themselves, crossing the intervals of space.

Consider proposition 10: "As long as we are not torn by affects contrary to our nature, we have the power of ordering and connecting the affections of the body according to the order of the intellect."[13] There is an immense rift or interval that appears here between the subordinate and the principal. For affects contrary to our nature above all prevent us from forming common notions, since they depend upon bodies that do not agree with our own; on the contrary, whenever a body agrees with our own and increases our power (joy), a common notion of the two bodies can be formed, from which an order and an active linking of the affections will ensue. In this voluntarily opened rift, the ideas of the agreement between bodies and of the restricted common notion have only an implicit presence, and they both appear only if one reconstitutes a missing chain: a double interval. If this reconstitution is not made, if this white space is not filled in, not only will the demonstration be inconclusive, but we will always remain undecided about the fundamental question: How do we come to form any common notion at all? And why is it a question of the least universal of notions (common to our body and *one* other)? The function of the interval or hiatus is to bring together to the maximum degree terms that are distant as such, and thereby to assure a speed of absolute survey. Speeds can be absolute and yet have a greater or lesser magnitude. The magnitude of an absolute speed is measured in precise terms by the distance it covers at one stroke, that is, by the number of intermediaries it envelops, surveys, or implies (here, at least two). There are always leaps, lacunae, and cuts as positive characteristics of the third kind.

Another example can be found in propositions 14 and 22, where one passes, this time by contraction, from the idea of God as the most universal common notion to the idea of God as the most singular essence. It is as if one jumped from a relative speed (the greatest) to an absolute speed. Finally, to limit ourselves to a few examples, demonstration 30 traces, but along a dotted line, a kind of sublime triangle whose summits are the figures of light (Self, World, and God), and whose sides, as distances, are traversed by an absolute speed that is in turn revealed to be the greatest. The peculiar characteristics of Book V, the way it surpasses the method of the preceding books, always come down to this: the absolute speed of figures of light.

The *Ethics* of the definitions, axioms and postulates, demonstrations and corollaries is a river-book that develops its course. But the *Ethics* of the scholia is a subterranean book of fire. The *Ethics* of Book V is an aerial book of light, which proceeds by flashes. A logic of the sign, a logic of the concept, a logic of essence: Shadow, Color, Light. Each of the three *Ethics* coexists with the others and is taken up in the others, despite their differences in kind. It is one and the same world. Each of them sends out bridges in order to cross the emptiness that separates them.

18

The Exhausted

Being exhausted is much more than being tired.[1] "It's not just tiredness, I'm not just tired, in spite of the climb."[2] The tired person no
longer has any (subjective) possibility at his disposal; he therefore cannot realize the slightest (objective) possibility. But the latter remains,
because one can never realize the whole of the possible; in fact, one
even creates the possible to the extent that one realizes it. The tired
person has merely exhausted the realization, whereas the exhausted
person exhausts the whole of the possible. The tired person can no
longer realize, but the exhausted person can no longer possibilize.
"That the impossible should be asked of me, good, what else could be
asked of me."[3] There is no longer any possible: a relentless Spinozism.
Does he exhaust the possible because he is himself exhausted, or is he
exhausted because he has exhausted the possible? He exhausts himself
in exhausting the possible, and vice-versa. He exhausts that which, in
the possible, *is not realized*. He has had done with the possible, beyond
all tiredness, "for to end yet again."[4]

God is the originary, or the sum total of all possibility. The possible is realized only in the derivative, in tiredness, whereas one is exhausted before birth, before realizing oneself, or realizing anything
whatsoever ("I gave up before birth").[5] When one realizes some of the
possible, one does so according to certain goals, plans, and preferences:
I put on shoes to go out, and slippers when I stay in. When I speak,
for example, when I say "it's daytime," the interlocutor answers, "it's
possible . . ." because he is waiting to know what purpose I want the
day to serve: I'm going to go out because it's daytime . . .[6] Language

states the possible, but only by readying it for a realization. And I can no doubt make use of the day to stay at home, or I can stay at home because of some other possibility ("it's night"). But the realization of the possible always proceeds through exclusion, because it presupposes preferences and goals that vary, always replacing the preceeding ones. In the end, it is these variations, these substitutions, all these exclusive disjunctions (daytime/nighttime, going out/staying in . . .) that are tiring.

Exhaustion is something entirely different: one combines the set of variables of a situation, on the condition that one renounce any order of preference, any organization in relation to a goal, any signification. The goal is no longer to go out or stay in, and one no longer makes use of the days and nights. One no longer realizes, even though one accomplishes something. Shoes, one stays in; slippers, one goes out. Yet one does not fall into the undifferentiated, or into the famous unity of contradictories, nor is one passive: one remains active, but for nothing. One was tired of something, but one is exhausted by nothing. The disjunctions subsist, and the distinction between terms may become ever more crude, but the disjointed terms are affirmed in their nondecomposable distance, since they are used for nothing except to create further permutations. It is enough to say about an event that it is possible, since it does not occur without merging with nothing, and abolishing the real to which it lays claim. There is no existence other than the possible. It is night, it is not night, it is raining, it is not raining.[7] "Yes, I was my father and I was my son."[8] The disjuction has become *inclusive*: everything divides, but into itself; and God, who is the sum total of the possible, merges with Nothing, of which each thing is a modification. "Simple games that time plays with space, now with these toys, and now with those."[9] Beckett's characters play with the possible without realizing it; they are too involved in a possibility that is ever more restricted in its kind to care about what is still happening. The permutation of "sucking stones" in *Molloy* is one of the most famous texts. In *Murphy*, the hero devotes himself to the combinatorial of five small biscuits, but on the condition of having vanquished all order of preference, and of having thereby conquered the hundred and twenty modes of total permutability: "Overcome by these perspectives Murphy fell forward on his face in the grass, beside those biscuits of which it could be said as truly as of the stars, that one differed from another, but of which he could not partake in their fullness until he had learnt not to prefer any one to any other."[10] *I would prefer not to,* following Bartleby's Beckettian formula. Beckett's entire oeuvre is pervaded by exhaustive series, that is, exhausting series—most notably *Watt,* with its series of footwear (sock-stocking; boot-shoe-slipper) or furniture (tall-boy—dressing table—night stool—wash stand; on its feet—on its head—on its face—on its back—on its side; bed-door-window-fire: fifteen thousand arrangements).[11] *Watt* is the great serial novel, in which Mr. Knott, whose only need is to be without need, does not earmark any combination for a particular use that would exclude the others, and whose circumstances would still be yet to come.

The combinatorial is the art or science of exhausting the possible through inclusive disjunctions. But only an exhausted person can exhaust the possible, because he has renounced all need, preference, goal, or signification. Only the exhausted person is sufficiently disinterested, sufficiently scrupulous. Indeed, he is obliged to replace his plans with tables and programs that are devoid of all meaning. For him, what matters is the order in which he does what he has to do, and in what combinations he does two things at the same time—when it is still necessary to do so, for nothing. Beckett's great contribution to logic is to have shown that exhaustion (exhaustivity) does not occur without a certain physiological exhaustion, somewhat as Nietzsche showed that the scientific ideal is not attained without a kind of vital degeneration—for example, in the Man with leeches, "the conscientious in spirit" who wanted to know everything about the leech's brain.[12] The combinatorial exhausts its object, but only because its subject is himself exhausted. The exhaustive *and* the exhausted. Must one be exhausted to give oneself over to the combinatorial, or is it the combinatorial that exhausts us, that leads us to exhaustion—or even the two together, the combinatorial and the exhaustion? Here again, inclusive disjunctions. And perhaps it is like the front and back side of a single thing: a keen sense or science of the possible, joined, or rather disjoined, with a fantastic decomposition of the self. What Blanchot says about Musil is equally true of Beckett: the greatest exactitude and the most extreme dissolution; the indefinite exchange of mathematical formulations and the pursuit of the formless or the unformulated.[13] These are the two meanings of exhaustion, and both are necessary in order to abolish the real. Many authors are too polite, and are content to announce the total work and the death of the self. But this remains an abstraction as long as one does not show "how it is": how one makes an "inventory," errors included, and how the self decomposes, stench and agony included, in the manner of *Malone Dies*. A double innocence, for as the exhausted person says, "the art of combining is not my fault. It's a curse from above. For the rest I would suggest not guilty."[14]

More than an art, this is a science that demands long study. The combiner is seated at his school desk: "In a learned school / Till the wreck of body / Slow decay of blood / Testy delirium / Or dull decrepitude . . ."[15] Not that the decrepitude or the wreck interrupts one's studies; on the contrary, they complete them, as much as they condition and accompany them: the exhausted person remains seated at his school desk, "bowed head resting on hands," hands sitting on the table and head sitting on the hands, the head level with the table.[16] This is the posture of the exhausted person, which *Nacht und Träume* will take up again and duplicate. Beckett's damned together present the most astonishing gallery of postures, gaits, and positions since Dante. Macmann had no doubt remarked that he felt "happier sitting than standing and lying down than sitting."[17] But this was a formula more suited to tiredness than to exhaustion. Lying down is never the end or the last word; it is the penultimate word. For if one is sufficiently rested, there is the risk that one will, if not get up, at least roll over or crawl. To be kept from crawling, one must be put in a ditch or stuck in a jar where, no longer able to stir one's limbs, one will nonetheless stir some memories. But exhaustion does not allow one to lie down; when night falls, one remains seated at the table, empty head in captive hands, "head sunk on crippled hands," "one night as he sat at his table head on hands . . . Lift his past head a moment to see his past hands . . . ," "skull alone in a dark place pent bowed on a board . . . ," "hands and head a little heap."[18] This is the most horrible position in which to await death: seated, without the strength either to get up or to lie down, watching for the signal that will make us stand up one last time and then lie down forever. Once seated, one cannot recover, one can no longer stir even a single memory. The rocking chair is still imperfect in this regard: it must come to a stop.[19] We should perhaps distinguish between Beckett's "lying down" work and his "seated" work, which alone is final. This is because there is a difference in nature between "seated" exhaustion and the tiredness that "lies down," "crawls," or "gets stuck." Tiredness affects action in all its states, whereas exhaustion only concerns an amnesiac witness. The seated person is the witness around which the other revolves while developing all the degrees of tiredness. He is there before birth, and before the other begins. "Was there a time when I too revolved thus? No, I have always been sitting here, at this selfsame spot . . ."[20] But why is the seated person on the lookout for words, for voices, for sounds?

Language names the possible. How could one combine what has no name, the object = x? Molloy finds himself before a small, strange thing, made up of "two crosses joined, at their point of intersection, by a bar," equally stable and indiscernible on its four bases.[21] Future archaeologists, if they find one in our ruins, will, as is their wont, probably interpret it as a religious object used in prayers or sacrifices. How could it enter into a combinatorial if one does not have its name, "knife holder"? Nonetheless, if the ambition of the combinatorial is to exhaust the possible with words, it must constitute a metalanguage, a very special language in which the relations between objects are identical to the relations between words; and consequently, words must no longer give a realization to the possible, but must themselves give the possible a reality that is proper to it, a reality that is, precisely, exhaustible: "Minimally less. No more. Well on the way to inexistence. As to zero the infinite."[22] Let us call this atomic, disjunctive, cut and chopped language in Beckett *language I*, a language in which enumeration replaces propositions and combinatorial relations replace syntactic relations: a language of names. But if one thereby hopes to exhaust the possible with words, one must also hope to exhaust the words themselves; whence the need for another metalanguage, a *language II*, which is no longer a language of names but of voices, a language that no longer operates with combinable atoms but with blendable flows. Voices are waves or flows that direct and distribute the linguistic corpuscles. When one exhausts the possible with words, one cuts and chops the atoms, and when one exhausts the words themselves, one drys up the flows. It is this problem, to have done now with words, that dominates Beckett's work from *The Unnamable* onward: a true silence, not a simple tiredness with talking, because "it is all very well to keep silence, but one has also to consider the kind of silence one keeps."[23] What will be the last word, and how can it be recognized?

To exhaust the possible, the *possibilia* (objects or "things") must be related to the words that designate them through inclusive disjunctions within a combinatorial. To exhaust words, they must be related to Others who pronounce them—or rather, who emit them, secrete them— following flows that sometimes intermingle and sometimes separate off. This second, very complex, moment is not unrelated to the first: it is always an Other who speaks, since the words have not waited for me, and there is no language other than the foreign; it is always an Other, the "owner" of the objects he possesses by speaking. It is still a question of the possible, but in a new fashion: the Others are *possible worlds,* on which the voices confer a reality that is always variable, depending on the force they have, and revocable, depending on the silences they create. Sometimes they are strong, sometimes they are weak, until a moment arrives when they fall silent (a silence of tiredness). Sometimes they separate and even oppose each other, sometimes they merge together. The Others—that is, the possible worlds, with their objects, with their voices that bestow on them the only reality to which they can lay claim—constitute "stories." The Others have no other reality than the one given to them in their possible world by their voices.[24] Such are Murphy, Watt, Mercier, and all the others— "Mahood and Co."[25] Mahood and Company: How can one have done with them, with both their voices and their stories? To exhaust the possible in this new sense, the problem of exhaustive series must be confronted anew, even if it means falling into an "aporia."[26] One would have to succeed in speaking of them—but how can one speak of them without introducing oneself into the series, without "prolonging" their voices, without passing through each of them, without being in turn Murphy, Molloy, Malone, Watt, and so on, and coming back once again to the inexhaustible Mahood? *Or else* one would have to succeed in arriving at the self, not as a term in the series, but as its limit: me, the exhausted one, the unnamable, me, sitting alone in the dark, having become Worm, "the anti-Mahood," deprived of any voice, so that I could speak of myself only through the voice of Mahood, and could only be Worm by becoming Mahood yet again.[27] The aporia lies in the inexhaustible series of all these exhausted beings. "How many of us are there altogether, finally? And who is holding forth at the moment? And to whom? And about what?"[28] How can one imagine a whole that holds everything together [*un tout qui fasse compagnie*]? How can one make a whole out of the series? By going up the series, by going down it, by mutiplying it by two if one speaks to the other, or by three if one speaks to the other of yet another?[29] The aporia will be solved if one considers that the limit of the series does not lie at the infinity of the terms but can be anywhere in the flow: between two terms, between two voices or the variations of a single voice—a point that is already reached well before one knows that the series is exhausted, and well before one learns that there is no longer any possibility or any story, and that there has not been one for a long time.[30] Long since exhausted, without our knowing it, without his knowing it. The inexhaustible Mahood and Worm the exhausted, the Other and myself, are the same character, the same dead foreign language.

There is therefore a *language III,* which no longer relates language to enumerable or combinable objects, nor to transmitting voices, but to immanent limits that are ceaselessly displaced—hiatuses, holes, or tears that we would never notice, or would attribute to mere tiredness, if they did not suddenly widen in such a way as to receive something from the outside or from elsewhere. "Blanks for when words gone. When nohow on. Then all seen as only then. Undimmed. All undimmed that words dim. All so seen unsaid."[31] This something seen or heard is called Image, a visual or aural Image, provided it is freed from the chains in which it was bound by the other two languages. It is no longer a question of imagining a "whole" of the series with language I (a combinatorial imagination "sullied by reason"), or of inventing stories or making inventories of memories with language II (imagination sullied by memory), although the cruelty of voices never stops piercing us with unbearable memories, absurd stories, or undesirable company.[32] It is extremely difficult to tear all these adhesions away from the image so as to reach the point of "Imagination Dead Imagine."[33] It is extremely difficult to make a pure and unsullied image, one that is nothing but an image, by reaching the point where it emerges in all its singularity, retaining nothing of the personal or the rational, and by ascending to the indefinite as if into a celestial state. *A* woman, *a* hand, *a* mouth, *some* eyes . . . some blue and some white . . . a little green with white and red patches, a small field with crocuses and sheep: "little scenes yes in the light yes but not often no as if a light went on yes as if yes . . . he calls that the life above yes . . . they are not memories no."[34]

To *make* an image from time to time ("it's done I've done the image"): Can art, painting, and music have any other goal, even if the contents of the image are quite meagre, quite mediocre?[35] In one of Lichtenstein's porcelain sculptures, sixty centimeters high, there stands a brown-trunked tree, topped with a ball of green, and flanked by a little cloud on the left and a patch of sky on the right, at different heights: what force! One asks nothing more, neither of Bram van Velde nor of

Beethoven. The image is a little ritornello, whether visual or aural, once the time has come: "the exquisite hour . . ."[36] In *Watt*, the three frogs intermingle their songs, each with its own cadence, Krak, Krek, and Krik.[37] Image-ritornellos run throughout Beckett's books. In *First Love*, "he" watches a patch of starry sky as it comes and goes, and "she" sings in a low voice. The image is not defined by the sublimity of its content but by its form, that is, by its "internal tension," or by the force it mobilizes to create a void or to bore holes, to loosen the grip of words, to dry up the oozing of voices, so as to free itself from memory and reason: a small, alogical, amnesiac, and almost aphasic image, sometimes standing in the void, sometimes shivering in the open.[38] The image is not an object but a "process." We do not know the power of such images, so simple do they appear from the point of view of the object. This is *language III*, which is no longer a language of names or voices but a language of images, resounding and coloring images. What is tedious about the language of words is the way in which it is burdened with calculations, memories, and stories: it cannot avoid them. Nevertheless, the pure image must be inserted into language, into the names and voices. Sometimes this will occur in silence, by means of an ordinary silence, when the voices seem to have died out. But sometimes it will happen at the signal of an inductive term, in the current of the voice, Ping: "Ping image only just almost never one second light time blue and white in the wind."[39] Sometimes this is a very distinctive flat-toned voice, as if it were predetermined or preexisting, that of an Announcer or Opener who describes all the elements of the image to come, but which still lacks form.[40] Sometimes, finally, the voice manages to overcome its repugnances, its loyalties, its ill will, and, carried along by the music, it becomes speech, capable in turn of making a verbal image, as in a lied, or of itself making the music and color of an image, as in a poem.[41] Language III, then, can bring together words and voices in images, but in accordance with a special combination: language I was that of the novels, and culminates in *Watt*; language II marks out its multiple paths throughout the novels (*The Unnamable*), suffuses the works for theater, and blares forth in the radio pieces. But *language III*, born in the novel (*How It Is*), passing through the theater (*Happy Days, Act without Words, Catastrophe*), finds the secret of its assemblage in television: a prerecorded voice for an image that in each case is in the process of taking form. There is a specificity to the works for television.[42]

This outside of language is not only the image, but also the "vastitude" of space. Language III does not operate only with images but also with spaces. And just as the image must attain the indefinite, while remaining completely determined, so space must always be an any-space-whatever, disused, unmodified, even though it is entirely determined geometrically (a square with these sides and diagonals, a circle with these zones, a cylinder "fifty metres round and sixteen high").[43] The any-space-whatever is populated and well-trodden, it is even that which we ourselves populate and traverse, but it is opposed to all our pseudoqualified extensions, and is defined as "neither here nor there where all the footsteps ever fell can never fare nearer to anywhere nor from anywhere further away."[44] Just as the image appears as a visual or aural ritornello to the one who makes it, space appears as a motor ritornello—postures, positions, and gaits—to the one who travels through it. All these images compose and decompose themselves.[45] The "Pings," which activate the images, are mixed together with the "Hups," which activate strange movements within the spatial directions.[46] A manner of walking is no less a ritornello than a song or a tiny colored vision: for example, the gait of Watt, who moves east by turning his bust toward the north and throwing the right leg toward the south, then the bust toward the south and the left leg toward the north.[47] We can see that this gait is exhaustive, since it invests all the cardinal points at the same time, the fourth obviously being the direction from which he comes, without ever moving away from it. It is a matter of covering every possible direction, while nonetheless moving in a straight line. There is an equality between the straight line and the plane, and between the plane and the volume: the consideration of space gives a new meaning and a new object to exhaustion—exhausting the potentialities of an any-space-whatever.

Space has potentialities inasmuch as it makes the realization of events possible; it therefore precedes realization, and potentiality itself belongs to the possible. But was this not equally the case for the image, which had already put forth a specific means for exhausting the possible? This time, it would seem that an image, inasmuch as it stands in the void outside space, and also apart from words, stories, and memories, accumulates a fantastic potential energy, which it detonates by dissipating itself. What counts in the image is not its meager content, but the energy—mad and ready to explode—that it has harnessed, which is why images never last very long. The images merge with the detonation, combustion, and dissipation of their condensed energy. Like ultimate particles, they never last very long, and Ping activates an "image only just almost never one second."[48] When the protagonist says, "Enough, enough . . . images,"[49] it is not only because he is disgusted by them, but also because their existence is purely ephemeral. "No more blue the blue is done."[50] We will not invent an entity that would be Art, capable of making the image endure: the image lasts only as long as the furtive moment of our pleasure, our gaze ("I stood for three minutes before Professor Pater's smile, to look at it.")[51] There is a time for images, a right moment when they can appear or insinuate themselves, breaking the combination of words and the flow of voices. There is a time for images, as when Winnie feels that she can sing L'heure exquise, but it is a moment very near the end, an hour close to the last. The rocking chair is a motor ritornello that tends toward its own end, pushing all the possible toward it, going "faster and faster," "shorter and shorter," until, quite suddenly, it abruptly stops.[52] The energy of the image is dissipative. The image quickly ends and dissipates because it is itself the means of having done with itself. It captures all the possible in order to make it explode. When one says, "I've done the image," it is because this time it is finished, *there is no more possibility.* The only uncertainty that makes us continue is that even painters, even musicians, are never sure they have succeeded in making the image. What great painter has not said to himself, on his deathbed, that he had failed to make a single image, even a small or simple one? It is, rather, the end, the end of all possibility, that teaches us that we have made it, that we have just made the image. And it is the same with space: if the image, by its very nature, has a very short duration, then space perhaps has a very restricted place, as restricted as the one that cramps Winnie, when she says, "la terre est juste" ["the earth is tight"] and Godard, "juste une image" ["just an image"].[53] No sooner is the space made than it contracts into a "pinhole," just as the image contracts into a microfraction of time: a singular darkness, "again that certain dark that alone certain ashes can," "ping silence ping over."[54]

There are thus four ways of exhausting the possible:

—forming exhaustive series of things,
—drying up the flow of voices,
—extenuating the potentialities of space,
—dissipating the power of the image.

The exhausted is the exhaustive, the dried up, the extenuated, and the dissipated. The last two ways are united in language III, the language of images and spaces. It maintains a relationship with language in its entirety, but rises up or stretches out in its holes, its gaps, or its silences. Sometimes it operates in silence, sometimes it presents itself through the use of a recorded voice; moreover, it forces speech to become image, movement, song, poem. No doubt this language is born in the novels and the novellas, and passes through the theater, but it is in television that it accomplishes its own mission, distinct from the first two. *Quad* will be Space with silence and eventually music. *Ghost Trio* will be Space with a presenting voice and music. . . . *But the clouds* . . . will be Image with voice and poetry. *Nacht und Träume* will be Image with silence, song, and music.[55]

Quad, without words, without voice, is *a* quadrilateral, *a* square. Nonetheless, it is perfectly determined, possessing certain dimensions; but it has no other determinations than its formal singularities, four equidistant vertices and a center, and no other contents or occupants than the four identical characters who ceaselessly traverse it. It is a closed, globally defined, any-space-whatever. Even the characters— short and thin, asexual, wrapped in their cowls—have no other singularities than the fact that each of them departs from a vertex as from a cardinal point, "any-characters-whatever" who traverse the square, each following a given course and direction. They can always be modified with a light, a color, a percussion, or a particular sound of footsteps, which would allow us to distinguish between them. But this is merely a means of recognizing them; in themselves, they are only determined spatially; in themselves, they are modified by nothing other than their order and position. They are unmodified protagonists in an unmodifiable space. *Quad* is a ritornello that is essentially motor, whose music is the shuffling of slippers—like the sound of rats. The form of the ritornello is the series, which in this case is no longer concerned with objects to be combined, but only with journeys having no object.[55] The series has an *order,* according to which the series increases and decreases, increases and decreases again, depending on the appearance and disappearance of the protagonists at the four corners of the square: it is a canon. It has a continuous *course,* depending on the succession of the segments that are traversed: one side, the diagonal, another side, and so on. It has a *set,* which Beckett describes as follows:

"Four possible solos all given. Six possible duos all given (*two twice*). Four possible trios all given *twice*";[56] four times a quartet. The order, the course, and the set render the movement all the more inexorable inasmuch as it has no object, like a conveyor belt that makes moving objects appear and disappear.

Beckett's text is perfectly clear: it is a question of exhausting space. There is no doubt that the characters will become tired, and will drag their feet more and more. Yet tiredness primarily concerns a minor aspect of the enterprise: the number of times one possible combination is realized (for example, two of the duos are realized twice, the four trios twice, the quartet four times). The protagonists become tired depending on the number of realizations. But the possible is accomplished, independently of this number, by the exhausted characters who exhaust it. The problem is: in relation to what is exhaustion (which must not be confused with tiredness) going to be defined? The characters realize and tire at the four corners of the square, and along the sides and diagonals. But they accomplish and exhaust at the center of the square, where the diagonals cross. This is where the potentiality of the square seems to lie. Potentiality is a double possible. It is the possibility that an event, in itself possible, might be realized in the space under consideration: the possibility that something is realizing *itself*, and the possibility that some place is realizing *it*. The potentiality of the square is the possibility that the four moving bodies that inhabit it will collide—two, three, or all four of them—depending on the order and the course of the series.[57] The center is precisely that place where they can run into each other; and their encounter, their collision is not one event among others, but the only possibility of an event—that is, the potentiality of the corresponding space. To exhaust space is to extenuate its potentiality by making any encounter impossible. Consequently, the solution to the problem lies in this slight dislocation at the center, this sway of the hips, this deflection, this hiatus, this punctuation, this syncope, this quick sidestep or little jump that foresees the encounter and averts it. The repetition takes nothing away from the decisive and absolute character of such a gesture. The bodies avoid each other respectively, but they avoid the center absolutely. They sidestep each other at the center in order to avoid each other, but each of them also sidesteps in solo in order to avoid the center. What is depotentialized is the space, a "track . . . just wide enough for one. On it no two ever meet."[58]

Quad is close to a ballet. The general similarities between Beckett's work and modern ballet are numerous: the abandonment of the privileging of vertical stature; the agglutination of bodies as a means of remaining upright; the substitution of an any-space-whatever for qualified and extended spaces; the replacement of all story and narration by a "gestus" as a logic of postures and positions; the quest for a minimalism; the introduction of walking and its various accidents into dance; the conquest of gestural dissonances. It is not surprising that Beckett asks that the walkers of *Quad* have "some ballet training." Not only does the walking require it, but so does the hiatus, the punctuation, and the dissonance.

It is also close to a musical work. A work by Beethoven, "Ghost Trio," appears in another of Beckett's pieces for television, and gives it its title. The second movement of the trio, which Beckett utilizes, presents us with the composition, decomposition, and recomposition of a theme with two motifs, with two ritornellos. It is like the increase and decrease of a more or less dense compound along melodic and harmonic lines, its sonorous surface traversed by a continual movement, obsessive and obsessional. But there is something else as well: a kind of central erosion that first arises as a threat among the bass parts and is expressed in the trill or wavering of the piano, as if one key were about to be abandoned for another, or *for nothing*, hollowing out the surface, plunging into a ghostly dimension where dissonances would appear only to punctuate the silence. And this is precisely what Beckett emphasizes whenever he speaks of Beethoven: a hitherto unknown art of dissonances, a wavering, a hiatus, "a punctuation of dehiscence," a stress given by what opens, slips away, and disappears, a gap that punctuates nothing other than the silence of a final ending.[59] But if the trio effectively displays these traits, why was it not used to accompany *Quad,* to which it is so well suited? Why is it used to punctuate another piece? Perhaps because there is no need for *Quad* to illustrate a piece of music that will take on a role elsewhere by developing its ghostly dimension in a different manner.

Ghost Trio is made up of both voice and music. It is still concerned with space, with exhausting its potentialities, but it does so in a completely different manner than does *Quad.* One might at first think it is an extended space qualified by the elements that occupy it: the floor, the walls, the door, the window, the pallet. But these elements are defunctionalized, and the voice names each of them successively while the camera shows them in close-up—homogenous, gray, rectangular parts homologous with a single space distinguished solely by nuances of gray: in the order of succession, *a* sample of the floor, *a* sample of the wall, *a* door without a knob, *an* opaque window, *a* pallet seen from above. These objects in space are strictly identical to the parts of space. It is therefore an any-space-whatever, in the previously defined sense: it is completely determined, but it is determined locally—and not globally, as in *Quad*—by a succession of even gray bands. It is an any-space-whatever in fragmentation, in close-ups, whose filmic vocation was indicated by Robert Bresson: fragmentation "is indispensable if one does not want to fall into representation. . . . Isolate the parts. Make them independent as a way of giving them a new dependence."[60] Disconnect them to allow for a new connection. Fragmentation is the first step in a depotentialization of space, through local paths.

To be sure, a global space had been given at the outset, in a long shot. But even here, it is not as in *Quad,* where the camera is fixed and elevated, exterior to the space of a closed shot, necessarily operating in a continuous manner. To be sure, a global space can be exhausted by the simple power of a fixed camera, immobile and continuous, operating with a zoom. One famous example is Michael Snow's *Wavelength:* a forty-five-minute zoom explores a rectangular any-space-whatever, and rejects the events it encounters as it moves forward by endowing them with little more than a ghostly existence (through negative superimposition, for example) until it reaches the far wall, on which is hung an image of the empty sea, into which the entire space is swallowed up. It is, as has been said, "the story of the diminishing area of pure potentiality."[61] But apart from the fact that Beckett does not like special effects, the conditions of the problem, from the point of view of a localized reconstruction, require that the camera be both mobile (with tracking shots) and discontinuous (with jump cuts): everything is written down and quantified. This is because the space of *Trio* is only determined on three sides, east, north, and west, the south being constituted by the camera as a mobile partition. This is not the closed space of *Quad,* with a single central potentiality, but a space with three potentialities: the door to the east, the window to the north, and the pallet to the west. And since these are the parts of space, the camera movements and cuts constitute the passage from one to the other, as well as their succession, their substitution, all these gray bands that compose the space in accordance with the demands of the local treatment. But moreover (and this is the most profound aspect of *Trio*), all these parts plunge into the void, each in its own way, each revealing the emptiness into which they are plunging: the door opening onto a dark corridor, the window looking out onto a rainy night, the flat pallet that reveals its own emptiness. So that the passage and the succession from one part to another *only serves to connect or link together unfathomable voids*. Such is the new connection, specifically ghostlike, or the second step of depotentialization. It corresponds to Beethoven's music when the latter succeeds in punctuating the silence, and when a "path of sound" no longer connects anything but "unfathomable abysses of silence."[62] This is particularly the case in Beethoven's "Trio," in which the wavering, the tremolo, already indicates holes of silence across which the sonorous connection passes, at the price of dissonances.

The situation is as follows: the voice of a woman, prerecorded, predetermined, prophetic, whose source is off-screen, announces in a whisper that the protagonist "will think he hears her."[63] Seated on a stool near the door and clutching a small cassette player, the protagonist gets up, sets the cassette player down, and like a ghostly night watchman or sentinel moves toward the door, then the window, then the pallet. There are startings-over, returns to the seated position, and the cassette player emits music only when the protagonist is seated, leaning over the machine. This general situation is not unlike the one in *Eh Joe,* which was Beckett's first piece for television.[64] But the differences between it and *Trio* are even greater. In *Eh Joe,* the female voice did not present the objects, and the objects were not identified with the flat and equivalent parts of the space. In addition to the door and the window, there was a cupboard that introduced an interior depth to the room, and the bed had a space beneath it, rather than simply being a pallet laid on the floor. The protagonist was tracked, and the function of the voice was not to name or to announce, but to remind, to threaten, to persecute. This was still language II. The voice had intentions and intonations, it evoked personal recollections that were unbearable to the protagonist, and sunk into this dimension of memory without being able to rise to the ghostly dimension of an indefinite impersonal. It is only in *Ghost Trio* that this latter dimension is attained: a woman, a man, and a child, without any personal coordinates. From *Eh Joe* to *Trio,* a kind of vocal and spatial purification takes place, which gives the first piece a preparatory value that serves to introduce the works for television, rather than being fully a part of them. In *Trio,* the whispering voice has become neutral, blank, without intentions, without resonance, and the space has become an any-space-whatever, without depth and with no underside, having no other objects than its own parts. This is the final step of depotentialization—a double step, since the voice dries up the possible at the same time as the space extenuates its potentialities. Everything indicates that the woman who speaks from the outside and the woman who could suddenly appear in this space are one and the same. Between the two, however, between the off-screen voice and the pure field of space, there is a scission, a line of separation, as in Greek theater, Japanese No, or the cinema of the Straubs and Marguerite Duras.[65] It is as if a radio piece and a silent film were being played simultaneously: a new form of the inclusive disjunction. Or rather, it is like a split frame, on one side of which are inscribed the silences of the voice, and on the other, the voids of space (jump cuts). It is onto this ghostly frame that the music is hurled, connecting the voids and the silences, following a ridge line like a limit to infinity.

There are numerous trios: voice, space, and music; woman, man, and child; the three principal positions of the camera; the door to the east, the window to the north, and the pallet to the west, three potentialities of space . . . The voice says: "He will now think he hears her."[66] But we should not think he is afraid and feels threatened; this was true in *Eh Joe,* but not here. He no longer wants or is waiting for the woman; on the contrary. He is merely waiting for the end, the latest end. The whole of *Trio* is organized in order to put an end to it, and the end so earnestly desired is at hand: the music (absent from *Eh Joe*), the music of Beethoven, is inseparable from a conversion to silence, from a tendency to abolish itself in the voids that it connects. In truth, the protagonist has extenuated all the potentialities of the space, inasmuch as he has treated the three sources as simple, identical, and blind parts, floating in the void: *he has made the arrival of the woman impossible.* Even the pallet is so flat that it bears witness to its emptiness. Why does the protagonist nevertheless start over again, long after the voice has fallen silent? Why does he again go to the door, to the window, to the head of the pallet? We have seen why: it is because the end *will have been,* long before he could know it: "everything will continue automatically, until the order arrives, to stop everything."[67] And when the little mute messenger suddenly appears, it is not to announce that the woman will not be coming, as if this were a piece of bad news, but to bring the long-awaited order to stop everything, everything being well and truly finished. At least the protagonist has a means of sensing that the end is at hand. Language III involves not only space but also the image. There is a mirror in *Ghost Trio* that plays an important role, and must be distinguished from the door-window-pallet series because it is not visible from the "camera position general view," and it does not figure in the presentations given at the beginning; moreover, it will be paired with the cassette player ("small gray rectangle, same dimensions as cassette") and not with the three objects.[68] Furthermore, the only time the prophetic voice is taken by surprise, caught off guard—"Ah!"—is when the protagonist leans over the mirror for the first time, before we are able to see it. When at last we see the mirror, in an extreme close-up, what suddenly appears in it is the Image, that is, the face of the abominable protagonist. The image will leave its support and become a floating close-up, while the final, amplified bars of the second movement of the "Trio" are being played. The face starts to smile, the astonishingly treacherous and cunning smile of someone who has reached the goal of his "testy delirium": he has *made* the image.[69]

Trio goes from the space to the image. The any-space-whatever already belongs to the category of possibility, because its potentialities make possible the realization of an event that is itself possible. But the image is more profound because it frees itself from its object in order to become a process itself, that is, an event as a "possible" that no longer even needs to be realized in a body or an object, somewhat like the smile without a cat in Lewis Carroll. This is why Beckett takes such care in making the image. Already in *Eh Joe*, the smiling face appeared in an image, but without our being able to see the mouth, the pure possibility of the smile being in the eyes and in the two upward-rising commisures, the rest not being included in the shot. A horrible smile without a mouth. In . . . *but the clouds* . . . , the female face "has almost no head, a face without head suspended in the void"; and in *Nacht und Träume,* the dreamed face seems as if it were wrested from the cloth which mops away its sweat, like a face of Christ, and is floating in space.[70] But if it is true that the any-space-whatever cannot be separated from an inhabitant who extenuates some of its potentialities, the image, with even greater reason, remains inseparable from the movement through which it dissipates itself: the head bows, turns away, fades, or disperses like a cloud or a puff of smoke. The visual image is carried along by the music, the sonorous image that rushes toward its own abolition. Both of them rush toward the end, all possibility exhausted.

The *Trio* leads us from space to the thresholds of the image. But . . . *but the clouds* . . . enters into the "sanctum." The sanctum is the place where the protagonist will make the image. Or rather, in a return to the post-Cartesian theories of *Murphy,* there are now two worlds, the physical and the mental, the corporeal and the spiritual, the real and the possible.[71] The physical world seems to be made up of a qualified, extended space: to the left, there is a door that opens onto some "back roads," and through which the protagonist leaves and returns; to the right, a closet in which he changes his clothes; and up above, the sanctum into which he disappears. But all this only exists in the voice, which is that of the protagonist himself. What we see, by contrast, is only an any-space-whatever, determined as a circle surrounded by black, which becomes darker as one moves toward the periphery and brighter as one moves toward the center. The door, the closet, and the sanctum are merely directions in the circle: west, east, north; and far to the south, outside the circle, lies the immobile camera. When the protagonist moves in one direction, he simply disappears into the shadow; when he *is* in the sanctum, he only appears in close-up, from behind, "sitting on invisible stool bowed over invisible table."[72] The sanctum, then, only has a mental existence; it is a "mental chamber," as Murphy said, and corresponds to the law of inversion as formulated by Murphy: "But motion in this world [of the mind] depended on rest in the world [of the body]."[73] The image is precisely this: not a representation of an object but a movement in the world of the mind. The image is the spiritual life, the "life above" of *How It Is.* One can exhaust the joys, the movements, and the acrobatics of the life of the mind only if the body remains immobile, curled up, seated, somber, itself exhausted: this is what Murphy called "collusion,"[74] the perfect accord between the needs of the body and the needs of the mind, the double exhaustion. The subject of . . . *but the clouds* . . . is this spiritual need, this life above. What matters is no longer the any-space-whatever but the mental image to which it leads.

Of course, it is not easy to make an image. It is not enough simply to think of something or someone. The voice says: "When I thought of her . . . No . . . No, that is not right . . ." What is required is an obscure spiritual tension, a second or third *intensio*, as the authors of the Middle Ages put it, a silent evocation that is also an invocation and even a convocation, and a revocation, since it raises the thing or the person to the state of an indefinite: *a* woman . . . "I call to the eye of the mind," exclaims Willie.[75] Nine hundred and ninety-eight times out of a thousand, one fails and nothing appears. And when one succeeds, the sublime image invades the screen, a female face with no outline; sometimes it disappears immediately, "in the same breath,"[76] sometimes it lingers before disappearing, sometimes it murmurs some words from Yeats's poem. In any case, the image answers to the demands of Ill seen Ill said, Ill seen Ill heard, which reigns in the kingdom of the mind. And as a spiritual movement, it cannot be separated from the process of its own disappearance, its dissipation, whether premature or not. The image is a pant, a breath, but it is an expiring breath, on its way to extinction. The image is that which extinguishes itself, consumes itself: a fall. It is a pure intensity, which is defined as such by its height, that is, by its level above zero, which it describes only by falling.[77] What is retained from Yeats's poem is the visual image of clouds moving through the sky and dispersing on the horizon, and the sonorous image of the bird's cry fading into the night. It is in this sense that the image concentrates within itself a potential energy, which it carries along in its process of self-dissipation. It announces that the end of the possible is at hand for the protagonist of . . . *but the clouds . . .* , just as it was for Winnie, who felt a "zephyr," a "breath,"[78] right before the eternal darkness, the dead end of the black night. There is no longer an image, any more than there is a space: beyond the possible there is only darkness, as in Murphy's third and final state, where the protagonist no longer moves in spirit but has become an indiscernible atom, abulic, "in the dark . . . of . . . absolute freedom."[79] This is the final word, "nohow."[80]

It is the entire last stanza of Yeats's poem that ties in with . . . *but the clouds . . .* : it takes two exhaustions to produce the end that carries off the Seated person. But Beckett's encounter with Yeats goes well beyond this piece; it is not that Beckett takes up Yeats's project of introducing Japanese No as the fulfillment of the theater. But the convergences between Beckett and No, even if involuntary, perhaps presuppose the theatre of Yeats, and appear for their part in the works for television.[81] This is what has been called a "visual poem," a theater of the mind that does not set out to recount a story but to erect an image: the words provide a decor for a network of circuits in an any-space-whatever; these finely detailed circuits are measured and recapitulated in space and time in relation to what must remain indefinite in the spiritual image; the characters are like "supermarionettes"; the camera, as a character, has an autonomous, furtive, or dazzling movement that is antagonistic to the movement of the other characters; artificial techniques (slow motion, superimposition) are rejected as being unsuited to the movements of the mind . . .[82] According to Beckett, only television is able to satisfy these demands.

Making the image is still the operation of *Nacht und Träume*. In this case, however, the protagonist has no voice with which to speak and does not hear any voices; he is unable to move about, seated, empty head in crippled hands, "clenched staring eyes."[83] This is a new purification, "Nohow less. Nohow worse. Nohow nought. Nohow on."[84] It is night, and he is about to dream. Are we supposed to think he is falling asleep? We would do better to believe Blanchot when he says that sleep betrays the night because it introduces an interruption between two days, permitting the following day to succeed the preceding one.[85] We are often content to distinguish between daydreams or waking dreams and the dreams of sleep. But these are questions of tiredness and repose. We thereby miss the third state, which is perhaps the most important one: insomnia, which alone is appropriate to night, and the dream of insomnia, which is a matter of exhaustion. The exhausted person is the wide-eyed person. We dreamed *in* sleep, but we dream *alongside* insomnia. The two exhaustions, the logical and the psychological, "the head and the lungs," as Kafka said, meet up behind our backs. Kafka and Beckett hardly resemble each other, but what they do have in common is the insomniac dream.[86] In the dream of insomnia, it is a question not of realizing the impossible but of exhausting the possible, either by giving it a maximal extension that allows it to be treated like a real waking day, in the manner of Kafka, or else by reducing it to a minimum that subjects it to the nothingness of a night without sleep, as in Beckett. The dream is the guardian of insomnia that keeps it from falling asleep. Insomnia is the crouching beast that stretches out as long as the days and curls up as tightly as the night. The terrifying posture of insomnia.

The insomniac of *Nacht und Träume* is preparing himself for what he has to do. He is seated, his hands seated on the table, his head seated on his hands: a simple movement of the hands, which could be placed on the head or simply separated from each other, is a possibility that can only appear in a dream, like a flying footstool . . . But this dream has to be *made*. The dream of the exhausted, insomniac, or abulic person is not like the dream of sleep, which is fashioned all alone in the depths of the body and of desire; it is a dream of the mind that has to be made, fabricated. What is "dreamed," the image, will be the same character in the same seated position, but inverted, left profile instead of right profile, above the dreamer. But in order for the dreamed hands to be released into an image, other hands, those of a woman, will have to flutter about and raise his head, make him drink abundantly from a chalice, and wipe his brow with a cloth—all in such a way that, with his head now raised, the dreamed character can extend his hands toward one of these other hands that condense and dispense the energy in the image. This image seems to attain a heartrending intensity until the head again sinks down onto three hands, the fourth resting gently on top of the head. And when the image is dissipated, we might imagine we heard a voice: the possible is accomplished, "it is done I've made the image." But there is no voice that speaks, any more than in *Quad*. There is only the male voice, which hums and sings the last bars of the humble ritornello carried along by the music of Schubert, "Soft dreams come again . . . ," once before the appearance of the image, and once after its disappearance. The sonorous image, the music, takes over from the visual image, and opens onto the void or the silence of the final end. In this case, it is Schubert, so admired by Beckett, who brings about a hiatus or a leap, a kind of uncoupling whose mode is very different from Beethoven's. The monodic, melodic voice leaps outside the harmonic support, here reduced to a minimum, in order to undertake an exploration of the pure intensities that are experienced in the way the sound fades. A vector of abolition straddled by music.

In his works for television, Beckett exhausts space twice over, and the image twice over. Beckett became less and less tolerant of words. And he knew from the outset the reason he became increasingly intolerant of them: the exceptional difficulty of "boring holes" in the surface of language so that "what lurks behind it" might at last appear. This can be done on the surface of a painted canvas, as in Rembrandt, Cézanne, or van Velde; or on the surface of sound, as in Beethoven or Schubert, so as to allow for the emergence of the void or the visible in itself, the silence or the audible in itself; but "is there any reason why that terrible materiality of the word surface should not be capable of being dissolved . . . ?"[87] It is not only that words lie; they are so burdened with calculations and significations, with intentions and personal memories, with old habits that cement them together, that one can scarcely bore into the surface before it closes up again. It sticks together. It imprisons and suffocates us. Music succeeds in transforming the death of *this* young girl into *a young girl dies;* it brings about this extreme determination of the indefinite like a pure intensity that pierces the surface, as in the "Concerto in Memory of an Angel." But words are unable to do this, given the adhesions that keep them bound to the general or the particular. They lack that "punctuation of dehiscence," that "disconnection" that comes from a groundswell peculiar to art. It is television that, in part, allows Beckett to overcome the inferiority of words: either by dispensing with spoken words, as in *Quad* and *Nacht und Träume;* or by using them to enumerate, to expound, or to create a decor, which loosens them and allows things and movements to be introduced between them (*Ghost Trio,* . . . *but the clouds* . . .); or by emphasizing certain words according to an interval or a bar, the rest passing by in a barely audible murmur, as at the end of *Eh Joe;* or by including some of the words in the melody, which gives them the accentuation they lack, as in *Nacht und Träume.* In television, however, there is always something other than words, *music or vision,* that makes them loosen their grip, separates them, or even opens them up completely. Is there then no salvation for words, like a new style in which words would at last open up by themselves, where language would become poetry, in such a way as to actually produce the visions and sounds that remained imperceptible behind the old language ("the old style")?[88] Visions or sounds: how can they be distinguished? So pure and so simple, so strong, they are said to be *ill seen ill said* whenever words pierce themselves and turn against themselves so as to reveal their own outside. A music proper to a poetry read aloud without music. From the beginning, Beckett employed a style that would at the same time proceed through a perforation and a proliferation of tissue ("a breaking down and multiplication of tissue").[89] It is worked out through the novels and theater pieces, shows itself in *How It Is,* and explodes in the splendor of his final texts. Sometimes short segments are ceaselessly added to the interior of the phrase in an attempt to break open the surface of words completely, as in the poem *What Is the Word*:

> folly seeing all this—
> this—
> what is the word—
> this this—
> this this here—
> all this this here—
> folly given all this—
> seeing—
> folly seeing all this this here—
> for to—
> what is the word—
> see—
> glimpse—
> seem to glimpse—
> need to seem to glimpse—
> folly for to need to seem to glimpse—
> what—
> ....[90]

And sometimes the phrase is riddled with dots or dashes [*traits*] in order to ceaselessly reduce the surface of words, as in the piece *Worstword Ho*:

> Less best. No. Naught best. Best worse. No. Not best worse. Naught not best worse. Less best worse. No. Least. Least best worse. Least never to be naught. Never to naught be brought. Never by naught be nulled. Unnullable least. Say that best worst. With leastening words say least best worst.
> ....Blanks
> for when words gone[91]

Notes

Introduction. "A Life of Pure Immanence": Deleuze's "Critique et Clinique" Project

1. Gilles Deleuze, "Coldness and Cruelty," in *Masochism*, trans. Jean McNeil (New York: Zone, 1989), p. 14. This essay is an expansion of ideas first developed in "De Sacher-Masoch au masochisme," in *Arguments* 5, no. 21 (January–April 1961): 40–46. See also the short but important interview with Madeleine Chapsal, "Mystique et masochisme," in *La quinzaine littéraire* 25 (April 1–15, 1967): 12–13.

2. Gilles Deleuze, *The Logic of Sense*, ed. Constantin V. Boundas, trans. Mark Lester with Charles Stivale (New York: Columbia University Press, 1990).

3. Gilles Deleuze and Félix Guattari, *Capitalism and Schizophrenia*, vol. 1, *Anti-Oedipus*, trans. Robert Hurley, Mark Seem, and Helen R. Lane (Minneapolis: University of Minnesota Press, 1983); vol. 2, *A Thousand Plateaus*, trans. Brian Massumi (Minneapolis: University of Minnesota Press, 1987).

4. Gilles Deleuze, *Proust and Signs*, trans. Richard Howard (New York: George Braziller, 1972); Gilles Deleuze and Félix Guattari, *Kafka: Toward a Minor Literature*, trans. Dana Polan (Minneapolis: University of Minnesota Press, 1986); "The Exhausted" (on Samuel Beckett), chapter 18 in this volume; "One Manifesto Less" (on Carmelo Bene), trans. Alan Orenstein, in *The Deleuze Reader*, ed. Constantin V. Boundas (New York: Columbia University Press, 1993), pp. 204–22.

5. Gilles Deleuze and Claire Parnet, *Dialogues*, trans. Hugh Tomlinson and Barbara Habberjam (New York: Columbia University Press, 1987), pp. 36–76.

6. Gilles Deleuze, "On Philosophy," in *Negotiations: 1972–1990*, trans. Martin Joughin (New York: Columbia University Press, 1995), p. 142: "I've dreamed about bringing together a series of studies under the general title *Critique et clinique*." For other explicit references to the project, see *Masochism*, p. 15; *Logic of Sense*, pp. 83, 92, 127–28, 237–38; and *Dialogues*, pp. 120, 141.

7. See Gilles Deleuze, preface to the English edition, *Difference and Repetition*, trans. Paul Patton (New York: Columbia University Press, 1994), p. xv: "A philosophical concept can never be confused with a scientific function or an artistic construction, but finds itself in *affinity* with these in this or that domain of science or style of art." Deleuze and Guattari analyze the precise relations between philosophy, art, science, and logic in *What Is Philosophy?* trans. Hugh Tomlinson and Graham Burchell (New York: Columbia University Press, 1994). On philosophy's need for such "intercessors" or mediators, see *Negotiations*, pp. 123–26.

8. Gilles Deleuze, "8 ans après: Entretien 1980" (interview with Catherine Clé-

ment), in *L'arc* 49 (rev. ed., 1980), special issue on Deleuze, p. 99. Deleuze's response to a question concerning the "genre" of *A Thousand Plateaus* is equally applicable to all his books.

9. *Negotiations,* p. 58.

10. Gilles Deleuze, *The Movement-Image,* trans. Hugh Tomlinson and Barbara Habberjam (Minneapolis: University of Minnesota Press, 1986), p. ix; *Negotiations,* p. 47.

11. Gilles Deleuze, *Francis Bacon: Logique de la sensation,* 2 vols. (Paris: Éditions de la Différence, 1981), vol. 1, p. 7.

12. Deleuze has established numerous such links in his works—between, for instance, Chekhov's short stories and Foucault's "Infamous Men" (*Negotiations,* pp. 108, 150); between Shakespeare's *Hamlet* and Kant's *Critique of Pure Reason* ("On Four Formulas That Might Summarize the Kantian Philosophy," chapter 5 in this volume); between Alfred Jarry and Martin Heidegger ("An Unrecognized Precursor to Heidegger: Alfred Jarry," chapter 11 in this volume); and in the cinema, between Kierkegaard and Dreyer, and between Pascal and Bresson (*The Movement-Image,* pp. 114–16). One might note that Stanley Cavell presents his own interest in the cinema in similar terms: "I discuss the blanket in *It Happened One Night* in terms of the censoring of human knowledge and aspiration in the philosophy of Kant; and I see the speculation of Heidegger exemplified or explained in the countenance of Buster Keaton." See "The Thought of Movies," in *Themes out of School: Effects and Causes* (Chicago: University of Chicago Press, 1984), pp. 6–7.

13. Gilles Deleuze, "Lettre-préface," in Mireille Buydens, *Sahara: L'esthétique de Gilles Deleuze* (Paris: Vrin, 1990), p. 5; and *Negotiations,* p. 143. The term *nonorganic life* is derived from Wilhelm Worringer, *Form in Gothic* (London: Putnam, 1927), pp. 41–42; Worringer used it to describe the vitality of the abstract line in Gothic art (see Deleuze and Guattari, *A Thousand Plateaus,* pp. 496–98).

14. Charles Dickens, *Our Mutual Friend,* book 3, chapter 3, in *The Oxford Illustrated Dickens* (London: Oxford University Press, 1952), p. 443.

15. Gilles Deleuze, "L'immanence: Une vie . . . ," *Philosophie* 47 (September 1, 1995): 5. "With a young child, one already has an organic, personal relationship, but not with a baby, which concentrates in its smallness the same energy that shatters paving stones. With a baby, one has nothing but an affective, athletic, impersonal, vital relation. *It is certain that the will to power appears in an infinitely more exact manner in a baby than in a man of war*" ("To Have Done with Judgment," chapter 15 in this volume, emphasis added).

16. "Literature and Life," chapter 1 in this volume.

17. Gilles Deleuze, *Nietzsche and Philosophy,* trans. Hugh Tomlinson (New York: Columbia University Press, 1981), p. 1: "We always have the beliefs, feelings, and thoughts we deserve, given our way of being or our style of life." On the distinction between ethics and morality, see *Negotiations,* pp. 100, 114–15, as well as "On the Difference between the *Ethics* and a Morality," in *Spinoza: Practical Philosophy,* trans. Robert Hurley (San Francisco: City Lights, 1988), pp. 17–29. *Règles facultatives* is a term Deleuze adopts from the sociolinguist William Labov to designate "functions of internal variation and no longer constants." See Gilles Deleuze, *Foucault,* trans. Seán Hand (Minneapolis: University of Minnesota Press, 1988), pp. 146–47, note 18.

18. Friedrich Nietzsche, *On the Genealogy of Morals,* essay 1, § 17, in *Basic Writings of Nietzsche,* trans. Walter Kaufmann (New York: Modern Library, 1968), p. 491.

19. *Negotiations,* p. 100.

20. *What Is Philosophy?* p. 172.

21. *Negotiations,* p. 134.

22. *What Is Philosophy?* p. 170.

23. *Negotiations,* p. 143, and *What Is Philosophy?* p. 171.

24. Deleuze was responding to a question posed to him during the Cerisy colloquium on Nietzsche in 1972; see *Nietzsche aujourd'hui* (Paris: Union Générale d'Éditions, 10/18, 1973), vol. 1, *Intensities,* pp. 186–87. Moreover, Deleuze and Guattari have distanced themselves from certain Heideggerian problematics that Derrida has taken up: "The death of metaphysics or the overcoming of philosophy has never been a problem for us" (*What Is Philosophy?* p. 9). Deleuze nonetheless cites Derrida on numerous occasions, and the many lines of convergence between their respective works remain to be explored.

25. See "Mystique et masochisme," p. 13: "I would never have permitted myself to write on psychoanalysis and psychiatry were I not dealing with a problem of symptomatology. Symptomatology is situated almost outside of medicine, at a neutral point, a zero point, where artists and philosophers and doctors and patients can encounter each other."

26. *Masochism,* p. 133. The history of medicine, Deleuze suggests, can therefore be regarded under at least two aspects. The first is the *history of diseases,* which may disappear, recede, reappear, or alter their form depending on numerous external factors (the appearance of new microbes or viruses, altered technological and therapeutic techniques, and changing social conditions). But intertwined with this is the *history of symptomatology,* which is a kind of "syntax" of medicine that sometimes follows and sometimes precedes changes in therapy or the nature of diseases: symptoms are isolated, named, and regrouped in various manners. While external factors can make new symptomatologies possible, they can never determine them as such. See, for instance, Deleuze's comments on post–World War II developments in symptomatology in *Negotiations,* pp. 132–33.

27. See *Logic of Sense,* p. 237: "From the perspective of Freud's genius, it is not the complex which provides us with information about Oedipus and Hamlet, but rather Oedipus and Hamlet who provide us with information about the complex."

28. *Logic of Sense,* p. 237, translation modified. See also *Masochism,* p. 14: "Symptomatology is always a question of art."

29. See, in particular, Friedrich Nietzsche, "The Philosopher as Cultural Physician" (1873), in *Philosophy and Truth,* ed. Daniel Brezeale (Atlantic Highlands, N. J.: Humanities Press, 1979), pp. 67–76, though the idea of the philosopher as a physician of culture occurs throughout Nietzsche's writings. For Deleuze's analysis of the symptomatological method in Nietzsche, see *Nietzsche and Philosophy,* pp. x, 3, 75, 79, 157.

30. "Mystique et masochisme," p. 13.

31. On all these points, see the important passage in *Anti-Oedipus,* pp. 132–36, especially on the status of psychosis in literature (Artaud). For Freud, the libido does not invest the social field as such except on the condition that it be "desexualized" and "sublimated"; any sexual libidinal investment having a social dimension therefore seems to him to bear witness to a pathogenic state, either a "fixation" in narcissism or a "regression" to pre-Oedipal states. For Deleuze's reflections on the present state of "the space of literature" and the fragile conditions for the literary production, see *Negotiations,* pp. 22–23, 128–31. On the effect of marketing on both literature and philosophy, see Deleuze's critique of the "new philosophers," "A propos des nouveaux philosophes et d'un problème plus général," *Minuit* 4, supplement (June 5, 1977): n.p.

32. "De Sacher-Masoch au masochisme," p. 40. For an analysis of the role of the "sexual instinct—whose various transformations and inversions were used to account for the "perversions"—in nineteenth-century psychiatry, see Arnold I. Davidson, "Closing Up the Corpses: Diseases of Sexuality and the Emergence of the Psychiatric Style of

Reasoning," in *Meaning and Method: Essays in Honor of Hilary Putnam,* ed. George Boolos (Cambridge: Cambridge University Press, 1990), pp. 295–325.

33. Deleuze summarizes the results of his clinical analyses in eleven propositions in the last paragraph of the book (*Masochism,* p. 134). For the analyses of the literary techniques, see chapter 2, "The Role of Descriptions," pp. 25–35. For the relation to minorities, see *Masochism,* pp. 9–10, 93; *Negotiations,* p. 142.

34. "Mystique et masochisme," pp. 12-13. Asked why he had treated only Sade and Masoch from this point of view, Deleuze replied, "There are others, in fact, but their work has not yet been recognized under the aspect of a creative symptomatology, as was the case with Masoch at the start. There is a prodigious table [*tableaux*] of symptoms corresponding to the work of Samuel Beckett: not that it is simply a question of identifying an illness, but the world as symptom, and the artist as symptomatologist" (p. 13).

35. *Dialogues,* p. 120.

36. Gilles Deleuze, *Expressionism in Philosophy: Spinoza,* trans. Martin Joughin (New York: Zone, 1990). See Deleuze's comments in his letter to the translator, p. 11.

37. *Negotiations,* p. 142: "The *Recherche* is a general semiology, a symptomatology of different worlds."

38. See Deleuze's discussion of the three components of the "critique et clinique" project in *Dialogues,* pp. 120–23; I discuss various aspects of the third component (lines of flight) in the latter sections of this essay.

39. *Anti-Oedipus,* p. 122.

40. Gilles Deleuze, "Schizophrénie et positivité du désir," in *Encyclopédia Universalis* (Paris: Éditions Encyclopédie Universalis France, 1972), vol. 14, p. 735.

41. The definition of schizophrenia as a process has a complex history. When Emile Kraepelin tried to ground his concept of *dementia praecox* ("premature senility"), he defined it neither by causes nor by symptoms but by a process, by an evolution and a terminal state; but he conceived of this terminal state as a complete and total disintegration, which justified the confinement of the patient in an asylum while awaiting his death. Deleuze and Guattari's notion is closer to that of Karl Jaspers and R. D. Laing, who formulated a rich notion of process as a rupture, an irruption, an opening (*percée*) that breaks the continuity of a personality, carrying it off in a kind of voyage through an intense and terrifying "more than reality," following lines of flight that engulf both nature and history, both the organism and the mind. See *Anti-Oedipus,* pp. 24–25.

42. Gilles Deleuze and Félix Guattari, "La synthèse disjonctive," *L'arc* 43, special issue on Pierre Klossowski (Aix-en-Provence: Duponchelle, 1970), p. 56, emphasis added.

43. *A Thousand Plateaus,* p. 4; *Negotiations,* p. 23. See also "Schizophrénie et positivité du désir," p. 735: "Let us resign ourselves to the idea that certain artists or writers have had more revelations concerning schizophrenia than the psychiatrists and psychoanalysts."

44. This text is included in the English translation under the title "Antilogos; or, the Literary Machine," in *Proust and Signs,* pp. 93–157.

45. *Proust and Signs,* pp. 128, 154; for the comparison with Joyce's epiphanies, see p. 138.

46. *Proust and Signs,* p. 129. The notion that "meaning is use" comes from Wittgenstein, though to my knowledge Deleuze makes only two references to Wittgenstein in his work. In the first, he writes approvingly that "Wittgenstein and his disciples are right to define meaning by use" (*Logic of Sense,* p. 146); in the second, he writes that Whitehead "stands provisionally as the last great Anglo-American philosopher, just before Wittgenstein's disciples spread their mists, their sufficiency, and their terror" (*The Fold: Leibniz and the Baroque,* trans. Tom Conley [Minneapolis: University of Minnesota Press, 1993], p. 76). His disapproval perhaps stems from the reintroduction, by cer-

tain of Wittgenstein's followers, of a form of "common sense" in the guise of a "grammar" that would be properly "philosophical" and a "form of life" that would be generically human.

47. *Anti-Oedipus*, p. 109.

48. *Proust and Signs*, p. 138. See also p. 128, where Deleuze cites Malcolm Lowry's description of the "meaning" of his novel: "It can be regarded as a kind of symphony, or in another way as a kind of opera—or even a horse opera. It is hot music, a poem, a song, a tragedy, a comedy, a farce, and so forth. It is superficial, entertaining and boring, according to taste. It is a prophecy, a political warning, a cryptogram, a preposterous movie, and a writing on the wall. *It can even be regarded as a sort of machine: it works too, believe me, as I have found out.*" *Selected Letters of Malcolm Lowry*, ed. Harvey Breit and Margerie Bonner Lowry (Philadelphia and New York: Lippincott, 1965), p. 66, emphasis added.

49. *Anti-Oedipus*, p. 324. See also "Balance-Sheet Program for Desiring Machines," in Félix Guattari, *Chaosophy*, ed. Sylvère Lotringer (New York: Semiotext[e], 1995), p. 145: "How can elements be bound together by the absence of any link? In a certain sense, it can be said that Cartesianism, in Spinoza and Leibniz, has not ceased to reply to this question. It is the theory of the real distinction, insofar as it implies a specific logic. It is because they are really distinct, and completely independent of each other, that ultimate elements or simple forms belong to the same being or to the same substance."

50. *Proust and Signs*, pp. 93–157. Thomas Wolfe, in his essay "The Story of a Novel," in *The Autobiography of an American Artist*, ed. Leslie Field (Cambridge, Mass.: Harvard University Press, 1983), describes his compositional technique in similar terms: "It was as if I had discovered a whole new universe of chemical elements and had begun to see certain relations between some of them but had by no means begun to organize and arrange the whole series in such a way that they would crystallize into a harmonious and coherent union. From this time on, I think my effort might be described as the effort to complete that organization."

51. *Negotiations*, p. 147; *A Thousand Plateaus*, p. 6.

52. See Ernst Mayr, "An Analysis of the Concept of Natural Selection," in *Toward a New Philosophy of Biology: Observations of an Evolutionist* (Cambridge, Mass.: Harvard University Press, 1988), p. 98: "Selection would not be possible without the continuous restoration of variability."

53. Gilles Deleuze, *The Time-Image*, trans. Hugh Tomlinson and Robert Galeta (Minneapolis: University of Minnesota Press, 1989), p. 129, translation modified, emphasis added. On the philosophical use of scientific functions, see *Negotiations*, pp. 123–26.

54. See "Klossowski, or Bodies-Language," in *The Logic of Sense*, esp. pp. 292–94, where Deleuze contrasts "the order of God" with "the order of the Anti-Christ."

55. *The Fold*, chapter 5, and *Logic of Sense*, pp. 110–11. For the distinction between the virtual and the actual, Deleuze relies on the model proposed in Albert Lautman's theory of differential equations in *Le problème du temps* (Paris: Hermann, 1946), p. 42. Lautman argues that a singularity can be grasped in two ways. The conditions of a *problem* are determined by the nomadic distribution of singular points in a virtual space, in which each singularity is inseparable from a zone of objective indetermination (ordinary points). The *solution* appears only with the integral curves and the form they take in the neighborhood of singularities within the field of vectors, which constitutes the beginning of the actualization of the singularities (a singularity is analytically extended over a series of ordinary points until it reaches the neighborhood of another singularity, etc.).

56. Jorge Luis Borges, "The Garden of Forking Paths," in *Ficciones* (New York:

Grove, 1962), p. 98, emphasis added. For Deleuze's various references to this story, see *The Fold*, p. 62; *Logic of Sense*, p. 114; *The Time-Image*, p. 131; *Difference and Repetition*, p. 73; *Foucault*, p. 145 n. 3.

57. *The Time-Image*, p. 303. For Leibniz's narrative, see *Theodicy*, §§ 414–17.

58. See *The Time-Image*, "The Powers of the False," pp. 126–55. The following themes are summaries of this chapter, some of which are developed in more detail in *The Fold*, where Deleuze makes use of Leibniz's work to develop a concept of the "baroque."

59. See *The Logic of Sense*, p. 174: "The whole question, and rightly so, is to know under what conditions disjunction is a veritable synthesis, instead of being a procedure of analysis which is satisfied with the exclusion of predicates from a thing by virtue of the identity of its concept (the negative, limitative, or exclusive use of disjunction). The answer is given insofar as the divergence or the decentering determined by the disjunction become objects of affirmation as such . . . an *inclusive disjunction* that carries out the synthesis itself by drifting from one term to another and following the distance between terms." For the concept of the rhizome, see "Introduction: Rhizome," in *A Thousand Plateaus*, pp. 3–25, esp. p. 7.

60. *Negotiations*, p. 126. See also *The Time-Image*, p. 133: "Narration is constantly being modified in each of its episodes, not according to subjective variations, but as a consequence of disconnected spaces and de-chronologized moments."

61. For Deleuze's analysis of the three types of portmanteau words in Lewis Carroll's work, see "Of Esoteric Words," in *The Logic of Sense*, pp. 42–47. Deleuze cites Carroll's explanation of the disjunctive portmanteau word: "If your thoughts incline ever so little towards 'fuming,' you will say 'fuming-furious'; if they turn, even by a hair's breadth, towards 'furious,' you will say 'furious-fuming'; but if you have the rarest of gifts, a perfectly balanced mind, you will say 'frumious'" (p. 46).

62. See Michel Foucault, *Death and the Labyrinth: The World of Raymond Roussel* (Garden City, N.Y.: Doubleday, 1986), especially chapter 2. For Deleuze's analyses, see *Difference and Repetition*, pp. 22, 121, and *Logic of Sense*, pp. 39, 85. Roussel's language rests not simply on the combinatorial possibilities of language—the fact that language has fewer terms of designation than things to designate, but nonetheless can extract an immense wealth from this poverty—but more precisely on the possibility of saying two things with the same word, inscribing a maximum of difference within the repetition of the same word.

63. On Gombrowicz, see *Difference and Repetition*, p. 123, and *Logic of Sense*, p. 39; on Joyce, see *Difference and Repetition*, pp. 121–23, and *Logic of Sense*, pp. 260–61, 264.

64. *Logic of Sense*, p. 60, translation modified.

65. *Logic of Sense*, p. 174, translation modified.

66. Joe Bousquet, *Les capitales* (Paris: Le Cercle du Livre, 1955), p. 103, as cited in *Logic of Sense*, p. 148. It is in the context of his discussion of Bousquet that Deleuze defines ethics in terms of the relation of the individual to the singularities it embodies: an active life is one that is able to affirm the singularities that constitute it, to become worthy of the events that happen to it ("Everything was in order with the events of my life before I made them mine," writes Bousquet. "To live them is to find myself tempted *to become their equal*"); a reactive life, by contrast, is driven by a *ressentiment* of the event, grasping whatever happens to it as unjust and unwarranted. "Either ethics makes no sense at all," writes Deleuze, "or this is what it means and has nothing else to say: not to be unworthy of what happens to us" (p. 149).

67. *Logic of Sense*, p. 178.

68. Antonin Artaud, "Here Lies," in *Selected Writings*, ed. Susan Sontag, trans. Helen Weaver (New York: Farrar Straus & Giroux, 1977), p. 540; and Vaslav Nijinsky, *Diary* (New York: Simon & Schuster, 1936), pp. 20, 156, as cited in *Anti-Oedipus*,

pp. 15, 77. On the role of included disjunctions in the schizophrenic process, see "La synthèse disjonctive," p. 59: "Schizophrenization: a disjunction that remains disjunctive, and which nonetheless affirms the disjoint terms, affirms them through all their distance, without limiting one by the other or excluding one from the other."

69. Deleuze, "The Exhausted," chapter 18 in this volume: "Beckett's great contribution to logic is to have shown that exhaustion (exhaustivity) does not occur without a certain physiological exhaustion. . . . Perhaps it is like the front and back side of a single thing: a keen sense or science of the possible joined, or rather disjoined, with a fantastic decomposition of the 'self.'" Deleuze himself, however, draws a sharp distinction between the virtual and the possible; see *Difference and Repetition,* pp. 211–14.

70. Deleuze and Guattari, "1730: Becoming-Intense, Becoming-Animal, Becoming-Imperceptible . . . ," in *A Thousand Plateaus,* pp. 232–309.

71. *What Is Philosophy?* p. 173. Deleuze's monographs in the history of philosophy all inhabit such a zone of indiscernibility, which accounts for the sense that they are fully "Deleuzian" despite the variety of figures he considers.

72. *A Thousand Plateaus,* p. 243.

73. Herman Melville, *Moby-Dick,* chapter 36, "The Quarter-Deck," as cited in *A Thousand Plateaus,* p. 245.

74. *Negotiations,* p. 137, translation modified.

75. Deleuze, "Bartleby; or, the Formula," chapter 10 in this volume.

76. *What Is Philosophy?* p. 168.

77. *The Movement-Image,* p. 102, We might note here a shift that seems to take place in Deleuze's terminology. In Spinoza, an "affection" (*affectio*) indicates the state of a body insofar as it is affected by another body, while an "affect" (*affectus*) marks the passage from one state to another as an increase or decrease in the body's power as a function of its affections. This terminology, which Deleuze analyzes in detail in *Expressionism in Philosophy: Spinoza,* is retained throughout *A Thousand Plateaus.* In *The Movement-Image* and *What Is Philosophy?,* however, Deleuze replaces these terms with *perception* and *affection* respectively, reserving the word *affect* for the pure qualities or powers that are extracted from affections and achieve an autonomous status.

78. *The Movement-Image,* p. 98; this text contains Deleuze's analysis of "Firstness" and "Secondness" in Peirce and makes the comparison with Biran.

79. *What Is Philosophy?* p. 177.

80. Cited in *The Movement-Image,* p. 99.

81. *The Movement-Image,* p. 103.

82. *The Movement-Image,* p. 106.

83. *The Movement-Image,* pp. 99-101.

84. *What Is Philosophy?* p. 174.

85. *A Thousand Plateaus,* p. 270.

86. Emily Brontë, *Wuthering Heights* (New York: Norton, 1990), chapter 9, pp. 62–64.

87. Gilles Deleuze and Félix Guattari, *Kafka: Toward a Minor Literature,* trans. Dana Polan (Minneapolis: University of Minnesota Press, 1986), p. 39.

88. *A Thousand Plateaus,* p. 174.

89. *What Is Philosophy?* p. 173.

90. "Bartleby; or, The Formula," chapter 10 in this volume.

91. François Zourabichvili, "Six Notes on the Percept (On the Relation between the Critical and the Clinical)," in *Deleuze: A Critical Reader,* ed. Paul Patton (Cambridge, Mass.: Blackwell, 1996), p. 190. Zourabichvili's article provides a profound analysis of the clinical status of the percept in Deleuze's work.

92. Virginia Woolf, *Mrs. Dalloway* (New York: Harcourt Brace & World, 1925),

p. 11; see *A Thousand Plateaus*, p. 263. For Deleuze's analysis of the role of affects and percepts in *Seven Pillars of Wisdom*, see "The Shame and the Glory: T. E. Lawrence," chapter 14 in this volume.

93. *A Thousand Plateaus*, p. 262.

94. *What Is Philosophy?* p. 169.

95. See Joachim Gasquet, *Cézanne: A Memoir with Conversations*, trans. Christopher Pemberton (London: Thames and Hudson, 1991), p. 160, translation modified: "man absent from but entirely within the landscape." Cézanne's phrase captures exactly the paradox of the percept.

96. Claude Samuel, *Conversations with Olivier Messiaen*, trans. Félix Aprahamian (London: Stainer and Bell, 1976), pp. 61–63.

97. Virginia Woolf, *The Diary of Virginia Woolf*, ed. Anne Olivier Bell (London: Hogarth, 1980), vol. 3, p. 209, as cited in *A Thousand Plateaus*, p. 280, and *What Is Philosophy?* p. 172.

98. *What Is Philosophy?* p. 170. One might note that it is in precisely this context that Deleuze considers the effects of drugs and alcohol on literary creation: though drugs can indeed open the "doors of perception," drug-induced works rarely if ever attain the level of the percept; the effects of such perceptive experimentations, Deleuze argues, must be brought about "by quite different means"—that is, in art. For Deleuze's discussions of drugs, see *A Thousand Plateaus*, pp. 282–86, which is an elaboration of an earlier article, "Deux questions" (Two questions), which appeared in *Recherches*, 39 bis (December 1979), pp. 231–34. The first question concerns the "specific causality" of drugs, which Deleuze locates in a "line of flight" that invests the system of perception directly: drugs "stop the world" and release pure auditory and optical percepts; they create microintervals and molecular holes in matter, forms, colors, sounds; and they make lines of speed pass through these intervals (see *The Movement-Image*, p. 85). The second question, however, concerns the inevitable "turning point": in themselves, drugs are unable to draw the plane necessary for the action of this "line of flight," and instead result in "erroneous perceptions" (Artaud), "bad feelings" (Michaux), dependency, addiction, and so on. Burroughs thus formulates the aesthetic problem posed by drugs in the following manner: How can one incarnate the power of drugs without becoming an addict? "Imagine that everything that can be attained by chemical means is accessible by other paths" (*Logic of Sense*, p. 161).

99. *A Thousand Plateaus*, p. 261.

100. See Deleuze and Guattari's comments in *A Thousand Plateaus*: "Is it not necessary to retain a minimum of strata, a minimum of forms or functions, a minimal subject from which to extract materials, affects, and assemblages?" (p. 270). "You don't reach the plane of consistency by wildly destratifying. . . . Staying stratified—organized, signified, subjected—is not the worst that can happen; the worst that can happen is if you throw the strata into demented or suicidal collapse, which brings them back down on us heavier than ever. This is how it should be done: Lodge yourself on a stratum, experiment with the opportunities it offers, find an advantageous place on it, find potential movements of deterritorialization, possible lines of flight, experience them, produce flow conjunctions here and there, try out continuums of intensities segment by segment, have a small plot of new land at all times" (pp. 160–61).

101. *A Thousand Plateaus*, p. 356. For the comparison between Goethe and Kleist, see pp. 268–69.

102. *What Is Philosophy?* pp. 188–89. This is how Deleuze defines Proust's project: to render visible the invisible force of time. "Time," writes Proust, "which is usually not visible, in order to become so seeks bodies and, wherever it finds them, seizes

upon them in order to project its magic lantern upon them" (cited in *Proust and Signs,* p. 142).

103. *Negotiations,* p. 6; *Dialogues,* p. 11, emphasis added.

104. *A Thousand Plateaus,* chapter 6, pp. 149–66.

105. On Deleuze's use of embryology and the model of the egg, see *Difference and Repetition,* pp. 214–17, 249–52.

106. William Burroughs, *Naked Lunch* (New York: Grove, 1966), pp. 8, 131, as cited in *A Thousand Plateaus,* pp. 153, 150.

107. George Büchner, *Lenz,* in *Complete Plays and Prose,* trans. Carl Richard Mueller (New York: Hill & Wang, 1963), p. 141, as cited in *Anti-Oedipus,* p. 2: "He thought that it must be a feeling of endless bliss to be in contact with the profound life of every form, to have a soul for rocks, metals, water, and plants, to take into himself, as in a dream, every element of nature, like flowers that breathe with the waxing and waning of the moon."

108. D. H. Lawrence, *Fantasia of the Unconscious* (New York: Viking, 1960).

109. See *Anti-Oedipus,* pp. 18–19.

110. See *Anti-Oedipus,* pp. 84–89.

111. Arthur Rimbaud, *A Season in Hell,* in *Rimbaud: Complete Works, Selected Letters,* trans. Wallace Fowlie (Chicago: University of Chicago Press, 1966), pp. 177, 179, 189, 193.

112. See Pierre Klossowski, "The Euphoria at Turin," in *Nietzsche and the Vicious Circle,* trans. Daniel W. Smith (Chicago: University of Chicago Press, 1997). Klossowski cites one of Nietzsche's final fragments, in which the two poles of delirium are mixed: "I touch here the question of race. I am a Polish gentleman, *pure blood,* in whom not a drop of impure blood is mixed, not the slightest. If I seek my most profound opposite . . .—I always find my mother and my sister: to see myself allied with such German riff-raff was a blasphemy against my divinity. The ancestry on the side of my mother and sister to this very day (—) was a monstrosity."

113. *Dialogues,* pp. 36–51. The Anglo-American writers that appear most frequently in Deleuze's writings include Samuel Beckett, William Burroughs, Lewis Carroll, Charles Dickens, F. Scott Fitzgerald, Allen Ginsberg, Thomas Hardy, Henry James, James Joyce, Jack Kerouac, D. H. Lawrence, T. E. Lawrence, H. P. Lovecraft, Malcolm Lowry, Herman Melville, Henry Miller, R. L. Stevenson, Virginia Woolf.

114. On the geography of American literature, see *A Thousand Plateaus,* pp. 19, 520 n. 18; on the process of demolition, see *Anti-Oedipus,* pp. 133, 277–78, and *Dialogues,* pp. 38–39, 140–41.

115. See, for example, Paul Klee, *On Modern Art,* trans. Paul Findlay (London: Faber, 1966), p. 55: "We have found parts, but not the whole. We still lack the ultimate power, for the people are not with us. But we seek a people."

116. On all these points, see the short section in *The Time-Image* (pp. 215–24) that analyzes the conditions of a modern political cinema. In a parallel section of the book that would deserve a separate discussion (pp. 262–70), Deleuze analyzes the conditions under which the cinema is capable of fighting an internal battle against informatics and communication (a "creation beyond information").

117. See *Negotiations,* pp. 171–72. For Deleuze and Guattari's critique of the concept of class, see *Anti-Oedipus,* pp. 252–62.

118. In *A Thousand Plateaus,* pp. 469–70, Deleuze and Guattari provide a set theoretical interpretation of the major/minor distinction. What defines a minority is not its number but rather relations internal to the number: a majority is constituted by a set that is *denumerable,* whereas a minority is defined as a *nondenumerable* set, no matter how many elements it has. The capitalist axiomatic manipulates only denumerable sets,

whereas minorities constitute fuzzy, nondenumerable, and nonaxiomizable sets, which implies a calculus of *problematics* rather than an *axiomatic*.

119. See *A Thousand Plateaus*, pp. 291, 106.

120. "1227: Treatise on Nomadology—The War Machine," in *A Thousand Plateaus*, pp. 351–423, which could be read as an attempt to set forth the type of political formation that would correspond with the "active" mode of existence outlined in Nietzsche's *Genealogy of Morals*.

121. *The Time-Image*, p. 219.

122. Pier Paolo Pasolini develops this notion of free indirect discourse in *L'expérience hérétique* (Paris: Payot, 1976), pp. 39–65 (in literature), and pp. 139–55 (in cinema). For Deleuze's analyses, see *The Movement-Image*, pp. 72–76.

123. See Herman Melville's essay on American literature, "Hawthorne and his Mosses," in *The Portable Melville*, ed. Jay Leyda (New York: Viking, 1952), pp. 411–14; and Franz Kafka's diary entry (December 25, 1911) on "the literature of small peoples," in *The Diaries of Franz Kafka: 1910–1913*, ed. Max Brod, trans. Joseph Kresh (New York: Schocken, 1948), pp. 191–98.

124. *Kafka: Toward a Minor Literature*, p. 18.

125. *Negotiations*, p. 174. Bergson develops the notion of fabulation in chapter 2 of *Two Sources of Morality and Religion*, trans. T. Ashley Audra and Cloudesley Brereton with W. Horsfall Carter (New York: Henry Holt, 1935).

126. *Dialogues*, p. 43. For the concept of "minority," see *A Thousand Plateaus*, pp. 105–6, 469–71. On the conditions for a political cinema in relation to minorities, and Bergson's notion of "fabulation," see *The Time-Image*, pp. 215–24.

127. Marcel Proust, *By Way of Sainte-Beuve*, trans. Sylvia Townsend Warner (London: Chatto & Windus, 1958), pp. 194–95: "Great literature is written in a sort of foreign language. To each sentence we attach a meaning, or at any rate a mental image, which is often a mistranslation. But in great literature all our mistranslations result in beauty."

128. "He Stuttered," chapter 13 in this volume.

129. Deleuze, "Avenir de linguistique," preface to Henri Gobard, *L'aliénation linguistique* (Paris: Flammarion, 1976), pp. 9–14. See also *Kafka: Toward a Minor Literature*, p. 23–27: "The spatiotemporal categories of these languages differ sharply: vernacular language is "here," vehicular language is "everywhere," referential language is "over there," mythic language is "beyond" (p. 23).

130. *A Thousand Plateaus*, p. 102.

131. On all these points, see *Kafka: Toward a Minor Literature*, pp. 15–16, 23. Pierre Perrault encountered a similar situation in Quebec: the impossibility of not speaking, the impossibility of speaking other than in English, the impossibility of speaking in English, the impossibility of settling in France in order to speak French (see *The Time-Image*, p. 217).

132. *Negotiations*, p. 133.

133. *Kafka: Toward a Minor Literature*, p. 18.

134. See *A Thousand Plateaus*, pp. 361–74.

135. *A Thousand Plateaus*, p. 101; cf. p. 76: "A rule of grammar is a power marker before it is a syntactical marker."

136. *Kafka: Toward a Minor Literature*, p. 19.

137. In addition to the essays collected in *Essays Critical and Clinical*, see Deleuze's essay "Of the Schizophrenic and the Little Girl," in *Logic of Sense*, pp. 82–93, which compares the procedures of Carroll and Artaud (especially p. 83, where Deleuze notes that the comparison must take place at both a "clinical" and a "critical" level).

138. See Gilles Deleuze, "One Manifesto Less," in *The Deleuze Reader*, ed. Constantin V. Boundas (New York: Columbia University Press, 1994).

139. *Negotiations*, pp. 140–41. With regard to this "outside" of language in philosophy, Deleuze writes that "style in philosophy tends toward these three poles: concepts, or new ways of thinking; percepts, or new ways of seeing and hearing; and affects, or new ways of feeling" (pp. 164–65, translation modified).

140. *Anti-Oedipus*, pp. 133, 370–71, 106. For this use of the term *experimentation*, see John Cage, *Silence* (Middletown, Conn.: Wesleyan University Press, 1961), p. 13: "The word *experimental* is apt, providing it is understood not as descriptive of an act to be later judged in terms of success and failure, but simply as of an act the outcome of which is unknown."

141. *Dialogues*, p. 50.

142. *Negotiations*, pp. 146–47. See also *A Thousand Plateaus*, p. 100: "Only continuous variation brings forth this virtual line, this continuum of life, 'the essential element of the real beneath the everyday.'"

143. "To Have Done with Judgment," chapter 15 in this volume. On the distinction between "transcendent judgment" and "immanent evaluation," see *The Time-Image*, p. 141: "It is not a matter of judging life in the name of a higher authority which would be the good, the true; it is a matter, on the contrary, of evaluating every being, every action and passion, even every value, in relation to the Life which they involve. Affect as immanent evaluation, instead of judgment as transcendent value."

144. On the notion of immanent criteria, see *Kafka*, pp. 87–88, and *A Thousand Plateaus*, pp. 70, 251: "Although there is no preformed logical order to becomings and multiplicities, there are *criteria*, and the important thing is that they not be used after the fact, that they be applied in the course of events."

145. *A Thousand Plateaus*, p. 187, translation modified.

146. *Dialogues*, p. 141.

1. Literature and Life

1. See André Dhôtel, *Terres de mémoire* (Paris: Delarge, 1978), on a becoming-aster in *La chronique fabuleuse* (Paris: Mercure de France, 1960), p. 225.

2. J.-M. G. Le Clezio, *Haï* (Paris: Flammarion, 1971), p. 5. In his first novel, *The Interrogation*, trans. Daphne Woodward (New York: Atheneum, 1964), Le Clezio presents in an almost exemplary fashion a character taken up in a becoming-woman, then a becoming-rat, then a becoming-imperceptible in which he effaces himself.

3. [Franz Kafka, as cited by Elias Canetti, *Kafka's Other Trial: The Letters to Felice*, trans. Christopher Middleton (New York: Schocken, 1974), p. 90.—Trans.]

4. Karl Philipp Moritz (1756–93), "Anton Reiser," in Jean-Christophe Bailly, *La légende dispersée: Anthologie du romantisme allemand* (Paris: Union Générale d'Éditions, 10–18, 1976), p. 38.

5. Marthe Robert, *Origins of the Novel*, trans. Sacha Rabinovitch (Bloomington: Indiana University Press, 1980).

6. D. H. Lawrence, letter to John Middleton Murry, May 20, 1929, in *The Letters of D. H. Lawrence*, ed. Keith Sagar and James T. Bolton (Cambridge: Cambridge University Press, 1993), vol. 7, letter 5095, p. 294.

7. Maurice Blanchot, *The Work of Fire*, trans. Charlotte Mandell (Stanford, Calif.: Stanford University Press, 1995), pp. 21–22, and *The Infinite Conversation*, trans. Susan Hanson (Minneapolis: University of Minnesota Press, 1993), pp. 384–85: "Something happens to [the characters] that they can only recapture by relinquishing their power to say 'I.'" Literature here seems to refute the linguistic conception, which finds in shifters, and notably in the two first persons, the very condition of enunciation.

8. On literature as an affair of health, but for those who do not have it or have

only a fragile health, see Henri Michaux, postface to "Mes propriétés," in *La nuit remue* (Paris: Gallimard, 1972), p. 193. And Le Clezio, *Haï*, p. 7: "One day, we will perhaps know that there wasn't any art but only medicine."

9. André Bay, preface to Thomas Wolfe, *De la mort au matin* (Paris: Stock, 1987), p. 12.

10. See Kafka's reflections on so-called minor literatures in his diary entry for December 25, 1911, in *The Diaries of Franz Kafka: 1910–1913*, ed. Max Brod, trans. Joseph Kresh (New York: Schocken, 1948), pp. 191–98, and Melville's reflections on American literature in his "Hawthorne and His Mosses," in *The Portable Melville*, ed. Jay Leyda (New York: Viking, 1952), pp. 411–14.

11. [Arthur Rimbaud, *A Season in Hell*, in *Rimbaud: Complete Works, Selected Letters*, trans. Wallace Fowlie (Chicago: University of Chicago Press, 1966), p. 193— Trans.]

12. Marcel Proust, *Correspondence avec Madame Straus*, letter 47 (1936; Paris: Livre de Poche, 1974), pp. 110–15 ("there are no certainties, not even grammatical ones").

2. Louis Wolfson; or, The Procedure

1. [This essay was first published as the preface to Louis Wolfson, *Le schizo et les langues* (Paris: Gallimard, 1970), pp. 5–23, under the title "Schizologie"; it appears here in revised form.—Trans.]

2. Louis Wolfson, *Le schizo et les langues; Ma mère musicienne est morte* (Paris: Navarin, 1984).

3. See not only Michel Foucault's *Death and the Labyrinth: The World of Raymond Roussel*, trans. C. Ruas (New York: Doubleday, 1986), but also his preface to the new edition of Brisset, in *Dits et écrits 1954–1988* (Paris: Gallimard, 1994), vol. 2, pp. 13–24, where he compares the three procedures of Roussel, Brisset, and Wolfson in terms of the distribution of three organs: the mouth, the eye, and the ear.

4. Alain Rey has provided an analysis of the conditional, both in itself and as it is used by Wolfson, in his article "Le schizolexe," in *Critique*, September 1970, pp. 681–82.

5. François Martel has made a detailed study of the disjunctions in Beckett's *Watt*, in "Jeux formels dans *Watt*," in *Poétique* 10 (1972). See also "Assez," in *Têtes-mortes* (Paris: Minuit, 1967), and Beckett's English version, "Enough," in *No's Knife* (London: Calder, 1967). A large part of Beckett's work can be understood in terms of the great formula of *Malone Dies* (New York: Grove, 1966), p. 4: "Everything divides into itself."

6. In Artaud, the famous breath-words are opposed to the maternal language and to broken letters; and the body without organs is opposed to the organism, to organs and larvae. But the breath-words are supported by a poetic syntax, and the body without organs by a vital cosmology that exceeds the limits of Wolfson's equation on all sides.

7. See Piera Castoriadis-Aulagnier's psychoanalytic interpretation of Wolfson in "Le sense perdu," in *Topique* 7–8. The conclusion of the study seems to open up a larger perspective.

8. On the "impossible" in language, and the means to render it possible, see Jean-Claude Milner, *For the Love of Language*, trans. Ann Banfield (New York: St. Martin's, 1990), especially his considerations of maternal languages and the diversity of languages. It is true that the author appeals to the Lacanian concept of *lalangue*, which links together language and desire, but this concept does not seem any more reducible to psychoanalysis than it is to linguistics.

4. The Greatest Irish Film (Beckett's "Film")

1. [This essay was originally published in *Revue d'esthétique,* 1986, pp. 381–82, under the title "Le plus grand film irlandais (en hommage à Samuel Beckett)"; it appears here in revised form.—Trans.]

2. [Beckett's original English phrasing is "all contentedly in *percipere* and *percipi,*" which we have modified in accordance with the French translation; see Samuel Beckett, *The Complete Dramatic Works* (London: Faber, 1986), p. 324.—Trans.]

5. On Four Poetic Formulas That Might Summarize the Kantian Philosophy

1. Shakespeare, *Hamlet,* Act 1, Scene 5. Shestov often used Shakespeare's formula as the tragic device of his own thought; see "The Ethical Problem in *Julius Caesar,*" trans. S. Konovalov, in *The New Adelphi,* June 1928, p. 348, and "Celui qui édifie et détruit des mondes (Tolstoï)," trans. Sylvie Luneau, in *L'homme pris au piége (Pouchkine, Tolstoï, Tchékhov)* (Paris: Union Générale d'Éditions, 1966), p. 29. [Deleuze follows Bonnefoy's French translation of this phrase as *le temps est hors de ses gonds,* literally, "time is off its hinges"; see *Hamlet,* trans. Yves Bonnefoy (Paris: Gallimard, Folio, 1992).—Trans.]

2. [This essay was first published as the preface to *Kant's Critical Philosophy: The Doctrine of the Faculties,* trans. Hugh Tomlinson and Barbara Habberjam (Minneapolis: University of Minnesota Press, 1984), pp. vii–xiii. The French text subsequently appeared as "Sur quatre formules qui pourraient résumer la philosophie kantienne," in *Philosophie 9* (1986): 29–34. The present essay is a revised and expanded version of this earlier text.—Trans.]

3. Eric Alliez, in *Capital Times: Tales from the Conquest of Time,* trans. George van den Abbeele (Minneapolis: University of Minnesota Press, 1996), has analyzed in ancient thought, this tendency toward the emancipation of time when movement ceases to be circular: for instance, in the "chrematism" and time as a monetary movement in Aristotle.

4. Jorge Luis Borges, "Death and the Compass," trans. Anthony Kerrigan, in *Ficciones* (New York: Knopf, 1993), p. 113, translation modified.

5. Friedrich Hölderlin, "Remarks on 'Oedipus,'" in *Essays and Letters on Theory,* ed. and trans. Thomas Pfau (Albany: State University of New York Press, 1988), pp. 101–8. See also Jean Beaufret's commentary, "Hölderlin et Sophocles," in Hölderlin, *Remarques sur Oedipe* (Paris: Union Générale d'Éditions, 10/18, 1965), which analyses the relation with Kant.

6. [Arthur Rimbaud, *Complete Works,* trans. Paul Schmidt (New York: Harper & Row, 1975), letter to Georges Izambard, May 13, 1871, p. 101; letter to Paul Demeny, May 15, 1871, p. 103, translation modified.—Trans.]

7. Nietzsche, *The Birth of Tragedy,* trans. Walter Kaufmann (New York: Random House, 1967), §9, pp. 67–72.

8. Samuel Beckett, *Murphy* (Paris: Bordas, 1948), chapter 6, p. 85. ["Metabulia" is a neologism coined by Beckett in his French translation of *Murphy: meta* combined with *abulia,* an abnormal lack of ability to act or to make decisions. In the original English version (1938), the term *will-lessness* was used; see *Murphy* (London: Picador, 1973), p. 66.—Trans.]

9. [Franz Kafka, "The Problem of Our Laws," in *The Complete Stories,* ed. Nahum Glatzer (New York: Schocken, 1983), p. 437, translation modified.—Trans.]

10. Franz Kafka, "Advocates," in *The Complete Stories,* ed. Nahum N. Glatzer (New York: Schocken, 1971), pp. 449–51.

11. Sigmund Freud, *Civilization and Its Discontents,* in *The Standard Edition of the Complete Psychological Works,* trans. James Strachey, vol. 21 (London: Hogarth, 1961), pp. 125–26.

12. [Arthur Rimbaud, *Complete Works,* letter to Georges Izambard, May 13, 1871, p. 101; and letter to Paul Demeny, May 15, 1871, p. 103.—Trans.]

6. Nietzsche and Saint Paul, Lawrence and John of Patmos

1. [This essay was originally published as the preface to D. H. Lawrence, *Apocalypse* (Paris: Balland, 1978), pp. 7–37, where its authorship is ascribed to "Fanny and Gilles Deleuze."—Trans.]

2. For the text of and commentaries on the Apocalypse, see Charles Brütsch, *La clarté de l'Apocalypse* (Geneva: Labor et Fides, 1967). On the question of the author or authors, see pp. 397–405; the scholarly reasons to assimilate the two authors seem very weak. [In the notes that follow, the page numbers refer to the definitive text established in the Cambridge edition of the works of D. H. Lawrence, *Apocalypse and the Writings on Revelation,* ed. Mara Kalnins (Cambridge: Cambridge University Press, 1980); the numbers in brackets refer to the pagination of the more readily available Viking edition of the Cambridge text, which does not include the critical apparatus (D. H. Lawrence, *Apocalypse* [1931], ed. Mara Kalnins [New York: Viking, 1982]). Citations of the Book of Revelation are from the Revised Standard Version.—Trans.]

3. [Friedrich Nietzsche, *The Antichrist,* in *The Portable Nietzsche,* trans. Walter Kaufmann (New York: Viking, 1954), §42, p. 618.—Trans.]

4. Friedrich Nietzsche, "Schopenhauer as Educator," in *Untimely Meditations,* trans. R. J. Hollingdale (Cambridge: Cambridge University Press, 1983), §7, p. 177.

5. *Apocalypse,* chapter 3, p. 69 [14].

6. D. H. Lawrence, *Aaron's Rod,* ed. Mara Kalnins (Cambridge: Cambridge University Press, 1988), pp. 77–78: "Don't you see that it's the Judas principle you really worship. Judas is the real hero. But for Judas the whole show would have been *manqué.* . . . When people say Christ they mean Judas. They find him luscious on the palate. And Jesus fostered him."

7. *Apocalypse,* chapter 9, p. 100 [52].

8. Nietzsche, *The Antichrist,* §17, p. 585: God is "at home anywhere, this great cosmopolitan. . . . Nevertheless, he remained a Jew, he remained the god of nooks, the god of all the dark corners and places. . . . His world-wide kingdom is, as ever, an underworld kingdom, a hospital, a *souterrain* kingdom."

9. D. H. Lawrence, *Etruscan Places* (New York: Viking, 1933), p. 22.

10. *Apocalypse,* chapter 6, p. 81 [28–29].

11. [Revelation 20:4.—Trans.]

12. *Apocalypse,* chapter 6, p. 80 [27].

13. [Deleuze is referring to the expression *La vengeance est un plat qui se mange froid*—"revenge is a dish best eaten cold."—Trans.]

14. Revelation 6:10–11: "O Sovereign Lord, holy and true, how long before thou wilt judge and avenge our blood on those who dwell on the earth? Then they were . . . told to rest a little longer, until the number of their brethren should be complete, who were to be killed as they themselves had been."

15. *Apocalypse,* chapter 6, p. 80 [27–28].

16. Nietzsche, *The Antichrist,* §42, p. 617: "Paul simply transposed the center of gravity of that whole existence *after* this existence—in the *lie* of the 'resurrected' Jesus.

At bottom, he had no use at all for the life of the Redeemer—he needed the death on the cross *and* something more."

17. *Apocalypse,* chapter 15, p. 119 [74].

18. *Apocalypse,* chapter 6, p. 82 [30].

19. [*Apocalypse,* chapter 6, p. 83 [31].—Trans.]

20. *Apocalypse,* chapter 6, p. 84 [32].

21. *Apocalypse,* chapter 2, p. 66 [7].

22. [*Apocalypse,* chapter 6, p. 86 [34–35].—Trans.]

23. Certain thinkers have today painted a properly "apocalyptic" picture, in which three characteristics can be identified: (1) the germs of an absolute worldwide State; (2) the destruction of the "habitable" world in favor of a sterile and lethal environment or milieu; (3) the hunt for the "unspecified" enemy. See Paul Virilio, *L'insécurité du territoire* (Paris: Stock, 1986).

24. Revelation 21:23, 27.

25. [Revelation 21:2.—Trans.]

26. *Apocalypse,* chapter 13, p. 112 [66].

27. *Apocalypse,* chapter 10, p. 102 [54]. The horse as a vibrant force and lived symbol appears in Lawrence's story "The Woman Who Rode Away," in *The Woman Who Rode Away and Other Stories* (London: Martin Secker, 1928), pp. 57–102.

28. *Apocalypse,* chapter 16, pp. 123–29 [78–86].

29. [Revelation 12:5.—Trans.]

30. *Apocalypse,* chapters 15 and 16, pp. 119 [74] and 126 [82].

31. *Apocalypse,* chapter 14, pp. 116–17 [70–71].

32. These different aspects of symbolic thought are analyzed by Lawrence throughout his commentary on the Apocalypse. For a more general exposition concerning the planes, centers, or foci, the parts of the soul, see *Fantasia of the Unconscious* (1921; New York: Viking, 1960).

33. *Apocalypse,* chapter 22, p. 144 [104].

34. D. H. Lawrence, *The Man Who Died* (London: Martin Secker, 1931), pp. 23, 41 (emphasis added), 51: the great scene of Christ with Mary Magdalene ("And in his heart he knew he would never go to live in her house. For the flicker of triumph had gleamed in her eyes; the greed of giving. . . . A revulsion from all the life he had known came over him again" [pp. 47–48]). There is an analogous scene in *Aaron's Rod,* chapter 11, in which Aaron returns to his wife, only to flee again, horrified by the glimmer in her eyes.

35. D. H. Lawrence, *Fantasia of the Unconscious* (1921; New York: Viking, 1960), pp. 176–78.

36. On the necessity of being alone, and of attaining the refusal to give—a constant theme in Lawrence—see *Aaron's Rod,* pp. 189–201 ("His intrinsic and central isolation was the very center of his being, if he broke this central solitude, everything would be broken. To cede is the greatest temptation, and it was the final sacrilege."), and p. 128 ("Let there be clean and pure division first, perfect singleness. That is the only way to final, living unison: through sheer, finished singleness.").

37. D. H. Lawrence, *Studies in Classic American Literature* (1923; New York: Viking, 1961), pp. 173–77.

38. On this conception of flows and the sexuality that follows from it, see one of Lawrence's last texts, "We Need One Another" (1930), in *Phoenix: The Posthumous Papers of D. H. Lawrence* (London: Heinemann, 1936), pp. 188–95.

39. *Apocalypse,* chapter 23, p. 149 [110–11]. It is this thought of false and true connections that animates Lawrence's political thought, notably in *Phoenix: The Posthumous Papers of D. H. Lawrence,* ed. Edward D. McDonald (London: Heinemann,

1961), and *Phoenix II: Uncollected, Unpublished, and Other Prose,* ed. Warren Roberts and Harry T. Moore (London: Heinemann, 1968).

7. Re-presentation of Masoch

1. [This essay was originally published in the French newpaper *Libération* on May 18, 1989. The title refers to Deleuze's book *Présentation de Sacher-Masoch* (Paris: Minuit, 1967), the theses of which are re-presented here.—Trans.]

2. In his biography of Sacher-Masoch, Bernard Michel shows that the very name of the hero of "The Metamorphosis," Gregor Samsa, is quite plausibly an *hommage* to Masoch: Gregor is the pseudonym that the hero of *Venus in Furs* takes on, and Samsa seems to be a diminutive or partial anagram of Sacher-Masoch. Not only are masochist themes numerous in Kafka, but the problem of minorities in the Austro-Hungarian Empire animates both oeuvres. Nonetheless, there are important differences between the juridicism of the tribunal in Kafka and the juridicism of the contract in Masoch. See Bernard Michel, *Sacher-Masoch: 1836–1895* (Paris: Laffont, 1989), p. 303.

3. Pascal Quignard, *L'être du balbutiement, essai sur S-M* (Paris: Mercure de France, 1969), pp. 21–22, 147–64.

8. Whitman

1. Friedrich Hölderlin, "Remarks on 'Oedipus,'" in *Essays and Letters on Theory,* ed. and trans. Thomas Pfau (Albany: State University of New York Press, 1988), pp. 101–8, and Jean Beaufret's commentaries in *Remarques sur Oedipe* (Paris: Union Générale d'Éditions, 10–18, 1965).

2. Walt Whitman, *Specimen Days,* in *The Portable Walt Whitman,* ed. Mark Van Doren (New York: Viking, 1973), "A Happy Hour's Command," pp. 387–88.

3. Whitman, *Specimen Days,* "A Happy Hour's Command," pp. 387–88.

4. Whitman, *Specimen Days,* "Convulsiveness," p. 480.

5. Franz Kafka, *Diaries 1910–1913,* ed. Max Brod, trans. Joseph Kresh (New York: Schocken, 1948), entry for December 25, 1911, pp. 191–98.

6. This is a constant theme of *Leaves of Grass,* in *Walt Whitman: Complete Poetry and Selected Prose and Letters,* ed. Emory Halloway (London: Nonesuch, 1964). See also Herman Melville, *Redburn: His Maiden Voyage* (Evanston and Chicago: Northwestern University Press and Newberry Library, 1969), chapter 33, p. 169.

7. Whitman, *Specimen Days,* "An Interviewer's Item," pp. 578–79.

8. Whitman, *Specimen Days,* "A Night Battle, over a Week Since," pp. 422–24, and "The Real War Will Never Get in the Books," pp. 482–84.

9. Herman Melville, "Hawthorne and His Mosses," in *Herman Melville,* ed. R. W. B. Leavis (New York: Dell, 1962), p. 48. In the same way, Whitman invokes the necessity of an American literature "without a trace or taste of Europe's soil, reminiscence, technical letter or spirit" (*Specimen Days,* "The Prairies and Great Plains in Poetry," p. 573).

10. Whitman, *Specimen Days,* "Bumble-Bees," pp. 488–91.

11. Whitman, *Specimen Days,* "Carlyle from American Points of View," pp. 602–11.

12. D. H. Lawrence, in *Studies in Classic American Literature* (New York: Viking, 1964), violently criticizes Whitman for his pantheism and his conception of an Ego-Whole; but he salutes him as the greatest poet because, more profoundly, Whitman sings of "sympathies," that is, of relations that are constructed externally, "on the Open Road" (pp. 174–75).

13. See Paul Jamati, *Walt Whitman: Une étude, un choix de poèmes* (Paris: Seghers, 1950), p. 77: the poem as polyphony.

14. Whitman, *Specimen Days*, "Mississippi Valley Literature," pp. 577-78.

15. Whitman, *Specimen Days*, "The Real War Will Never Get in the Books," pp. 482-84.

16. Whitman, *Specimen Days*, "The Oaks and I," pp. 515-16.

17. Whitman, *Specimen Days*, "The Real War Will Never Get in the Books," pp. 482-84. On camaraderie, see Whitman, *Leaves of Grass*, "Calamus."

18. Whitman, *Specimen Days*, "The Death of President Lincoln," p. 467.

19. Whitman, *Specimen Days*, "Nature and Democracy," pp. 639-40.

9. What Children Say

1. [*Trajets*. Throughout this essay, *trajet* has been translated as "trajectory" or "pathway"; *trajectoire* has been translated uniformly as "trajectory"; and *parcours* has been translated variously as "route," "journey," or "distance" (as in "distance covered"), depending on the context. *Parcourir* has been rendered as "to travel through."—Trans.]

2. Sigmund Freud, "Analysis of a Phobia in a Five-Year-Old Boy" (1909), in *The Standard Edition of the Complete Psychological Works*, trans. James Strachey, vol. 10 (London: Hogarth, 1953).

3. Fernand Deligny, "Voix et voir," in *Cahiers de l'immuable* I (Fontenay-sous-Bois: Recherches, 1975).

4. Pierre Kaufmann, *Kurt Lewin: Une théorie du champ dans les sciences de l'homme* (Paris: Vrin, 1968), 170–73: the notion of path.

5. [In English in the original.—Trans.]

6. Melanie Klein, *Narrative of a Child Analysis* (New York: Free Press, 1984).

7. See Barbara Glowczewski, *Du rêve à la loi chez les Aborigènes* (Paris: PUF, 1992), chapter 1.

8. Félix Guattari, *Les années d'hiver* (Paris: Barrault, 1986). And *Cartographies schizo-analytiques* (Paris: Galilée, 1989).

9. Elie Faure, *History of Art*, vol. 2, *Medieval Art*, trans. Walter Pach (New York: Harper & Brothers, 1922), pp. 12–14: "There at the shore of the sea, at the base of a mountain, they encountered a great wall of granite. Then they all entered the granite. . . . Behind them they left the emptied granite, its galleries hollowed out in every direction, its sculptured, chiseled walls, its natural or artificial pillars."

10. Jean-Claude Polack and Danielle Sivadon, *L'intime utopie* (Paris: PUF, 1991) (the authors oppose the "geographical" method to a "geological" method like that of Gisela Pankow, p. 28).

11. See Sándor Ferenczi, "A Little Chanticleer," in *Sex in Psychoanalysis*, trans. Ernest Jones (New York: Basic Books, 1950), pp. 240–42.

12. Robert Louis Stevenson, "My First Book, *Treasure Island*'" in *Treasure Island* (London: Oxford University Press, 1955).

13. Svetlana Alpers, *The Art of Describing: Dutch Art in the Seventeenth Century* (Chicago: University of Chicago Press, 1983), p. 122.

14. Eugène Fromentin, *Un été dans le Sahara*, in *Oeuvres* (Paris: Gallimard, Pléiade, 1984), p. 18.

15. On an art of paths that opposes itself to the monumental or commemorative, see *Voie suisse: L'itinéraire genevois* (analyses by Carmen Perrin). See also *Bertholin* (Vassivière), with the text by Patrick Le Nouène, "Chose d'oubli et lieux de passage." The center of Vassivière, or that of Crestet, are the sites of this *nouvelle sculpture*, whose principles refer to the great conceptions of Henry Moore.

16. Cf. the multiplicity of courses in Boulez, and the comparison with "the street-map of a town" (p. 82), in works like *The Third Piano Sonata, Eclat*, or *Domaines*, in

Pierre Boulez: Conversations with Celestin Deliege (London: Eulenburg, 1976), chapter 12 ("the course of a work ought to be multiple," p. 81).

10. Bartleby; or, The Formula

1. Nicolas Ruwet, "Parallélismes et déviations en poésie," in *Langue, discours, société*, ed. Julia Kristeva and Nicholas Ruwet (Paris: Seuil, 1975), pp. 334–44 (on "portmanteau-constructions").

2. Philippe Jaworski, *Melville, le désert et l'empire* (Paris: Presses de l'Ecole Normale, 1986), p. 19.

3. See Viola Sachs, *La contre-Bible de Melville* (Paris: Mouton, 1975).

4. On Bartleby and Melville's silence, see Armand Farrachi, *La part du silence* (Paris: Barrault, 1984), pp. 40–45.

5. Mathieu Lindon, "Bartleby," *Delta* 6 (May 1978): 22.

6. Kafka's great text almost reads like another version of "Bartleby." See Franz Kafka, *The Diaries of Franz Kafka: 1910–1913,* ed. Max Brod, trans. Joseph Kresh (New York: Schocken, 1948), p. 26.

7. Blanchot demonstrates that Musil's character is not only without qualities, but "without particularities," since he has no more substance than he does qualities. See *Le livre à venir* (Paris: Gallimard/Folio, 1963), pp. 202–3. This theme of the man without particularities, the modern-day Ulysses, arises early in the nineteenth century, and in France appears in the rather strange book of Ballanche, a friend of Chateaubriand; see Pierre Simon Ballanche, *Essais de palingénésie sociale,* notably "La ville des expiations" (1827), in *Oeuvres complètes* (Geneva: Slatkine Reprints, 1967).

8. Herman Melville, "Bartleby the Scrivener," in *Billy Budd, Sailor and Other Stories,* ed. Harold Beaver (London: Penguin Classics, 1967), p. 89.

9. Régis Durand, in his *Melville, signes et métaphores* (Paris: L'Age d'Homme, 1980), pp. 103–7, has pointed out the role played by loose lines aboard a whaler, as opposed to the formalized riggings. Both Durand's and Jaworski's books are among the most profound analyses of Melville to have appeared recently.

10. George Dumézil, preface to Georges Charachidzé, *Prométhée ou le Caucase: Essai de mythologie contrastive* (Paris: Flammarion 1986): "The Greek myth of Prometheus has remained, through the ages, an object of reflection and reference. The god who does not take part in his brothers' dynastic struggle against their cousin Zeus, but who, on personal grounds, defies and ridicules this same Zeus . . . this *anarchist,* affects and stirs up dark and sensitive zones in us."

11. On this conception of the two Natures in Sade (the theory of the pope in the *New Justine*), see Pierre Klossowski, *Sade My Neighbor,* trans. Alphonso Lingis (Evanston, Ill.: Northwestern University Press, 1991), pp. 99 ff.

12. Herman Melville, *Moby-Dick; or, the Whale,* chapter 36 (New York: Penguin Classics, 1992), p. 178.

13. See Schopenhauer's conception of sainthood as the act by which the Will denies itself in the suppression of all particularity. Pierre Leyris, in his second preface to the French translation of *Billy Budd* (Paris: Gallimard, 1980), recalls Melville's profound interest in Schopenhauer. Nietzsche saw Parsifal as a type of Schopenhauerian saint, a kind of Bartleby. But after Nietzsche, man still preferred being a demon to being a saint: "man would rather will *nothingness* than *not* will." Friedrich Nietzsche, *On the Genealogy of Morals,* trans. Walter Kaufmann and R. J. Hollingdale (New York: Random House, 1967), third essay, § 28, p. 163.

14. See Heinrich Kleist's letter to H. J. von Collin, December 1808, in *An Abyss Deep Enough: The Letters of Heinrich Von Kleist,* ed. Philip B. Miller (New York: Dut-

ton, 1982). Catherine Heilbronn had her own formula, close to that of Bartleby's: "I don't know" or simply "Don't know."

15. The comparison between Musil and Melville would pertain to the following four points: the critique of reason ("Principle of insufficient reason"), the denunciation of psychology ("the great hole we call the soul"), the new logic ("the other state"), and the hyperborean Zone (the "Possible").

16. See Francis Bacon and David Sylvester, *The Brutality of Fact: Interviews with Francis Bacon* (New York: Thames and Hudson, 1975), p. 22. And Melville said: "For the same reason that there is but one planet to one orbit, so can there be but one such original character to one work or invention. Two would conflict to chaos." Herman Melville, *The Confidence-Man*, ed. Stephen Matterson (London: Penguin Classics, 1990), p. 282.

17. See R. Durand, p. 153. Mayoux writes: "On the personal plane, the question of the father is momentarily postponed, if not settled. . . . But it is not only a question of the father. We are all orphans. Now is the age of fraternity." Jean-Jacques Mayoux, *Melville*, trans. John Ashbery (New York: Grove, 1960), p. 109, translation modified.

18. Emily Brontë, *Wuthering Heights* (London: Penguin, 1985), p. 122.

19. Kafka, *Diaries 1910–1913*, p. 28.

20. Herman Melville, *Redburn: His Maiden Voyage* (Evanston and Chicago: Northwestern University Press and Newberry Library, 1969), p. 169.

21. Jaworski has analyzed this world-as-archipelago or this patchwork experiment. These themes are to be found throughout Pragmatism, and notably among William James's most beautiful pages: the world as "shot point blank with a pistol." This is inseparable from the search for a new human community. In *Pierre; or, The Ambiguities*, Plotinus Plinlimmon's mysterious tract already seems like the manifestation of an absolute pragmatism. On the history of pragmatism in general, philosophical and political, see Gérard Deledalle, *La philosophie américaine* (Paris: L'Age d'Homme, 1983): Royce is particularly important, with his "absolute pragmatism" and his "great community of Interpretation" that unites individuals. There are many Melvillian echoes in Royce's work. His strange trio of the Aventurer, the Beneficiary, and the Insurer seems in certain ways to derive from Melville's trio of the Monomaniac, the Hypochondriac, and the Prophet, or even to refer to characters in *The Confidence-Man*, who would already prefigure the trio's comic version.

22. [In English in the original.—Trans.]

23. D. H. Lawrence, "Whitman," in *Studies in Classic American Literature* (New York: Viking, 1953). This book also includes two famous studies on Melville. Lawrence criticizes both Melville and Whitman for having succumbed to the very things they denounced; nonetheless, he says, it was American literature that, thanks to them, marked out the path.

24. [See Henry David Thoreau, *Walden and Civil Disobedience*, ed. Owen Thomas (New York: Norton, 1966), p. 233: "Under a government which imprisons any unjustly, the true place for a just man is also a prison."—Trans.]

25. See Alexander Mitscherlich's *Society without the Father: A Contribution to Social Psychology*, trans. Eric Musbacher (New York: J. Aronson, 1974), which is written from a psychoanalytic point of view that remains indifferent to the movements of History and invokes the benefits of the paternal English Constitution.

26. See Melville's text on American literature, "Hawthorne and His Mosses," in *The Portable Melville*, ed. Jay Leyda (New York: Viking, 1952), pp. 411–14, which should be compared with Kafka's text on "the literature of small peoples," in *The Diaries of Franz Kafka: 1910–1913*, entry for December 25, 1911, pp. 210 ff.

11. An Unrecognized Precursor to Heidegger: Alfred Jarry

1. Alfred Jarry, *Exploits and Opinions of Doctor Faustroll, Pataphysician*, in *Selected Works of Alfred Jarry*, ed. Roger Shattuck and Simon Watson Taylor (New York: Grove, 1965), p. 192.

2. Martin Heidegger, *Being and Time*, trans. John Macquarrie and Edward Robinson (New York: Harper & Row, 1962), §7, p. 60 ("Only as phenomenology is ontology possible," although Heidegger uses the Greeks as his authority more than Husserl).

3. Jarry, *Faustroll*, p. 192.

4. Alfred Jarry, *Être et vivre* (*Being and Living*), in *Oeuvres complètes* (Paris: Gallimard, Pléiade edition, 1972), vol. 1, p. 342: "Being, clubbed to death by Berkeley's cudgel [*être, défublé du bât de Berkeley*] . . ."

5. Jarry, *Faustroll* and *Être et vivre*, in *Oeuvres complètes*, vol. 1, p. 343 ("Living is the carnival of Being . . .").

6. On anarchy according to Jarry, see not only *Être et vivre*, but above all "Visions Present and Future," in *Selected Works*, pp. 109–13.

7. The appeal to science (physics and mathematics) appears above all in *Faustroll* and in *The Supermale*, trans. Barbara Wright (London: Jonathan Cape, 1968); the theory of machines is specifically developed in a text supplementary to *Faustroll*, "How to Construct a Time Machine," in *Selected Works*, pp. 114–21.

8. Alfred Jarry, "The Passion Considered as an Uphill Bicycle Race," in *Selected Works*, pp. 122–24.

9. Martin Heidegger, "The Question Concerning Technology," in *The Question Concerning Technology*, trans. William Lovitt (New York: Harper & Row, 1977), p. 28.

10. Marlène Zarader has shown this double turning in Heidegger, one toward the rear, the other toward the front, particularly well, in *Heidegger et les paroles de l'origine* (Paris: Vrin, 1990), pp. 260–73.

11. Martin Heidegger, "Time and Being," in *On Time and Being*, trans. Joan Stambaugh (New York: Harper & Row, 1972): "without regard to metaphysics," or even "the intention to overcome metaphysics" (p. 24).

12. See Henri Bordillon, preface to *Oeuvres complètes* (Paris: Gallimard, Pléiade, 1972), vol. 2, pp. xix–xx: Jarry "almost never utilizes the word pataphysics between 1900 and his death," except in the texts related to Ubu. In *Être et vivre*, Jarry said, "Being is the sub-supreme of the Idea, for it is less comprehensible than the Possible . . . ," *Oeuvres complètes*, vol. 1, p. 342.

13. See the definition of pataphysics in *Faustroll*, p. 193: science "symbolically attributes the properties of objects, described by their virtuality, to their lineaments." On the frame, see "How to Construct a Time Machine," in *Selected Works*, pp. 118–19.

14. Jarry, "How to Construct a Time Machine," in *Selected Works*, pp. 114–21, which sets forth the whole of Jarry's theory of time, is an obscure and very beautiful text, which must be related to Bergson as much as to Heidegger.

15. See the description of Jarry's machines, and their sexual content, in Michel Carrouges's *Les machines célibataires* (Paris: Arcanes, 1954). See also Jacques Derrida's commentary, in which he suggests that Dasein, according to Heidegger, implies a sexuality, but one that is irreducible to the duality that appears in the animal or human being: "Geschlecht: Sexual Difference, Ontological Difference," *Research in Phenomenology* 13 (1983): 65–83.

16. According to Heidegger, the withdrawal concerns not only Being, but in another sense *Ereignis* itself: "Ereignis is withdrawal not only as a mode of giving, but *as* Ereignis" ("Time and Being," p. 22, translation modified). On the More and the Less, the "Less-in-More" and "More-in-Less," see *César-Antechrist*, in *Oeuvres complètes*, vol. 1, p. 290.

17. On the transitions from technique to art, art being related to the essence of technique while functioning differently, see "The Question Concerning Technology," pp. 34–35.

18. See *Visions Present and Future* and *Être et vivre*: Jarry's interest in anarchy is reinforced by his relations with Laurent Tailhade and Fénéon; but he criticizes anarchy for substituting "science for art," and for entrusting "the Beautiful Gesture" to the machine (see *Oeuvres complètes*, vol. 1, esp. p. 338). Could one also say that Heidegger sees a transition toward art in the national socialist machine?

19. Martin Heidegger, "The Thing," in *Poetry, Language, Thought*, trans. Albert Hofstadter (New York: Harper & Row, 1971), pp. 179–81.

20. In the theater of *César-Antechrist*, the mise-en-scène of the world is assured by the coats of arms, and the decor by the shields: the theme of the *Quadriparti* is clearly evident (*Oeuvres complètes*, vol. 1, pp. 286–88). In all Jarry's work, the fourfold Cross appears as the great sign. The value of the Bike comes from Jarry's invocation of an original bicycle, struck with forgetting, whose frame is a cross, "two tubes soldered together at right angles" ("The Passion Considered as an Uphill Bicycle Race," in *Selected Works*, p. 122).

21. Michel Arrivé in particular has insisted on the theory of the sign in Jarry; see his introduction in *Oeuvres complètes*, vol. 1, pp. ix–xxvi.

22. See Henri Béhar, *Les cultures de Jarry* (Paris: PUF, 1988), especially chapter 1 on "Celtic culture." Ubu provides only a limited idea of Jarry's style: a style with a sumptuous flavor, such as one hears, at the beginning of *César-Antechrist*, in the three Christs and the four Golden birds.

23. See the article contained in *La chandelle verte* (The green candle), "Ceux pour qui il n'y eut point de Babel" ("Those for whom there was no Babel whatsoever), in *Oeuvres complètes*, vol. 2, pp. 441–43. Jarry is reviewing a book by Victor Fournié, from which he extracts this principle: "the same sound or the same syllable always has the same meaning in all languages." But Jarry, for his part, does not exactly adopt this principle; instead, like Heidegger, he works with two languages, one dead and the other living, a language of Being and a language of beings, which are not really distinct, but nonetheless are eminently different from each other.

24. See the analyses of Henri Meschonnic, *Le langage Heidegger* (Paris: PUF, 1990).

25. Jarry, *Almanach illustré du Père Ubu* (Illustrated Almanac of Father Ubu, 1901), in *Oeuvres complètes*, vol. 1, p. 604.

26. Heidegger frequently cites this phrase from a poem by Stephan George in his essay "Words," in *On the Way to Language*, trans. Peter D. Hertz (New York: Harper & Row, 1971).

12. The Mystery of Ariadne according to Nietzsche

1. [Friedrich Nietzsche, *Dithyrambs of Dionysus*, trans. R. J. Hollingdale (Redding Ridge, Conn.: Black Swan, 1984), p. 59, translation modified.—Trans.]

2. [The original version of this essay was published in *Etudes Nietzschéennes* (1963), pp. 12–15, under the title "Mystère d'Ariane." A revised version, from which the present essay was adapted, appeared in *Magazine littéraire* 298 (April 1992): 21–24—Trans.]

3. Friedrich Nietzsche, *Ecce Homo*, trans. Walter Kaufmann (New York: Random House, 1969), "Why I Write Such Good Books," "Thus Spoke Zarathustra," § 8, p. 308.

4. [In *Nietzsche and Philosophy*, trans. Hugh Tomlinson (New York: Columbia University Press, 1983), Deleuze suggests that the French term *qui* be rendered in English as "which one" in order to avoid any "personalist" references (see p. xi and p. 207, note

3). We have chosen to render *qui* as "who" in this instance so as to echo the question "Who besides me . . . ?"—Trans.]

5. Friedrich Nietzsche, *Thus Spoke Zarathustra*, trans. Walter Kaufmann, in *The Portable Nietzsche* (New York: Viking, 1954), third part, "On the Spirit of Gravity," pp. 303–7. And *Beyond Good and Evil*, trans. Walter Kaufmann (New York: Random House, 1966), § 213, p. 139: "'Thinking' and taking a matter 'seriously,' considering it 'grave'—for them all this belongs together: that is the only way they have 'experienced' it."

6. Nietzsche, *Zarathustra*, second part, "On Those Who Are Sublime," pp. 229–30.

7. Ibid., p. 230.

8. Herman Melville, *The Confidence-Man*, ed. Stephen Matterson (London: Penguin Classics, 1990).

9. Friedrich Nietzsche, *Samtliche Werke. Kritische Studienausgabe*, ed. Giorgio Colli and Mazzino Montinari (Berlin: Walter de Gruyter, 1980), vol. 13, 23[3], p. 602.

10. Henri Jeanmaire, *Dionysos, histoire du culte de Bacchus* (Paris: Payot, 1970), p. 223.

11. Nietzsche, *Zarathustra*, second part, "On Those Who Are Sublime," p. 231, translation modified.

12. Nietzsche, fragment of a preface for *Human, All Too Human*. See also Ariadne's intervention in *Kritiche Studienausgabe*, vol. 11, p. 579, B7[4], June–July 1885.

13. Nietzsche, *Zarathustra*, second part, "The Night Song," pp. 217–19.

14. Nietzsche, *Dithyrambs of Dionysus*, "Fame and Eternity," p. 67, translation modified.

15. Nietzsche, *Dithyrambs of Dionysus*, "Ariadne's Complaint," p. 57, translation modified.

16. Friedrich Nietzsche, *The Case of Wagner*, trans. Walter Kaufmann (New York: Vintage, 1967).

17. See Marcel Detienne, *Dionysus at Large*, trans. Arthur Goldhammer (Cambridge, Mass.: Harvard University Press, 1989), pp. 51–52.

18. Concerning the eternal return, Zarathustra asks his own animals: "Have you already made a hurdy-gurdy song of this?" Nietzsche, *Zarathustra*, third part, "The Convalescent," p. 330.

19. See the different stanzas of "The Seven Seals" in Nietzsche, *Zarathustra*, pp. 340–43.

20. On the question of "sanctuary," that is, of God's territory, see Jeanmaire, *Dionysos*, p. 193 ("One encounters him everywhere, yet he is nowhere at home. . . . He insinuates himself more than he imposes himself").

21. Nietzsche, *Zarathustra*, fourth part, "The Welcome," p. 395.

13. He Stuttered

1. [Herman Melville, "Billy Budd, Sailor," in *Billy Budd, Sailor and Other Stories*, ed. Harold Beaver (London: Penguin Classics, 1967), pp. 317–409.—Trans.]

2. [*Quand dire, c'est faire*. This is an allusion to the title of the French translation of J. L. Austin's *How to Do Things with Words* (New York: Oxford University Press, 1962): *Quand dire c'est faire*, trans. Oswald Ducrot (Paris: Hermann, 1972.—Trans.]

3. Osip Mandelstam, *The Noise of Time: The Prose of Osip Mandelstam*, trans. Clarence Brown (San Francisco: North Point, 1986), pp. 109–10, translation modified.

4. See Gustave Guillaume, *Foundations for a Science of Language*, trans. W. Hirtle and J. Hewson (Philadelphia: Benjamins, 1984). It is not only articles in general, or verbs

in general, that have dynamisms as zones of variation, but also each verb, and each particular substantive.

5. Osip Mandelstam, *Entretien sur Dante* (Geneva: Dogana, 1989), p. 8.

6. Pierre Blanchaud is one of the rare translators of Kleist who has been able to raise this question of style; see Heinrich von Kleist, *Le duel* (Paris: Press-Pocket, 1985). This problem can be extended to every translation of a great writer: it is obvious that translation is a betrayal if it takes as its model the norms of equilibrium of the standard language into which it is translated.

7. These remarks refer to Gherasim Luca's famous poem "Passionnément," in *Le chant de la carpe* (Paris: J. Corti, 1986).

8. Samuel Beckett, "Comment dire," in *Poèmes* (Paris: Minuit, 1978); translated by Beckett as "What Is the Word," in *As the Story Was Told* (London: Calder, 1990), p. 132.

9. On this procedure used in *Impressions of Africa*, see Michel Foucault, *Death and the Labyrinth: The World of Raymond Roussel* (New York: Doubleday, 1986), pp. 129–30.

10. On the problem of style, its relation with language and its two aspects, see Giorgio Passerone, *La ligna astratta: Pragmatico dello stile* (Milan: Angelo Guerini, 1991).

11. Andrei Biely, *Carnets d'un toqué* (Geneva: L'Age d'Homme, 1991), p. 50. And Andrei Biely, *Kotik Letaiev,* trans. A.-M. Tatsis-Botton (from the Russian) (Geneva: L'Age d'Homme, 1973). For both these books, see the commentaries of Georges Nivat, especially on language and the procedure of "variation on a semantic root"; cf. *Kotik Letaiev,* p. 284.

12. Lyotard calls "childhood" this movement that sweeps away language and traces an always-repressed limit of language: "Infatia, what does not speak to itself. A childhood is not a period of life and does not pass on. It haunts discourse. . . . What does not allow itself to be written, in writing, perhaps calls forth a reader who no longer knows how to read, or not yet . . ." See Jean-François Lyotard, *Lectures d'enfance* (Paris: Galilée, 1991), p. 9.

14. The Shame and the Glory: T. E. Lawrence

1. T. E. Lawrence, *Seven Pillars of Wisdom: A Triumph* (Garden City, N.Y.: Doubleday, Doran 1935), book IV, chapter 54, p. 308. On the God of the Arabs, Colorless, Unformed, Untouchable, embracing everything, see *Introduction,* chapter 3.

2. Book III, chapter 38, pp. 221–22.

3. On the haze or "mirage," see book I, chapter 8, p. 65. A beautiful description can be found in book IX, chapter 104. On the revolt as gas or vapor, see book III, chapter 33.

4. See *Introduction,* chapter 2.

5. Book V, chapter 62, p. 350.

6. Book IV, chapter 40, p. 236.

7. Book V, chapters 62 and 67.

8. Book IV, chapter 39, p. 230; book IV, chapter 41, p. 238; book V, chapter 57, p. 323; book IX, chapter 99, p. 546.

9. Herman Melville, "Benito Cereno," in *Billy Budd, Sailor and Other Stories,* ed. Harold Beaver (London: Penguin Classics, 1967), pp. 221–22.

10. Marcel Proust, *Remembrance of Things Past,* trans. C. Scott Moncrieff and Terence Kilmartin (New York: Random House, 1981), vol. 2, *Cities of the Plain,* part two, chapter 2, p. 976.

11. On the two possible behaviors of the English in relation to the Arabs, see book V, chapter 61, pp. 346–47; and *Introduction,* chapter 1.

12. Note how Jean Genet describes this tendency in *Prisoner of Love,* trans. Barbara Bray (Hanover, N.H., and London: Wesleyan University Press, University Press of New England, 1992), pp. 261–63. There are numerous resemblances between Genet and Lawrence, and it is still a subjective disposition that Genet lays claim to when he finds himself in the desert among the Palestinians, ready for another Revolt. See Félix Guattari's commentary, "Genet retrouvé," in *Cartographies schizoanalytiques* (Paris: Galileé, 1989), pp. 272–75.

13. *Introduction:* "diurnal dreamers, dangerous men . . ." On the subjective characters of his perception, see book I, chapter 15; book II, chapter 21; book IV, chapter 48.

14. See book X, chapters 119, 120, 121 (the deposition of the pseudogovernment of the nephew of Abd-el-Kader).

15. Book IX, chapter 99, p. 549: "At last accident, with perverted humor, in casting me as a man of action had given me a place in the Arab Revolt, a theme ready and epic to a direct eye and hand, thus offering me an outlet in literature . . ."

16. Book VI, chapters 80 and 81. And *Introduction,* 1.

17. Book IX, chapter 99.

18. See E. M. Forster, letter to T. E. Lawrence, mid-February 1924, in *Letters to T. E. Lawrence* (London: Jonathan Cape, 1962). Forster notes that movement has never been rendered with so little mobility, through a succession of immobile points.

19. Book VI, chapter 7, p. 412.

20. Book IX, chapter 103, p. 563: "I was very conscious of the bundled powers and entities within me; it was their character which hid." And also on the spiritual beast, will or desire. Orson Welles insisted on the particular use of the word *character* in English; see André Bazin, *Orson Welles* (Paris: Cerf, 1972), pp. 178–80: in the Nietzschean sense, a will to power that unites diverse forces.

21. Book VII, chapter 91, p. 503 (and passim).

22. Book IX, chapter 99. (And see book V, chapter 57, where Aouda has all the more charm when he secretly negotiates with the Turks "through compassion").

23. Book V, chapter 59. And book X, chapter 118, p. 638: "the essence of the desert was the lonely moving individual."

24. Book X, chapter 118.

25. [This is the concluding line of Franz Kafka, *The Trial,* trans. Willa and Edwin Muir (New York: Knopf, 1948), p. 288.—Trans.]

26. Book IX, chapter 100, p. 551.

27. Book III, chapter 32.

28. Book III, chapter 32.

29. [T. E. Lawrence, *The Mint: Notes Made in the R. A. F. Depot between August and December 1922, and at Cadet College in 1926 by 352087 A/C Ross. Regrouped and copied in 1927 and 1928 at Aircraft Depot, Karachi* (Garden City, N.Y.: Doran, 1936).—Trans.]

30. See book IX, chapter 103. Lawrence complains that he has not found a master capable of subjecting him, even Allenby.

31. Book VII, chapter 83, p. 466: "These lads took pleasure in subordination; in degrading the body: so as to throw into greater relief their freedom in equality of mind. . . . They had a gladness of abasement, a freedom of consent to yield to their master the last service and degree of their flesh and blood, because their spirits were equal to his and the contract voluntary." Forced servitude is, on the contrary, a degradation of the spirit.

32. *Introduction,* chapter 3, p. 43.

33. Book VII, chapter 83, p. 468: "The conception of antithetical mind and matter,

which was basic in the Arab self-surrender, helped me not at all. I achieved surrender (as far as I did achieve it) by the very opposite road . . ."

34. Book VII, chapter 83, p. 468.

35. Book VI, chapter 80; book X, chapter 121.

36. Book IX, chapter 103, p. 564: "I liked the things underneath me and took my pleasures and adventures downward. There seemed a certainty in degradation, a final safety. Man could rise to any height, but there was an animal level beneath which he could not fall."

37. Book III, chapter 33, p. 188.

38. See William James, *Principles of Psychology* (London: Macmillan, 1890).

39. There are thus at least three "parts," as Lawrence says in part VI, chapter 81, p. 452: the one that goes on riding with the body or flesh; another "hovering to the right bent down curiously"; and "a third garrulous one talked and wondered, critical of the body's self-inflicted labor."

40. Book VI, chapter 78, p. 431.

41. *Introduction,* chapter 1, p. 29.

42. See Alain Milianti, "Le fils de la honte: Sur l'engagement politique de Genet" (The son of shame: On Genet's political engagement), in *Revue d'études palestiniennes* 42 (1992); in this text, everything said of Genet can be applied equally to Lawrence.

15. To Have Done with Judgment

1. See Elias Canetti, *Kafka's Other Trial: The Letters to Felice,* trans. Christopher Middleton (New York: Schocken, 1974), p. 68, translation modified.

2. Friedrich Nietzsche, *On the Genealogy of Morals,* trans. Walter Kaufmann and R. J. Hollingdale (New York: Random House, 1967), essay 2, § 20, p. 90.

3. Friedrich Nietzsche, *The Antichrist,* trans. Walter Kaufmann, in *The Portable Nietzsche* (New York: Viking Penguin, 1982), § 42, p. 618.

4. D. H. Lawrence, *Apocalypse,* ed. Mara Kalnins (New York: Viking, 1982), chapter 6, p. 27.

5. Franz Kafka, *The Trial,* trans. Willa and Edwin Muir (New York: Schocken, 1956), Titorelli's explanations.

6. Friedrich Nietzsche, *Genealogy of Morals,* essay 2. This extremely important text can be evaluated only in relation to later ethnographic texts, notably those on the potlatch. Despite a limitation in material, it constitutes a prodigious advance.

7. See Louis Gernet, *Anthropologie de la Grèce antique* (Paris: Maspero, 1976), pp. 215–17, 241–42 (the oath "only functions between single parties. . . . It would be anachronistic to say that it takes the place of judgment: given its original nature, it excludes the notion of judgment), and 269–70.

8. See Ismaël Kadaré, *Eschyle ou l'éternal perdant* (Paris: Fayard, 1984), chapter 4.

9. Antonin Artaud, *To Have Done with the Judgment of God* (1947), in *Antonin Artaud: Selected Writings,* ed. Susan Sontag, trans. Helen Weaver (New York: Farrar, Straus & Giroux, 1976), "The Abolition of the Cross," p. 559. For a comparison of the system of cruelty in Artaud and Nietzsche, see Camille Dumoulié, *Nietzsche et Artaud* (Paris: PUF, 1992).

10. Friedrich Nietzsche, *The Birth of Tragedy,* trans. Walter Kaufmann (New York: Random House, 1967), §§ 1 and 2, pp. 33-41.

11. See Antonin Artaud, *Oeuvres complètes* (Paris: Gallimard, 1978), vol. 3, "A propos du cinéma," pp. 61–87 (critique of the dream from the viewpoint of cinema and the functioning of thought). [An extract from this text is included in *Selected Writings,* pp. 181–82.—Trans.]

12. D. H. Lawrence, *The Plumed Serpent* (London: Cambridge University Press, 1987), chapter 22.

13. It is Blanchot who suggests that sleep is not appropriate to the night, but only insomnia; see Maurice Blanchot, *The Space of Literature*, trans. Ann Smock (Lincoln: University of Nebraska Press, 1982), pp. 266–67. René Char is not being contradictory when he invokes the rights of sleep beyond the dream, since he is concerned with a state of sleep in which one is not asleep, and that produces a lightning flash; see Paul Veyne, "René Char et l'expérience de l'extase," in *Nouvelle revue française* (November 1985).

14. Franz Kafka, "Wedding Preparations in the Country," in *Franz Kafka: The Complete Stories*, ed. Nahum N. Glatzer (New York: Schocken, 1971), pp. 55–56. See also *The Diaries of Franz Kafka: 1910–1913*, ed. Max Brod (New York: Schocken Books, 1948), entry for July 21, 1913, p. 291: "I cannot sleep. Only dreams, no sleep."

15. Antonin Artaud, *To Have Done with the Judgment of God*, in *Selected Writings*, pp. 555–71.

16. D. H. Lawrence, *Fantasia of the Unconscious* (New York: Viking, 1960).

17. D. H. Lawrence, *Aaron's Rod* (Cambridge: Cambridge University Press, 1988), p. 13.

18. Kafka, *The Trial*, p. 222, translation modified.

19. See Kafka's allusions in *Letters to Milena*, ed. Willi Haas, trans. Tania and James Stern (New York: Schocken, 1953), pp. 218–19.

20. On the combat of principles, the Will, the masculine and the feminine, see Artaud, *A Voyage to the Land of the Tarahumara* (1936), "The Peyote Dance," in *Selected Writings*, pp. 382–91; and *Heliogabalus; or, The Anarchist Crowned*, "The War of Principles," "Anarchy," in *Oeuvres complètes*, vol. 7, pp. 11–137 (the combat "of the ONE that divides while remaining ONE. Of the man who becomes woman and remains man in perpetuity"). [A translation of the second half of "Anarchy" is included in *Selected Writings*, pp. 317–34.—Trans.]

21. D. H. Lawrence, passim and, notably, "We Need Each Other," in *Phoenix: The Posthumous Papers of D. H. Lawrence*, ed. Edward D. McDonald (New York: Viking, 1968), pp. 188–95.

22. See Artaud, *Le Mexique et la civilization*, in *Oeuvres complètes*, vol. 8 (Paris: Gallimard, 1978): the invocation of Heraclitus, and the allusion to Lawrence.

23. See Artaud, the beginning of *To Have Done with the Judgment of God*; and Lawrence, the beginning of *Etruscan Places* (New York: Viking, 1933).

24. D. H. Lawrence, *Complete Poems*, ed. Vivian de Sola Pinto and Warren Roberts (New York: Heinemann, 1964), vol. 1, pp. 352–54: the very beautiful poem "Baby Tortoise."

25. Franz Kafka, cited by Canetti in *Kafka's Other Trial*, p. 94: "Two possibilities: making oneself infinitely small or being so. The second is perfection, that is to say, in activity, the first is beginning, that is to say, action." It was Dickens who turned miniaturization into a literary procedure (the crippled little girl); Kafka takes up the procedure, both in *The Trial* where the two detectives are beaten in the closet like small children, and in *The Castle* where the adults bathe in the tub and splash the children.

26. D. H. Lawrence, *Studies in Classic American Literature* (New York: Viking, 1953), pp. 189–90.

16. Plato, the Greeks

1. [This essay was first published in *Nos Grecs et leur modernité*, ed. Barbara Cassian (Paris: Seuil, 1992), pp. 249–50, under the title "Remarques"; it appears here in revised form.—Trans.]

17. Spinoza and the Three "Ethics"

1. [Anton Chekhov, "The Wedding," in *Complete Plays,* trans. Julius West (London: Duckworth, 1915), p. 61, translation modified.—Trans.]

2. Yvonne Toros, in *Spinoza et l'éspace projectif* (thesis, University of Paris-VIII, St.-Denis), makes use of various arguments to show that the geometry that inspires Spinoza is not that of Descartes or even Hobbes, but a projective optical geometry closer to that of Desargues. These arguments seem decisive, and entail, as we shall see, a new comprehension of Spinozism. In an earlier work, *Éspace et transformation: Spinoza* (Paris-I), Toros compared Spinoza with Vermeer, and sketched out a projective theory of color in accordance with the *Treatise on the Rainbow.*

3. Johann Wolfgang von Goethe, *Goethe's Color Theory,* ed. Rupprecht Matthaei, trans. Herb Aach (New York: Van Norstrand Reinhold, 1971), §494. And on the tendency of each color to reconstitute the whole, see §§ 803–15.

4. See Giuseppe Ungaretti, *Vermeer,* trans. Phillipe Jaccottet (Paris: Echoppe, 1990) unpaginated: "color that he sees as a color in itself, as light, and in which he also sees—and isolates when he sees it—the shadow . . ." See also Gilles Aillaud's theater piece *Vermeer and Spinoza* (Paris: Bourgois, 1987).

5. Aeschylus, *Agamemnon,* ll. 495–500.

6. [*Les sombres précurseurs.* The French phrase *signes précurseurs* ("precursory signs") usually refers to the ominous meteorological signs that portend a coming storm. Deleuze develops the notion of "the dark precursor" as a philosophical concept in *Difference and Repetition,* trans. Paul Patton (New York: Columbia University Press, 1994), pp. 119 ff.—Trans.]

7. See Robert Sasso, "Discours et non-discours de l'Ethique," in *Revue de synthèse* 89 (January 1978).

8. Science confronts this problem of geometrical figures and figures of light. (Thus Bergson can say, in chapter 5 of *Duration and Simultaneity* [trans. Leon Jacobson (Indianapolis: Bobbs-Merrill, 1965)], that the theory of Relativity reverses the traditional subordination of figures of light to solid, geometrical figures.) In art, the painter Delaunay opposes figures of light to the geometrical figures of cubism as well as abstract art.

9. Yvonne Toros, in chapter 6 of *Spinoza et l'éspace projectif,* marks in precise terms two aspects or two principles of Desargues's geometry: the first, homology, concerns propositions; the second, which will be named "duality," concerns the correspondence of the line with the point, and of the point with the plane. This is a new understanding of parallelism, since it is established between a point in thought (the idea of God) and an infinite development [*déroulement*] in extension.

10. Jules Lagneau, *Célèbres leçons et fragments,* 2d ed., revised and expanded (Paris: PUF, 1964) pp. 67–68 (the "rapidity of thought," to which one finds an equivalent only in music, and which rests less on the absolute than on the relative).

11. Aristotle, *Prior Analytics,* II, 27: the enthymeme is a syllogism of which one or the other premise is assumed, hidden, suppressed, or elided. Leibniz takes up the question in *New Essays,* I, chapter 1, §4 and §19, and shows that the hiatus is made not only in the exposition, but in our thought itself, and that "the strength of the conclusion consists in part in what one suppresses."

12. See the texts by Galois in André Dalmas, *Evariste Galois* (Paris: Fasquelle, 1956), p. 121, as well as p. 112 ("one must constantly indicate the progress of the calculations and foresee the results without ever being able to carry them out . . .") and p. 132 ("in these two memoirs, and especially in the second, one often finds the formula, *I don't know* . . ."). There thus exists a style, even in mathematics, that would be defined by modes of hiatus, elision, and contraction in thought as such. In this regard, some invalu-

able comments can be found in Gilles-Gaston Granger, *Essai d'une philosophie du style,* 2d ed. (Paris: Odile Jacob, 1988), though the author has a completely different conception of style in mathematics (pp. 20–21).

13. Spinoza, *Ethics,* in *The Collected Works of Spinoza,* ed. and trans. Edwin Curley (Princeton, N.J.: Princeton University Press, 1985), p. 601.

18. The Exhausted

1. [This essay was originally published as a postface to Samuel Beckett, *Quad et autres pièces pour la télévision,* trans. Edith Fournier (Paris: Minuit, 1992). The translation, by Anthony Uhlmann, first appeared in *Sub-stance* 78 (1995), pp. 3–28, and is here published in revised form.—Trans.]

2. Samuel Beckett, *Texts for Nothing,* in *Collected Shorter Prose 1945–1980* (London: Calder, 1984), p. 72.

3. Samuel Beckett, *The Unnamable* (New York: Grove, 1958), p. 70.

4. [Samuel Beckett, *For to End Yet Again,* in *Collected Shorter Prose: 1945–1980,* pp. 179–182.—Trans.]

5. Samuel Beckett, *I Gave Up Before Birth,* in *Collected Shorter Prose: 1945–1980,* pp. 197–98.

6. See Brice Parain, *Sur la dialectique* (Paris: Gallimard, 1953): language "does not say what is, it says what might be. . . . You say there is thunder, and in the country someone answers you: 'it's possible, that might be . . .' When I say that it is daytime, it is not at all because it is daytime . . . [but] because I have an intention to realize, one which is particular to me, and which makes use of the day only as an occasion, a pretext, or an argument" (pp. 61, 130).

7. [See Samuel Beckett, *Molloy* (New York: Grove, 1955), pp. 125, 241.—Trans.]

8. Beckett, *Texts for Nothing,* in *Collected Shorter Prose,* p. 74.

9. Samuel Beckett, *Watt* (London: Picador, 1988), p. 71.

10. Samuel Beckett, *Murphy* (London: Picador, 1973), p. 57.

11. Beckett, *Watt,* pp. 200–201, 204–6. François Martel has made a very rigorous study of the combinatorial science, of the series and disjunctions in *Watt:* "Jeux formels dans Watt," *Poétique* 10 (1972). See Samuel Beckett, *Malone Dies* (New York: Grove, 1956), p. 4: "Everything divides into itself."

12. [Friedrich Nietzsche, *Thus Spoke Zarathustra,* fourth part, section 4, "The Leech," in *The Portable Nietzsche,* ed. and trans. Walter Kaufmann (New York: Viking, 1954), p. 362.—Trans.]

13. Maurice Blanchot, *Le livre à venir* (Paris: Gallimard, 1959), p. 211. The exacerbation of the meaning of the possible is a constant theme in Musil's *The Man without Qualities.*

14. Beckett, *Enough,* in *Collected Shorter Prose,* p. 140.

15. See Yeats's poem "The Tower," which inspired Beckett's piece for television, . . . *but the clouds . . . ,* in *Selected Poems and Two Plays of William Butler Yeats,* ed. M. L. Rosenthal (New York: Collier, 1966), pp. 101–2.

16. [Samuel Beckett, *Nacht und Träume,* in *Complete Dramatic Works* (London: Faber, 1986), p. 465.—Trans.]

17. [Beckett, *Malone Dies,* p. 70.—Trans.]

18. Samuel Beckett, "Worstward Ho," in *Nohow On* (London: Calder, 1989), p. 103; *Stirrings Still,* in *As the Story Was Told* (London: Calder, 1990), pp. 113, 118; *For to End Yet Again,* in *Collected Shorter Prose,* p. 179; *Afar a Bird,* in *Collected Shorter Prose,* p. 195.

19. [See Samuel Beckett, *Rockaby*, in *Complete Dramatic Works*, pp. 431–42.—Trans.]

20. Beckett, *The Unnamable*, p. 269.

21. Beckett, *Molloy*, p. 59.

22. Beckett, *Ill Seen, Ill Said*, in *Nohow On*, p. 93.

23. Beckett, *The Unnamable*, p. 28. Cf. Edith Fournier, in *Samuel Beckett, Revue d'esthétique* (Paris: Privat, 1986), p. 24: "Beckett breaks the necessary bone, neither the sentence nor the word, but their incoming tide; his greatness lies in having known how to dry it up."

24. It is here that the great "theory" of *The Unnamable* seems to become circular. Whence the idea that the voices of the protagonists perhaps refer to "masters" who are different from the protagonists themselves.

25. [Beckett, *The Unnamable*, p. 82.—Trans.]

26. [See Beckett, *The Unnamable*, p. 3: "What am I to do, what shall I do, what should I do, in my situation, how proceed? By aporia pure and simple? Or by affirmations and negations invalidated as uttered, or sooner or later?"—Trans.]

27. Beckett, *The Unnamable*, p. 84.

28. [Beckett, *The Unnamable*, p. 114.—Trans.]

29. Samuel Beckett, *How It Is* (New York: Grove, 1964), pp. 128–29, and *Company*, in *Nohow On*, pp. 5–52.

30. Beckett, *The Unnamable*, p. 115.

31. Beckett, *Worstward Ho*, p. 124. And already in a letter of 1937, written in German (in *Disjecta: Miscellaneous Writings and a Dramatic Fragment*, ed. Ruby Cohen [London: Calder, 1984], p. 172), Beckett had written: "As we cannot eliminate language all at once, we should at least leave nothing undone that might contribute to its falling into disrepute. To bore one hole after another in it, until what lurks behind it—be it something or nothing—begins to seep through." (*Worstward Ho*, on the contrary, would say: "No ooze then.")

32. Often the image does not fully succeed in disengaging itself from a memory-image, notably in *Company*. And sometimes the voice is animated by a perverse desire to impose a particularly cruel memory: for example, in the television piece *Eh Joe*.

33. [See *Imagination Dead Imagine* and *All Strange Away*, both in *Collected Shorter Prose*.—Trans.]

34. Beckett, *How It Is*, p. 97 (and concerning a little blue and a little white, and the "life above," pp. 70, 72, 75).

35. [Samuel Beckett, *The Image*, in *As the Story Was Told*, p. 40 (and *How It Is*, p. 27: "a fine image fine I mean in movement and colour").—Trans.]

36. [See Samuel Beckett, *Happy Days/Oh les beaux jours* (London: Faber, 1978), esp. pp. 52–53 and 82–83. In *Happy Days*, Winnie possesses a small music box that "plays the Waltz Duet 'I love you so' from The Merry Widow" (pp. 52–53); in *Oh les beaux jours*, the lyrics of "I Love You So" are replaced by those of the French song "L'heure exquise," "The Exquisite Hour" (pp. 82–83). This is the song Winnie refers to throughout the play, carefully awaiting the right time to sing it, which she does at the very end.—Trans.]

37. [Beckett, *Watt*, pp. 135–37.—Trans.]

38. Samuel Beckett, "Le monde et le pantalon," in *Disjecta*, p. 118 (and on the two types of image in Bram and Geer van Velde, the congealed and the shuddering image).

39. Beckett, *Ping*, in *Collected Shorter Prose*, p. 150. Ping activates a murmur or a silence, usually accompanied by an image.

40. Cf. the voice in the television piece *Ghost Trio*, in *Complete Dramatic Works*,

pp. 405–14. In *Catastrophe,* pp. 455–61, the voice of the Assistant and that of the Director respond to one another so as to describe the image to be made and to make it.

41. In *Words and Music* (piece for radio, in *Complete Dramatic Works*) we witness the ill will of Words, too attached to the rehashing of personal memory, who refuses to follow Music.

42. The works for television consist of *Ghost Trio,* 1975, . . . *but the clouds* . . . , 1976, *Nacht und Träume,* 1982, *Quad,* 1982, as well as *Eh Joe,* 1965, which are all contained in *Complete Dramatic Works.* We will see below why *Eh Joe* is considered separately from the others.

43. [See *The Lost Ones,* in *Collected Shorter Prose,* p. 159.—Trans.]

44. Beckett, *For to End Yet Again,* in *Collected Shorter Prose,* p. 181.

45. Already with animals, ritornellos are made up not only of cries and chants, but also of colors, postures, and movements, as can be seen in the marking of territories and mating displays. This is also true of human ritornellos. Félix Guattari has studied the role of the ritornello in the work of Proust, in "Les ritournelles du temps perdu," in *L'inconscient machinique* (Paris: Encres, 1979), for example, the combination of Vinteuil's little phrase with colours, postures, and movements.

46. [In the original French version of *Bing,* Beckett makes use of the words *bing* and *hop,* both of which are rendered as *ping* in his English translation. Since Deleuze here maintains the French distinction, I have translated *hop* as *hup.* The French term is an interjection used to get someone to leap into action, as in "Allez, hop!" or "Hop là!"—Trans.]

47. Beckett, *Watt,* p. 28.

48. [Beckett, *Ping,* in *Collected Shorter Prose,* 150.—Trans.]

49. Beckett, *Nouvelles et textes pour rien* (Paris: Minuit, 1991), p. 109 [Beckett's English rendition of this phrase reads, "enough, enough . . . visions," in *The End,* in *Collected Shorter Prose,* p. 68.—Trans.]; *How It Is,* p. 106.

50. Beckett, *How It Is,* p. 106; cf. pp. 103–6.

51. Beckett, "La peinture des van Velde ou le Monde et le Pantalon," in *Disjecta,* p. 123.

52. Beckett, *Murphy,* pp. 141–42. [The French term *la berceuse* means both "rocking chair" and "lullaby," and can also refer to the female protagonist rocking herself in the chair.—Trans.]

53. [Beckett, *Happy Days/Oh les beaux jours,* pp. 40–41; the original English version reads, "the earth is very tight today." The second reference is to Jean-Luc Godard's famous formula, "pas une image juste, juste une image" ("not a correct image, just an image").—Trans.]

54. Beckett, *For to End Yet Again,* p. 182; and *Ping,* p. 151.

55. In novels like *Watt,* the series might already put movements into play, but always in relation to objects or behaviors.

56. [Beckett, *Quad,* in *Complete Dramatic Works,* pp. 451–52.—Trans.]

57. *Molloy* and *The Unnamable* both include, in their first pages, meditations on the encounter of two bodies.

58. Beckett, *Closed Space,* in *Collected Shorter Prose,* pp. 199–200.

59. See *Dream of Fair to Middling Women* (1932; New York: Arcade, 1993), and the letter of 1937 to Axel Kaun. Beckett emphasizes, in Beethoven, "a punctuation of dehiscence, flottements, the coherence gone to pieces . . ." (*Disjecta,* p. 49). André Bernold has commented on these texts by Beckett on Beethoven in a very beautiful article, "Cupio dissolvi, note sur Beckett musicien," in *Détail* 3/4 (Royaumont: Atelier de la Fondation Royaumont, 1991). Musicologists analyzing the second movement of Beethoven's trio

emphasize the notation in tremolo for the piano, which is followed by a finale "that soars straight towards the wrong key and stays there . . ." (Anthony Burton).

60. Robert Bresson, *Notes on Cinematography,* trans. Jonathan Griffen (New York: Urizen, 1977), p. 46, translation modified.

61. On Snow's film, see P. Adams Sitney, "Structural Film," in *Visionary Film: The American Avant-Garde* (New York: Oxford University Press, 1979), p. 375. Before Snow, Beckett had undertaken an analogous operation, but in purely radiophonic conditions: *Embers.* The protagonist, who we hear walking on pebbles close to the sea, evokes sound-memories that respond to his call. But soon they stop responding, the potentiality of the sonorous space being exhausted, and the sound of the sea engulfs everything.

62. See *Disjecta,* letter to Axel Krun, p. 172. On punctuation, the musical connection of silences, and the conversion of music into silence, see André Bernold, pp. 26, 28.

63. [Beckett, *Ghost Trio,* p. 410.—Trans.]

64. [Beckett, *Eh Joe,* in *Complete Dramatic Works.*—Trans.

65. The visual voice-image scission can have opposite consequences: in Beckett, there is a depotentialization of space, while in the Straubs or Marguerite Duras, on the contrary, there is a potentialization of matter. A voice is raised to speak of what has happened in the empty space, which is currently being shown. Voices are raised to speak of an ancient ball that took place in the same hall as the silent ball being put on today. The voice is raised to evoke what is buried in the earth as a still-active potential.

66. [Beckett, *Ghost Trio,* p. 410.—Trans.]

67. Beckett, *The Unnamable,* p. 115.

68. Beckett, *Ghost Trio,* p. 413.

69. "Testy delirium" appears in Yeats's poem "The Tower," as cited in . . . *but the clouds . . .*

70. Jim Lewis, Beckett's cameraman for the pieces for television produced in Stuttgart, speaks of the technical problems corresponding to these three cases in "Beckett et la camera," in *Revue d'esthéthique,* pp. 371 ff. Notably for *Eh Joe,* Beckett wanted the corners of the lips to enter into the image a quarter of a centimeter, and not half a centimeter.

71. This is from the great sixth chapter of *Murphy,* "Amor intellectualis quo Murphy se ipsum amat," p. 63.

72. [Beckett, *. . . but the clouds . . . ,* p. 417.—Trans.]

73. [Beckett, *Murphy,* p. 64.—Trans.]

74. [Beckett, *Murphy,* p. 65.—Trans.]

75. Beckett, *Happy Days/Oh les beaux jours,* pp. 74–75. This is a phrase borrowed from Yeats's play *At the Hawk's Well.* Similar phrases can be found in Klossowski: "instead of naming the spirit to Roberte, the reverse took place . . . Suddenly Roberte becomes the object of a pure spirit . . ." Pierre Klossowski, *Roberte ce soir,* trans. Austryn Wainhouse (New York: Grove, 1969), p. 24, translation modified. Klossowski, for his part, links together invocation and revocation, in relation to voices and breaths.

76. [Beckett, *. . . but the clouds . . . ,* p. 420.—Trans.]

77. The problem of the dissipation of the image, or the Figure, appears in very similar terms in Francis Bacon's paintings.

78. [Beckett, *Happy Days,* pp. 78–79.—Trans.]

79. Beckett, *Murphy,* p. 66.

80. [See Beckett, *Worstward Ho.*—Trans.]

81. See Jacqueline Genet, "Yeats et le Nô"; she draws the connections with Beckett in her book *William Butler Yeats* (Paris: L'Herne, 1981), pp. 336–53. On the possible relationships between Beckett and Japanese No, see Takahashi Yasunari, "Qu'est-ce qui arrive? Some Structural Comparisons of Beckett's Plays and Nô" in *Samuel Beckett: Hu-*

manistic Perspectives, ed. M. Beja, S. E. Gontarski, and P. Astier (Columbus: Ohio State University Press, 1983), pp. 99–106); and Kishi Tetsuo, "Des voix de nulle part: Langage et espace dans le theatre de Beckett et le No," in *Cahiers Renaud-Barrault* (Paris: Numero 102, 1981), pp. 85–92.

82. It is in *Film* that the camera acquires the maximum of antagonistic movement; but cinema has greater need of "trickery" than does television (cf. the technical problem of *Film,* in *Complete Dramatic Works,* p. 331), and control of the image here is much more difficult.

83. [Beckett, *Worstward Ho,* p. 103.—Trans.]

84. Beckett, *Worstward Ho,* p. 128.

85. Maurice Blanchot, *The Space of Literature,* trans. Ann Smock (Lincoln: University of Nebraska Press, 1982), p. 266: "night, the essence of night, does not let us sleep."

86. See Franz Kafka, "Wedding Preparations in the Country," trans. Ernst Kaiser and Eithne Wilkins, in *Wedding Preparations in the Country and Other Stories* (Harmondsworth: Penguin, 1978), p. 10. "I don't even need to go to the country myself, it isn't necessary. I'll send my clothed body. . . . For I myself am meanwhile lying in my bed, smoothly covered over with the yellow-brown blanket, exposed to the breeze that is wafted through that seldom-aired room." See also Bernard Groethuysen, "A propos de Kafka," in *Obliques* 3 (Paris, n.d.), special issue on Kafka, pp. 1, 88: "They remained awake during their sleep; they had kept their eyes open while they slept. . . . It is a world without sleep. The world of the waking sleeper. Everything, with a frightening clarity, is clear."

87. Cf. the two texts reprinted in *Disjecta,* p. 172.

88. [Cf. *Happy Days,* where this phrase recurs throughout the text.—Trans.]

89. [In English in the original.—Trans.]

90. Beckett, *What Is the Word,* in *As the Story Was Told* (London: Calder, 1990), p. 132.

91. Beckett, *Worstword Ho,* in *Nohow On,* pp. 118, 124.

Index

poetry, 97, 170, 173; in Melville, 72; in
  Whitman, 58–59
politics, in antiquity, 31; in Greece, 136;
  and literature, *xlvi–li*; minorization of,
  xli–xlv; Nietzsche's "grand politics,"
  xxxix
polyphony, *xxvii,* 59
pornography, 126
portmanteau words, *xxviii,* 69
portrait: and identification, 75; role of in
  Melville's writings, 77
possessive article, 3; in psychoanalysis, 65
possible, possibility, 94, 156, 161, 168;
  subjective vs. objective, 152; ways of
  exhausting, 168
Pound, Ezra, *xl*
power (*pouvoir*): in the Apocalypse, 48;
  Christianity as a religion of, 39, 43,
  127; and figure of the despot, 145;
  judgment as a new image of, 39;
  linguistic mechanisms of, *xlvii;* in
  Spinoza, 145
power(s) (*puissance*), 3, 124, 140; to
  affect and be affected, 131; as aspects
  of milieus, 61; and the body, 131; vs.
  claim, 136–37; of the mind, 124; variations of, 141
pragmatism, 86–88
Prague, *xlviii*
precursors, dark, 144
predication, *xxv,* 52, 115
preference, 71; Ahab's, 79; logic of, 73
presence, 95
pre-Socratics, 45
presuppositions, 83; logic of, 73
priest(hood), Christian, 39–40; Jewish,
  38–40; in Nietzsche, 37; psychology
  of, 127; in Spinoza, 145
prison, 89
procedure, 80; amplified, 8–9; in Brisset,
  9; as event, 11; evolved, 8–9; and literature, 72; pushes language to its limit,
  20; in Roussel, 9; its three operations,
  72; in Wolfson, 19–20. *See also* formula
process, *xxvi, xliii,* 11, 159, 168; as delirium, *lv;* interruptions of, 3, 5; liberatory, 128; life as, 3; world as, 86
processes, stationary, 119
programming, in the Apocalypse, 40–41
projection, 119; in T. E. Lawrence, 117

proletariat, *xli,* 74, 86, 88
property, 84; proprietorship, 84–85, 128
prophet(s), 42, 139–40; in Melville,
  79–82
prophetism, Jewish, 40–41; vs. apocalyptic, 41
Proust, Marcel, *xi, xix, xx, xxxvi, xlvi,* 5;
  A la recherche du temps perdu, xix,
  xxi, xxiii; and the "literary machine,"
  xxi–xxii; and "plane of composition,"
  xxxvi; and voyages, 62–63; on writing, *lv*
psychiatry, 53, 126; and literature, *xix*
psychoanalysis, 53, 117, 130; archaeological conception of the unconscious
  in, 63–64; on art, *xvii–xviii;* misconstrues the nature of forces, 65;
  misunderstands human-animal relationships, 54; misunderstands signs
  and symptoms, *xx;* primary error of,
  17; and psychotic procedures, 19; as
  rationalistic, 81
psychology, 81, 83
psychosis, 3, 17, 20, 71–72, 74, 78; inseparable from a linguistic procedure,
  9, 19; in Melville, 78

qualities, 84; as aspects of milieus, 61–62
Quignard, Pascal, 55

race, *xxxix;* pure vs. bastard, *xli,* 4
rationalism, psychology as, 81
reaction, 102; and force, 100–101
real, 153; and imaginary, 62–63
realization, process of, 152–53, 160
reason, 81–82, 145; as dominant faculty,
  33
reference, 71, 73, 77; referent, 141
reflection, 52; tragic, 56
relation(s): of counterpoint, 59; external
  to their terms, *xxiii,* 58; finite,
  127–28; living, 60; logic of, 52,
  58–59; of movement and rest, 142;
  must be invented, *xlii;* nonpreexistent,
  lii; in Spinoza, 142; and the whole,
  58–60
religion, *xlv,* 36, 49–51; religious ideal,
  101
Rembrandt van Rijn, 143, 172
Renan, Joseph Ernest, 54, 96
repetition, 55, 68, 163; in Péguy, 111

Gilles Deleuze was emeritus professor of philosophy at the University of Paris VIII, Vincennes-St. Denis, until his suicide at age seventy in 1995. He is the author of numerous books, including *Kant's Critical Philosophy: The Doctrine of the Faculties, Cinema 1: The Movement-Image, Cinema 2: The Time-Image, Foucault, The Fold: Leibniz and the Baroque,* and, with Félix Guattari, *Anti-Oedipus, A Thousand Plateaus,* and *Kafka: Toward a Minor Literature,* all published in translation by the University of Minnesota Press.

Daniel W. Smith is a Ph.D. candidate in the Department of Philosophy at the University of Chicago. He has also translated Deleuze's *Francis Bacon: The Logic of Sensation* and Pierre Klossowski's *Nietzsche and the Vicious Circle.*

Michael A. Greco is a photographer and freelance translator based in Paris.